VIEWPOINT

STUDENT'S BOOK 2

MICHAEL MCCARTHY

JEANNE MCCARTEN

HELEN SANDIFORD

CAMBRIDGE
UNIVERSITY PRESS

CAMBRIDGE UNIVERSITY PRESS
Cambridge, New York, Melbourne, Madrid, Cape Town,
Singapore, São Paulo, Delhi, Mexico City

Cambridge University Press
32 Avenue of the Americas, New York, NY 10013-2473, USA

www.cambridge.org
Information on this title: www.cambridge.org/9780521131896

First published 2014

Printed in Hong Kong, China, by Golden Cup Printing Company Limited

A catalog record for this publication is available from the British Library.

ISBN 978-0-521-13189-6 Student's Book
ISBN 978-1-107-60631-9 Workbook
ISBN 978-1-107-60156-7 Teacher's Edition with Assessment CD/CD-ROM
ISBN 978-1-107-66132-5 Class Audio CDs (4)
ISBN 978-1-107-67577-3 Presentation Plus
ISBN 978-1-107-65967-4 Blended Online Pack (Student's Book + Online Workbook)

Additional resources for this publication at
www.cambridge.org/viewpoint

Cover and interior design: Page 2, LLC
Layout/design services and photo research: Cenveo Publisher Services/Nesbitt Graphics, Inc.
Audio production: New York Audio Productions

Authors' acknowledgements

The authors would like to thank the entire team of professionals who have contributed their expertise to creating *Viewpoint 2*. We appreciate you all, including those we have not met. Here we would like to thank the people with whom we have had the most personal, day-to-day contact through the project. In particular, Michael Poor, who skillfully and sensitively edited the material and dedicated so much time and professional expertise to help us improve it; Mary Vaughn for her usual sage advice on our syllabus and her excellent contributions to the pronunciation materials; Dawn Elwell for her superb production skills; copy editor Karen Davy for checking through the manuscripts; Sue Aldcorn and Arley Gray for their work on creating the Teacher's Edition; Helen Tiliouine, Therese Naber and Janet Gokay, for creating and editing the testing program; Cristina Zurawski and Graham Skerritt for their comments on some of the early drafts, Mary McKeon, for her series oversight and project management; Melissa Struck for her help on the workbook and project management; Rossita Fernando and Jennifer Pardilla for their roles on the Workbook, Class Audio, and Video Program; Catherine Black for her support on the answer keys and audio scripts and deft handling of the Online Workbook; Tyler Heacock and Kathleen Corley, and their friends and family for the recordings they made, which fed into the materials; Ann Fiddes for corpus support and access to the English Profile wordlists; Dr. Cynan Ellis Evans for the interview on page 45, and Kristen Ulmer for the interview which is reported on page 55.

We would also like to express our deep appreciation to Bryan Fletcher and Sarah Cole, who started the *Viewpoint* project with incredible vision and drive; and Janet Aitchison for her continued support.

Finally, we would like to thank each other for getting through another project together! In addition, Helen Sandiford would like to thank her husband, Bryan, and her daughters for their unwavering support.

In addition, a great number of people contributed to the research and development of *Viewpoint*. The authors and publishers would like to extend their particular thanks to the following for their valuable insights and suggestions.

Reviewers and consultants:
Elisa Borges and Samara Camilo Tomé Costa from **Instituto Brasil-Estados Unidos**, Rio de Janeiro, Brazil; Deborah Iddon from **Harmon Hall** Cuajimalpa, México; and Chris Sol Cruz from **Suncross Media LLC**. Special thanks to Sedat Cilingir, Didem Mutçalıoğlu, and Burcu Tezvan from **İstanbul Bilgi Üniversitesi**, İstanbul, Turkey for their invaluable input in reviewing both the Student's Book and Workbook.

The authors and publishers would also like to thank our design and production teams at Nesbitt Graphics, Inc., Page 2, LLC, and New York Audio Productions.

Cambridge University Press staff and advisors:
Mary Lousie Baez, Jeff Chen, Seil Choi, Vincent Di Blasi, Julian Eynon, Maiza Fatureto, Keiko Hirano, Chris Hughes, Peter Holly, Tomomi Katsuki, Jeff Krum, Christine Lee, John Letcher, Vicky Lin, Hugo Loyola, Joao Madureira, Alejandro Martinez, Daniela A. Meyer, Devrim Ozdemir, Jinhee Park, Gabriela Perez, Panthipa Rojanasuworapong, Luiz Rose, Howard Siegelman, Satoko Shimoyama, Ian Sutherland, Alicione Soares Tavares, Frank Vargas, Julie Watson, Irene Yang, Jess Zhou, Frank Zhu.

Viewpoint Level 2 *Scope and sequence*

	Functions / Topics	Grammar	Vocabulary	Conversation strategies	Speaking naturally
Unit 1 **A great read** pages 10–19	• Talk about types of literature, reading habits, and favorite authors. • Discuss the pros and cons of reading and writing blogs. • Analyze and interpret a poem.	• Use auxiliary verbs, *to*, *one*, and *ones* to avoid repeating words and phrases.	• Idiomatic expressions for understanding (*I can't make heads or tails of it*) and remembering (*It's on the tip of my tongue*) • Synonyms (*enduring - lasting*)	• Use stressed auxiliary verbs (*do, does*) before main verbs to add emphasis. • Use *if so* to mean "if this is true", and *if not* to mean "if this is not true."	• Stressing auxiliaries for emphasis *page 138*
Unit 2 **Technology** pages 20–29	• Talk about technology and its impact on your life. • Discuss the issue of privacy vs. security. • Evaluate the pros and cons of modern conveniences. • Discuss how you respond to new technologies.	• Add information to nouns with different types of expressions. • Use two-part conjunctions like *either . . . or* to combine ideas.	• Compound adjectives to describe technology (*high-speed, energy-efficient*) • Suffixes (*innovation, radical*)	• Use adverbs like *predictably* and *apparently* to express what you predict, expect, etc. • Emphasize that something is impossible with *can't / couldn't possibly*.	• Stress in noun phrases *page 138*
Unit 3 **Society** pages 30–39	• Talk about different social pressures that you and others face. • Discuss the challenges of starting college and other new experiences. • Discuss how children put pressure on parents. • Evaluate gender differences in language.	• Use participle clauses to link events and add information about time or reason. • Add emphasis with *so . . . that*, *such . . . that*, *even*, and *only*.	• Expressions with *take* (*take advantage of, take credit for*) • Synonyms (*often – frequently; show – reveal*)	• Express a contrasting view with expressions like *having said that* and *then again*. • Use *even so* and *even then* to introduce a contrasting idea.	• Stress in expressions of contrast *page 139*
Checkpoint 1 Units 1–3 pages 40–41					
Unit 4 **Amazing world** pages 42–51	• Talk about the natural world. • Present information about a member of the animal kingdom. • Consider the impact that humans have on nature.	• Use future perfect forms to talk about the past in the future. • Use prepositions and prepositional phrases to combine ideas.	• Expressions to describe the behavior of wildlife (*hibernate, predator*) • Suffixes with *-able* (*remarkable, valuable*)	• Use expressions like *What's more* to add and focus on new ideas. • Use *in any case* and *in any event* to strengthen arguments and reach conclusions.	• Stress in adding expressions *page 139*

Listening	Reading	Writing	Vocabulary notebook	Grammar extra
The blogosphere • A presenter shares statistics about blogging. *My interpretation is . . .* • Someone gives an interpretation of a poem.	*A brief history of poetry* • An article about different types of poetry through history	• Write a review of a book you have enjoyed. • Describe, evaluate, and recommend a book. • Coordinate adjectives. • Avoid errors with *yet*.	*Heads or tails* • Think of situations when you can use certain idioms.	• More on auxiliary verbs to avoid repetition • *too, either, so, neither,* and *(to) do so* • More on using *to* to avoid repeating verb phrases • More on *one/ones* to avoid repeating countable nouns *pages 144–145*
Privacy or convenience? • Two friends discuss privacy and fingerprinting. *How do you multitask?* • Three conversations about multitasking	*As technology changes, so do adoption life cycles.* • An article about the willingness of consumers to invest in new technology	• Write a report about Internet use. • Describe graphs, charts, and tables. • Describe and compare statistics. • Avoid errors with *as can be seen*, etc.	*High-tech gadgets* • Use compound adjectives with nouns to say something true about your life.	• Adjectives after nouns • Negative phrases after nouns • More on two-part conjunctions • Two-part conjunctions with phrases and clauses *pages 146–147*
It's an issue . . . • Two people discuss the challenges when kids become more independent. *Language and gender* • A professor introduces a course on language and gender.	*Spring semester courses in Language and Society* • Course outlines of classes about language and society	• Write an evaluation of a course. • Plan and write an evaluative report. • Express results in writing. • Avoid errors with *therefore*.	*Take credit!* • Write sentences that paraphrase the meaning of new expressions.	• Clauses with prepositions and conjunctions + *-ing* • Passive forms of participle and time clauses • More on *so* and *such* • More on *even* and *only* *pages 148–149*
Checkpoint 1 Units 1–3 pages 40–41				
The Antarctic • An expert answers questions about Antarctica. *The genius of the natural world* • A presenter shares ideas about how biomimicry could solve problems.	*How nature inspires science – a look at some notable inventions* • An article about how nature inspires innovation	• Write a persuasive essay about an environmental concern. • Use academic prepositions and impersonal *one*. • Avoid errors with *upon*.	*Golden eggs* • Notice the use of specialized vocabulary in general English or in idioms.	• More on the future perfect • The future perfect for predictions and assumptions • Formal prepositional expressions • More on *the fact that*; prepositions + perfect forms *pages 150–151*

	Functions / Topics	Grammar	Vocabulary	Conversation strategies	Speaking naturally
Unit 5 **Progress** pages 52–61	• Talk about inventions, progress, and human achievements. • Evaluate the motivation of people who are driven to perform dangerous feats. • Discuss the pros and cons of research. • Discuss inventions and innovations.	• Use adverbs with continuous and perfect forms of the passive. • Use past modals with the passive.	• More formal adjectives (*obsolete, portable*) • Adjectives into nouns (*convenient – convenience; easy – ease*)	• Use expressions like *Let's put it this way* to make a point. • Use expressions like *Maybe (not), Absolutely (not),* and *Not necessarily* in responses.	• Stress in expressions *page 140*
Unit 6 **Business studies** pages 62–71	• Talk about business and retail. • Consider the motivations behind shopping habits. • Evaluate the benefits of online and instore shopping. • Present the advantages of big business and small business.	• Use relative clauses that begin with pronouns or prepositions. • Use *some, any, other, others,* and *another* to refer to people and things.	• Verbs that mean *attract* and *deter* (*entice, discourage*) • Adjectives (*malicious, vulnerable*)	• Use negative and tag questions to persuade others of your point of view. • Use *granted* to concede points.	• Prepositions in relative clauses *page 140*
Checkpoint 2 Units 4–6 pages 72–73					
Unit 7 **Relationships** pages 74–83	• Talk about relationships, marriage, and family life. • Discuss the most important issues to consider before getting married. • Talk about the best ways to meet people. • Evaluate the pros and cons of monitoring family members.	• Use conditional sentences without *if* to hypothesize. • Use *wh-* clauses as subjects and objects.	• Binomial expressions with *and, or, but* (*give and take, sooner or later, slowly but surely*) • Building synonyms (*see – perceive; improve – enhance*)	• Use expressions like *in the end* and *in a word* to summarize or finish your points. • Use *then* and *in that case* to draw a conclusion from something someone said.	• Binomial pairs *page 141*
Unit 8 **History** pages 84–93	• Talk about people and events in history. • Determine what makes a historical event "world-changing." • Talk about the importance of one's family history.	• Use the perfect infinitive to refer to past time. • Use cleft sentences beginning with *It* to focus on certain nouns, phrases, and clauses.	• Adjective antonyms (*lasting – temporary; superficial – profound*) • Metaphors (*sift, bring to life*)	• Use expressions like *Let's not go there* to avoid talking about a topic. • Respond with *That's what I'm saying* to focus on your viewpoint.	• Saying perfect infinitives *page 141*

Listening	Reading	Writing	Vocabulary notebook	Grammar extra
Kristen Ulmer – a world-class extreme skier • A reporter relates her conversation with Kristen Ulmer. *What's the point of research?* • Two people discuss the benefits and drawbacks of research.	*Invention: inspired thinking or accidental discovery?* • An article about how inventions come about	• Write an opinion essay about technological progress. • Compare and contrast arguments. • Use *it* clauses + passive to say what people think. • Avoid errors with *affect* and *effect*.	*Old or ancient?* • Learn synonyms to express basic concepts in formal writing.	• Adverbs in present and past passive verb phrases • Adverbs in perfect verb phrases • Adverbs and past modal verb phrases • Questions with passive past modals *pages 152–153*
Too good to be true? • Four consumer experts talk about special promotions. *The top threats* • A business expert discusses the risks of running a business.	*Data leakage – Are you protected?* • An article about keeping a business's information secure	• Write a report on data security. • Use modals to avoid being too assertive and to make recommendations. • Use expressions to describe cause (*This may be the result of . . .*). • Avoid errors with *can* and *could*.	*It's tempting.* • Write word family charts.	• Pronouns and numbers in relative clauses • Nouns in relative clauses • *other, every other, other than* • More on *another* *pages 154–155*
Checkpoint 2 Units 4–6 pages 72–73				
Bringing up baby? • A student talks about his experience with a "baby simulator." *Keeping tabs on the family* • A family counselor discusses using technology to keep track of family members.	*Technology – is it driving families apart?* • An article about how technology impacts family dynamics	• Write a magazine article about how to enhance friendships. • Express number and amount with expressions like *a number of, a great deal of.* • Avoid errors with *a number of*, etc. • Use expressions like *affect, have an effect on* to describe effects.	*Now or never* • Use expressions in sentences that are personally meaningful.	• More on inversions • More on *what* clauses • *what* clauses with passive verbs and modals in writing *pages 156–157*
Tracing family histories • Two friends talk about their family backgrounds. *Citizen participation projects* • A lecturer describes projects that help uncover the past.	*The Ancient Lives Project* • An article about the collaboration between experts and volunteers in piecing together the past	• Write a narrative essay about your family or someone you know. • Order events in the past. • Avoid errors with *in the end* and *at the end.*	*Deep, low, high* • Look up the synonyms and antonyms of new words.	• More on perfect infinitives • The perfect infinitive after adjectives and nouns • More on cleft sentences with *it + be* • *it + be* + noun phrase in writing *pages 158–159*

	Functions / Topics	Grammar	Vocabulary	Conversation strategies	Speaking naturally
Unit 9 **Engineering wonders** pages 94–103	• Talk about feats, challenges, and developments in engineering. • Evaluate the priorities in research and development. • Discuss the usefulness of robots.	• Use -*ever* words in talking about unknown people or things. • Use negative adverbs (*never, not only*) + inversion to start a sentence for emphasis.	• Vocabulary of engineering projects (*erect, install*) • Verbs (*interact, determine*)	• Use expressions like *given* or *considering* to introduce facts that support your opinions. • Emphasize negative phrases with *at all* and *whatsoever*.	• Intonation of background information *page 142*

Checkpoint 3 Units 7–9   pages 104–105

	Functions / Topics	Grammar	Vocabulary	Conversation strategies	Speaking naturally
Unit 10 **Current events** pages 106–115	• Talk about the news, who reports it, and how. • Discuss if speed or accuracy is more important in news reporting. • Evaluate how much you trust what you hear or read in the news.	• Use continuous infinitive forms to report events in progress. • Use the subjunctive to describe what should happen, what is important, and to refer to demands and recommendations.	• Noun and verb collocations (*undergo surgery, contain an oil spill*) • Vocabulary to express truth or fiction (*verify, fabricate*)	• Highlight topics by putting them at the start or end of what you say. • Use *this* and *these* to highlight information and *that* and *those* to refer to known information.	• Stress and intonation *page 142*
Unit 11 **Is it real?** pages 116–125	• Talk about whether information is true or not. • Consider how you would handle an emergency. • Talk about white lies and if they're ever acceptable. • Discuss if art forgers are still true artists.	• Use *be to* to refer to fixed or hypothetical future events. • Use passive verb complements.	• Idioms and phrasal verbs with *turn* (*turn over a new leaf, turn around*) • Words in context (*lucrative, laborious*)	• Use expressions like *That doesn't seem right* to express concerns. • Use *to me, to her,* etc. to introduce an opinion.	• Stress in longer idioms *page 143*
Unit 12 **Psychology** pages 126–135	• Talk about being independent, the psychology of attraction, and the brain. • Discuss the differences between online and in-person relationships. • Discuss stereotypes.	• Use objects + -*ing* forms after prepositions and verbs. • Use reflexive pronouns — including to add emphasis — and *each other / one another*.	• Phrasal verbs (*go by, pick up on*) • Expressions with *be, do, go, have, take* (*be close to, have to do with*)	• Use expressions like *I can see it from both sides* and *by the same token*. • Use *to put it* + adverb to indicate your meaning behind an opinion.	• Stress with reflexive pronouns *page 143*

Checkpoint 4 Units 10–12   pages 136–137

Listening	Reading	Writing	Vocabulary notebook	Grammar extra
Other amazing feats • Three documentaries describe marvels of engineering. *Is she for real?* • A radio interview about a robot.	*Robots* • An article about the widespread use of robots in society	• Write an essay about whether robots can replace humans. • Express alternatives. • Avoid errors with *would rather / rather than*.	*How do you do it?* • Ask yourself questions using new vocabulary.	• *whatever, whichever,* and *whoever* as subjects and objects • Patterns with *however* and *whatever* • More on inversion • Inversion with modals and in passive sentences *pages 160–161*

Checkpoint 3 Units 7–9   pages 104–105

Listening	Reading	Writing	Vocabulary notebook	Grammar extra
Journalism • A guest on a radio program discusses trends in journalism.	*Establishing the truth: How accurate are news reports?* • An article about issues in news reporting	• Summarize an article. • Use subject-verb agreement. • Avoid subject-verb agreement errors in relative clauses.	*Trust your instincts* • Find multiple verbs that collocate with the same noun.	• Simple vs. continuous infinitives • More on perfect continuous infinitives • More on the subjunctive • The subjunctive and conditional sentences *pages 162–163*
Online lies • Two friends talk about the lies that people tell about themselves online. *Fakes of art!* • A radio program profiles artist John Myatt.	*Authenticating art* • An article about the techniques used to identify art forgeries	• Write an essay about fake designer goods. • Share your views and those of others. • Use academic conjunctions and adverbs. • Avoid errors with *provided that*.	*Use it or lose it.* • Use new vocabulary in imaginary conversations with a friend.	• More on *be to; be due to, be meant to* • *be to* for orders and instructions • More on passive perfect infinitives • *would rather* *pages 164–165*
"Helicopter" parents • A mother and son talk about overprotective parents. *Understanding the brain – outcomes* • Four professionals lecture about the impact of brain research on their fields.	*The developing brain* • An article about how brain development relates to behavior	• Write a report using statistics. • Compare statistics. • Use expressions like *twice as likely, four times more often*. • Avoid errors with *twice*.	*Pick and choose* • Create a thesaurus.	• Common verbs, adjectives, and nouns + object + *-ing* • More on reflexive pronouns • Referring to unknown people *pages 166–167*

Checkpoint 4 Units 10–12   pages 136–137

Unit

1

A great read

In Unit 1, you . . .

- talk about literature, reading habits, and favorite authors.
- avoid repeating words by using auxiliary verbs, *to*, and *one(s)*.
- use auxiliary verbs for emphasis.
- use *if so* and *if not* instead of repeating ideas.

Lesson A *Memoirs*

1 Grammar in context

A Read the six-word memoirs below. Can you guess the story behind each memoir?

Who are you – in six words? Our readers wrote their autobiographies in just six words.

ⓐ **Lindsay**
Former accountant now wears chef's apron.

ⓒ **Yoshio**
Traveled everywhere. Saw everything. Sadly, broke.

ⓔ **Tim**
Every 10 years, I reinvent myself.

ⓑ **Dave**
Happily raising three beautiful kids. Exhausted!

ⓓ **Sasha**
Studied hard. Good degree. No job.

ⓕ **Stella**
The good child – until I wasn't!

B ◀》 CD 1.02 Listen. Which memoir is each person talking about? Write the letters a–f.

1. _____ "Like me he seems family oriented. He's obviously enjoying family life – as I am. But he finds it hard. Most people do. I know my sister does. She has three children – all under six!"

2. _____ "Well, she obviously changed careers – a lot of people do these days. But it sounds like she took a risk by choosing a career that's not as lucrative, which is what I did, too. I hope it works out for her. It did for me, but for some people it doesn't."

3. _____ "I'd say this person worked hard in college, which most students do. But it's too bad he or she hasn't gotten any work. I know a lot of graduates who haven't. It's so discouraging."

4. _____ "Sounds like me. I was the perfect kid – made my bed, ate my vegetables, and my brothers never did. At college I went wild, as a lot of kids do. Dyed my hair pink . . ."

5. _____ "This person clearly likes change. Actually, I'm thinking of making a big change in my life. I'm contemplating volunteering. I think it's a great idea, but my family doesn't for some reason."

6. _____ "He must have traveled all over. I'd love to do that. I haven't been abroad once. Most of my friends haven't either. I'm saving up for a trip, and so is one of my friends. So maybe soon."

About you **C** Pair work Discuss the questions below. Do you agree?

Which memoir writer in your view . . .

- seems happiest?
- might be least satisfied?
- has had the best experiences?
- has taken the most risks?

- has had the best education?
- is the most successful?
- seems the most interesting person?
- is most like someone you know?

2 Grammar Avoiding repetition 1

Figure
it out

A **How do the speakers in Exercise 1B avoid repeating the same or similar words? Rewrite the underlined parts of the sentences. Then read the grammar chart.**

1. Well, she obviously changed careers – a lot of people change careers these days.
2. I hope it works out for her. It worked out for me, but for some people it doesn't work out.
3. She still hasn't gotten any work. I know a lot of graduates who haven't gotten any work.

Auxiliary verbs

Grammar extra
See page 144.

You can avoid repeating words by using auxiliary verbs (e.g., *be, have, do*).

The auxiliary can be in the same tense as the first verb.	*He's obviously enjoying it – as I **am**.* (= am enjoying it) *I think it's a great idea, but my family **doesn't**.* (= doesn't think it's a great idea) *She took a risk, which is what I **did**, too.* (= took a risk) *I haven't been abroad. My friends **haven't** either.* (= haven't been abroad)
The auxiliary can also be in a different tense	*She obviously changed careers – a lot of people **do** these days.* (= change careers) *I hope it works out. It **did** for me.* (= worked out)

B **Complete the conversations. Use auxiliary verbs. Then practice with a partner.**

1. *A* Have you ever taken any risks in life?
   B No, I suppose I haven't really. I went to college, as my brother _____. It was expected, I guess. And I went into dentistry, which is what my dad _____, too. I guess I don't like taking risks. My brother _____, though. He gave up a good career to go into music.

2. *A* So, what's one of the best experiences you've had in life?
   B Well, I guess I've been lucky. I met the perfect guy. And you know, a lot of people _____. And we don't have any financial worries. That's nice. Many couples _____ these days.

3. *A* Have you ever made a decision you regret?
   B Well, let's see. I had the opportunity to go to China on a school trip, but I didn't go. Some of my friends _____, either. But I wish I had. I think they're planning a trip for next year – I hope they _____, anyway. I won't say no next time.

4. *A* Have you traveled much? I mean, where have you been?
   B Well, I haven't traveled much, though all my friends _____. I think it's good to travel, but my parents _____. They worry about me being safe.

About
you

C **Pair work** **Ask and answer the questions in Exercise B. Give your own answers.**

3 Viewpoint My life

Group work **Write your own six-word "memoir" on a piece of paper. Then mix up the papers and take turns reading each one aloud. What can you guess about the writer? Make comparisons with other people. Can you guess who wrote it?**

> Loving life. School. Family. Friends. Basketball.

In conversation . . .

You can use *-ly* adverbs to show your attitude to what you say.

"This person is obviously enjoying life – as I am."

Lesson B *Favorite books*

1 Vocabulary in context

A What are some classic works of literature? Who wrote them? Make a list.

> War and Peace by Leo Tolstoy
> The Tale of Genji by Murasaki Shikibu
> Iracema by José de Alencar

B 🔊 CD 1.03 Listen to people talk about their reading habits. What does each person like to read?

They say young people don't read literature anymore, so we interviewed people to find out.

Who's your favorite author?

"Well, let's see. . . . I love Isabel Allende's novels. Her best one was . . . oh, wait. **It's on the tip of my tongue**, um, . . . *The Stories of Eva Luna*. I would love to write like her, but I'll never be able to. She's so talented, and she tells these amazing, magical stories. I've read every book she's ever written. I hope she writes a new one soon." — *Michael*

What classic literature have you read?

"I enjoy reading Shakespeare. We had to read his plays in college – well, we were supposed to – but they were too difficult, and I **couldn't make heads or tails of** them. It can be hard to **get your head around** the language. But actually, once you **come to grips** with it, you can see how the plots and characters are still relevant today." — *Maiko*

What's your favorite piece of literature?

"Interestingly enough, it's actually a poem. It's one I **learned by heart** when I was a kid. It's about cats, and I can still recite the whole thing. I can't remember who wrote it, though. As kids we used to love reading poems out loud. I still like to, actually." — *Anita*

What did you read most recently?

"**Off the top of my head**, I can't think of anything. Um, let's think. No, nothing **comes to mind**. I don't read a lot of books, but the ones I like tend to be things like biographies, um, nonfiction, where you learn something and **get something out of** it. I don't **see the point** of reading stories that are just made up." — *Carlos*

Is it important to read classic literature?

"Not really. **It's beyond me** why people think you should read the classics. You don't have to. I know I probably shouldn't read trashy novels, and I try not to, but some of my favorite books are just cheap romance novels by unknown authors. They're the ones that **stick in my mind**." — *Sierra*

What are you reading right now?

"Actually, to tell the truth, I don't read much nowadays. I used to. In fact, I was an avid reader; I used to read a lot, but these days I prefer not to. I listen to the radio more, or podcasts, because with, um, sorry . . . **I lost my train of thought**. Um, yeah." — *Jackson*

Word sort

C Complete the idioms in the chart. Use the interviews above to help you. Then ask and answer the questions in Exercise B. Use at least six idioms in your answers.

Understanding	Remembering
I **can't make** _heads or tails of_ it!	It's _____ my tongue.
It's hard to **get your** _____ around it.	We have to **learn it by** _____.
You have to **come to** _____ it.	I don't know **off** _____ my head.
You want to **get something** _____ it.	Nothing **comes** _____.
It's _____ me.	Sometimes I **lose my** _____.
I don't **see** _____ it.	Her stories _____ in my mind.

"I have lots of favorite authors, but one that comes to mind is Paulo Coelho."

Vocabulary notebook

See page 19.

2 Grammar Avoiding repetition 2

Figure it out

A How might the people in the interviews continue this first sentence without repeating words? Choose words to delete or change. Then read the grammar chart.

I used to read a lot of trashy novels, but . . .

these days I'm not able to read a lot of trashy novels.   I haven't read a trashy novel in ages.
I wasn't supposed to read a lot of trashy novels.   the trashy novels I like have gotten too trashy.
I prefer not to read a lot of trashy novels nowadays.

Infinitive verb phrases; *one, ones*

Grammar extra
See page 145.

You can avoid repeating infinitive verb phrases by using *to* when it is clear what you mean.
*I would love to write like her, but I'll never be able **to**. I mean, I'd like **to**, but . . .*
*We had to read Shakespeare's plays in college. Well, we were supposed **to**.*

Notice the negatives with *try* and *prefer*.
*I shouldn't read trashy novels, and I try **not to**, but . . .*
*I used to read a lot, but these days I prefer **not to**.*

You can use *one* or *ones* to avoid repeating countable nouns. Don't use them after *my, your, his,* etc., *some, any,* or *both* unless there is an adjective.
*I've read all her books. Her best **one** is . . .*
*Of the books I read, the **ones** I like best are nonfiction.*

Common errors

You can omit *one / ones* after *first, second, next, best,* but not after *new, big, small, long,* etc.
*I hope she writes a **new one**.* (NOT . . . *a new.*)

B How can you avoid repetition in some of these sentences? Delete words or use *one / ones*. Write *one* or *ones* in parentheses where they are optional.

1. These days I hardly ever pick a book up. Well, I tend not to pick up a book. I'd rather read a magazine.
2. There's a lot of literature I haven't read. I've never read *Moby Dick*, but I'd like to read *Moby Dick* one day.
3. I read plays, especially modern plays. My favorite playwright is Arthur Miller. I've read all his plays. His best play is *The Crucible*. Though you have to *see* it performed to really get something out of it.
4. In elementary school, we had to learn poems by heart. At least we were supposed to learn poems by heart.
5. I read for half an hour in bed every night before I go to sleep. Well, I try to read for half an hour in bed every night.
6. I can't see the point of going into bookstores to buy print books. I tend not to go into bookstores to buy print books. My books are all downloaded onto a tablet. It's cheaper.
7. It's beyond me why people don't listen to audio books more. I love autobiographies, and it's a great way to "read," especially long autobiographies. I always get new audio books if I'm able to get them.
8. I still go to the library to borrow books. The books I get are usually historical novels. They're the best books.
9. I haven't read much classic literature, but I like the work of Jane Austen. Some of her books are also movies, like *Emma* and *Pride and Prejudice*. Both movies are good, but the best movie is *Emma*. That sticks in my mind.

About you

C **Pair work** Discuss the sentences in Exercise B. Are any of them true for you?

Lesson C *I do like it.*

① Conversation strategy Emphasizing ideas

A In the last day, how many different things have you read and written? Make two lists.

"I read a friend's blog. I wrote a comment on my friend's social network page."

B ◀))) CD 1.04 **Listen. What views are mentioned about reading and writing today?**

Professor	Not long ago, they were predicting that because of the increase in phone and computer use, people would stop reading and writing. But we haven't. In fact, we're reading and writing more than we did. So, are there implications of this for literature? And if so, what?
Yolanda	Yes, well, it does seem that with social media everybody's writing something these days, like blogs and check-ins and status updates. I know I am.
Elena	Which is a good thing. I mean, I do like the fact that anyone can write a blog. It makes writing, well, . . . more democratic somehow.
Professor	I do think, though, that it gives the impression that anybody can be a writer. But doesn't it take talent to be a good writer? And if not, then does that mean anything goes?
Tariq	Yes, nowadays anyone can publish a novel online, but how do you know if it's any good? How do we evaluate it?
Yolanda	Do you need to, though? I think the real problem is with nonfiction. I mean, how do you determine what information you read on the Internet is accurate and reliable?
Professor	Yes, indeed. That's just as important, if not more important.

C **Notice** how the speakers add a stressed auxiliary verb (*do, does*) before a main verb to add emphasis to what they say. Find more examples in the conversation.

> It **does** seem that everyone's writing something these days.

D ◀))) CD 1.05 **Read the conversations. Add the auxiliary verbs *do* or *does* to add emphasis where possible, and make any other necessary changes. Then listen and check.**

> **In conversation . . .**
>
> The most common phrases with **I do** are:
> *I do think, I do like, I do know, I do want, I do enjoy, I do believe, I do feel, I do agree.*

1. *A* The problem with many of the blogs you read is that they're very poorly written.
   B Yeah. I think it's hard to find ones that are well written. Some have good content, though.

2. *A* You know what I hate? Microblogs. I feel they're a waste of time and not worth reading.
   B Well, I follow some celebrities. I enjoy reading their thoughts on life.

3. *A* I believe that people are much less afraid of writing now. I know I am. It used to be so hard to get your work published, but not anymore. The Internet really makes a difference.
   B But it seems like that's the problem. Anyone can get their work out there.

4. *A* It's interesting how new kinds of writing have come about in recent years. Like those cell phone novels that started in Japan. It makes you wonder why they became so popular.
   B Yeah. It seems unlikely that people would want to read books on a cell phone.

About you **E** **Pair work** Discuss the conversations in Exercise D. Do you agree with the views presented? What other views do you have about each topic?

2 Strategy plus *If so, if not*

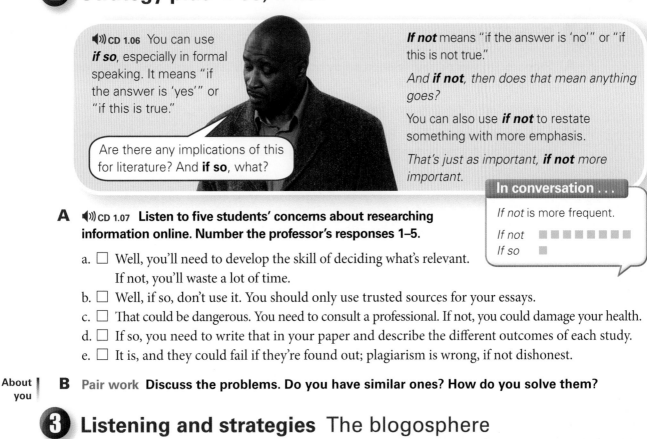

CD 1.06 You can use *if so*, especially in formal speaking. It means "if the answer is 'yes'" or "if this is true."

Are there any implications of this for literature? And **if so**, what?

If not means "if the answer is 'no'" or "if this is not true."

And **if not**, then does that mean anything goes?

You can also use **if not** to restate something with more emphasis.

That's just as important, **if not** more important.

In conversation . . .

If not is more frequent.

If not ■ ■ ■ ■ ■ ■ ■ ■
If so ■

A **CD 1.07** **Listen to five students' concerns about researching information online. Number the professor's responses 1–5.**

a. ☐ Well, you'll need to develop the skill of deciding what's relevant. If not, you'll waste a lot of time.

b. ☐ Well, if so, don't use it. You should only use trusted sources for your essays.

c. ☐ That could be dangerous. You need to consult a professional. If not, you could damage your health.

d. ☐ If so, you need to write that in your paper and describe the different outcomes of each study.

e. ☐ It is, and they could fail if they're found out; plagiarism is wrong, if not dishonest.

About you

B **Pair work Discuss the problems. Do you have similar ones? How do you solve them?**

3 Listening and strategies *The blogosphere*

A **CD 1.08** **Guess the missing words and numbers on the slide. Then listen to part of a presentation. Write a word or number in each space.**

> **Blogging and social media — the "blogosphere"**
>
> ■ 2/3 of blogs are written by _____
> ■ ____% of bloggers are between the ages of ____ and ____
> ■ Bloggers are also more _____
> ■ ____% of bloggers spend _____ hours or more a day blogging
> ■ 72% say they don't receive any _____

B **CD 1.09** **Listen to the next part of the presentation. Complete the notes on the reasons for blogging.**

1. "Bloggers' main motivation for writing blogs does appear to be more about _____."

2. ". . . the motivation to blog in a professional environment does seem to be _____."

3. "Bloggers do say that blogging makes them more committed to, if not passionate about, _____."

4. "There is a sense that bloggers are blogging because they really do _____."

5. ". . . those people who do derive supplementary income from their blog sites tend to _____."

About you

C **Pair work Discuss the questions.**

- Do you read or write blogs?
- Are you more likely to now?
- Did the presentation change your views about blogging?
- Did it give you any new information?

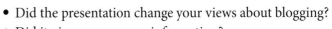

A Well, to be honest, I don't read many blogs, but it does seem that they could be interesting.
B Yes. I do think that they might be a useful way of promoting yourself at work, for example.

Speaking naturally

See page 138.

Lesson D *Poetry*

1 Reading

A **Prepare** Do you or your friends enjoy reading poetry? Who are some of the famous poets you know of? Make a list.

"Octavio Paz is a well-known poet here."

B **Read for main ideas** Read the article and the extracts from some poems. What kinds of poetry does it refer to? What are the features of each type?

A brief history of *poetry*

1 In the Museum of the Ancient Orient in Istanbul, Turkey, there is a small tablet with ancient Sumerian script on it. Few people have been able to read it, but Turkish historian and archaeologist Muazzez İlmiye Çığ believed that the words on the tablet are those of a lover from 4,000 years ago and that it is the oldest love poem ever found.

2 Of course, love has been one of the enduring themes of poetry for centuries. Additionally, in pre-literate society, poetry was often used as a means of keeping oral history alive, for storytelling, or simply as a way of recording family history or law, for example. Indeed, these societies had no other means of registering important events or cultural information, and reciting poetry was a way to pass what they held dear from generation to generation.

3 Poetry was also valued in religion as a way of remembering teachings and prophecies. Many of the world's sacred scriptures are written in poetic verse. Early agrarian societies used poetry in rituals to encourage a good harvest, while early Chinese poetry evolved from folk songs.

4 One of the earliest known Western poems is Homer's *The Iliad*, written in the eighth century BCE. It is typical of an epic poem and consists of 15,000 lines in a strict rhythmic structure. It tells of the war between the Acheans and Trojans and talks of gods and heroes like Achilles and Patroclus. With themes of war and fate, it is believed that *The Iliad* was learned by heart and repeated as part of passing on cultural values and educational messages.

An extract from *The Iliad*
Patroclus asks his friend Achilles for permission to join the battle, which Achilles has left.

"Give me your armor to put on your shoulders;
The Trojans might suppose I was you,
Hold back, and give the Acheans' sons a breather,
For breathing spells in war are very few.
Then, with a shout, fresh men might easily
Turn tired men from the ships toward the city."

5 During the European Renaissance, (late 15th to early 17th century), a poetic form that became popular was the sonnet. This has only 14 lines of verse. William Shakespeare, who was one of the many Renaissance poets, composed 154 of them.

An extract from Shakespeare's Sonnet 18

Shakespeare is praising the lasting beauty of a woman.

Shall I compare thee to a summer's day?
Thou art more lovely and more temperate:
Rough winds do shake the darling buds of May,
And summer's lease hath all too short a date:

6 In other cultures, there are different forms of traditional poetry. Japanese *haiku* is structured with 17 syllables in a 5-7-5-syllable pattern. Haiku often describes nature and communicates an abstract idea or a feeling in a moment in time. One eighteenth-century master *haiku* poet – Kobayashi Issa – wrote about his sadness on the death of his third child and then his wife.

Haiku by Kobayashi Issa

*Ikinokori
ikinokoritaru
samusa kana.*

7 While the forms of poetry have changed over time, it has generally retained a style and rhythm that make it different from other forms of writing such as novels, essays, letters, or articles. Nevertheless, one of the continuing debates centers around the issue of "What is poetry?" – a debate that still goes on with the rise of rap culture in the United States. Some see rap as the return of poetry as a performance art – poetry that should be heard rather than read – while critics say that rap should not be considered as poetry at all because it does not use "correct" English. Regardless of the ongoing debate, many rappers do consider themselves as poets. Certainly, the topics of rap songs are those of love, war, life, and death – something that hasn't changed since poetry first established itself as an art form.

Reading tip

In the last sentence or paragraph, writers often return to the theme raised at the start of the piece.

C Read for main ideas Find the ideas below in the article. Write the paragraph number.

Which paragraph mentions the following?   Paragraph
1. the belief that poetry could improve crop yields   _____
2. how poetry was used to register births and family relationships   _____
3. the controversy surrounding a definition of what poetry actually is   _____
4. how certain poetic forms express ideas that are difficult to define   _____
5. the notion of poets as teachers   _____
6. an example of how romantic poetry has existed for thousands of years   _____
7. the spiritual applications of poetry   _____

❷ Focus on vocabulary Synonyms

Tip

Writers use synonyms to avoid repeating the same word. The more synonyms you know, the easier a text is to understand.

A In each question, circle the two words in bold that are similar in meaning. Use the article to help you. Paragraph numbers are given in parentheses.

1. What are some of the **abstract (6)** / **enduring (2)** / **lasting (5)** themes of poetry?
2. Why was poetry **retained (7)** / **held dear (2)** / **valued (3)** in early societies?
3. In early societies, poetry was used for **recording (2)** / **consisting of (4)** / **registering (2)** what?
4. What famous poem describes a **war (4)** / **values (4)** / **battle (4)**?
5. Who **wrote (6)** / **evolved (3)** / **composed (5)** sonnets?
6. Which cultures used poetry as a **way (3)** / **fate (4)** / **means (2)** of educating audiences?
7. What is the nature of the **ongoing (7)** / **continuing (7)** / **communicating (6)** debate about rap?
8. Do you have a favorite **verse (3)** / **poem (1)** / **prophecy (3)**?

B Pair work Discuss the questions in Exercise A. Use the article to help you. Also add your own ideas and views.

❸ Listening My interpretation is . . .

A ◀)) CD 1.10 Read and listen to the poem. Who is the poet talking about?

B ◀)) CD 1.11 Listen to one person's interpretation of the poem. How does the person answer these questions?

1. What do you think of the poem?   *She thinks . . .*
2. What image does it bring to mind?
3. How do you think the poet feels?
4. How does it make you feel?

About you

C Pair work Discuss the questions in Exercise B. Do you agree?

PRIME by Amy Lowell

Your voice is like bells over roofs at dawn

When a bird flies

And the sky changes to a fresher color.

Speak, speak, Beloved.

Say little things

For my ears to catch

And run with them to my heart.

Writing *A short yet powerful novel . . .*

In this lesson, you . . .
- write a book review.
- link adjectives.
- avoid errors with *yet*.

Task | **Write a review of a book.**
Choose a book that you have enjoyed and write a review of it for the "Book Club" section of a magazine.

A **Look at a model** Look at the review of a novel. What does the writer think of the novel? Underline adjectives that are linked together.

> A <u>short yet powerful</u> novel, John Steinbeck's *Of Mice and Men* is set in California during the Depression of the 1930s. It tells the story of the friendship of two ranch workers and their hopes and dreams. Lennie, a physically large but gentle man of limited intelligence, and George, his tough yet compassionate and caring friend, share a dream that will be difficult, if not impossible, to fulfill: owning a piece of land.
>
> Throughout the novel, Steinbeck creates an atmosphere that is dark and menacing. It is clear from the start that this is a story that is not going to have a happy ending. Its dramatic, though not entirely unexpected, ending leaves the reader feeling sad but perhaps hopeful that the values of friendship and trust remain stronger than the desperate reality that George and Lennie inhabit.
>
> Brilliantly written, *Of Mice and Men* is compelling, if at times depressing, with themes that are as relevant today as they were then. It is a magnificent work of fiction.

B **Focus on language** Read the chart. Then choose the best options to complete the sentences below. Sometimes all are correct.

Linking adjectives in writing

You can link two related or compatible adjectives with *and* or use a comma before a noun.
*George is a **compassionate and caring** friend.* OR *George is a **compassionate, caring** friend.*

Use *but, yet,* or *though* to link adjectives with a contrasting meaning. *If* can introduce a negative idea.
*Lennie is a physically **large but gentle** man . . .*   *A **short yet powerful** novel, . . .*
*Its **dramatic, though not unexpected**, ending . . .*   *It is **compelling, if** at times **depressing**.*

You can use *if not* or (*or*) *even* to add a stronger adjective.
*Their dream will be **difficult, if not / (or) even impossible**, to fulfill.*

Common errors

Use *yet* in academic writing. Use *but* in most other cases.
*I enjoyed the book, **but** it was a little long.* (NOT . . . ~~yet it was~~ . . .)

1. It is an engaging **and** / **,** / **but** thought-provoking story about two men.
2. The novel has several scenes that are unbearably tense **and** / **,** / **if not** disturbing.
3. The lives of the characters are hard, **if not** / **even** / **though** desperate.
4. Their dreams are understandable **yet** / **but** / **though** / **if** ultimately unrealistic.
5. The writing is simple **yet** / **but** / **,** deeply symbolic.
6. The ending is moving, **if not** / **even** / **but** poignant, with an act that is compassionate, **even** / **though** / **if** brutal.

C **Write and check** Write a short review of a book. Exchange reviews with your classmates.

Writing a book review

Describe the setting, plot, characters, and themes. Evaluate the book. Write a recommendation.

Vocabulary notebook *Heads or tails*

You're trying to follow some instructions to put together a bookshelf.

"I can't make heads or tails of these instructions."

A   Match the situations with the expressions. Write the letters a–f.

1. You're taking a class, but you're not sure you're learning anything. _____
2. Someone has just unfriended you on your social networking site – you have no idea why. _____
3. You're trying to remember the name of the author of a book you've just read. _____
4. You have to give a short presentation in class without using any notes. _____
5. You're telling someone a story, but you get distracted. _____
6. You're telling someone about something memorable that happened to you when you were little. _____

a. *It's beyond me* why he did that.

b. *I have to learn it by heart*.

c. *Sorry. I lost my train of thought*.

d. *I hope I get something out of this*.

e. *That really sticks in my mind*.

f. *It's on the tip of my tongue*.

B   Look at these idioms. Think of a situation when you might use each idiom. Write the situations.

1. _____   "It's hard to get your head around."
2. _____   "I can't come to grips with it."
3. _____   "I really don't see the point of it."
4. _____   "Gosh, I don't know off the top of my head."
5. _____   "Well, nothing really comes to mind."

C   Word builder   Find the meanings of these idioms. Then write a situation for each one.

1. jog your memory
2. go in one ear and out the other
3. ring a bell
4. get the message
5. miss the point
6. it's a no-brainer

D   (Focus on vocabulary)   Write one word from the box that has a similar meaning to the words in bold. Then write answers to the questions. Refer to Exercise 2A on page 17 to help you.

battle	continuing	composed	lasting
means of	register	value	verse

OF COURSE YOU CAN'T MAKE HEADS OR TAILS OF THE BOOK. YOU'RE HOLDING IT UPSIDE DOWN.

1. What is something that you **hold dear**?
2. What's one of your **enduring** memories from childhood?
3. What information do you have to **record** on a birth certificate?
4. What famous **war** have you learned about in history?
5. When was the last time you **wrote** a poem?
6. What's the best **way of** recording your family history?
7. Do you have any **ongoing** ambitions?
8. Have you ever learned a **poem** by heart?

Technology

In Unit 2, you . . .

- talk about technology and its impact.
- add information to nouns.
- use conjunctions such as *both . . . and . . .* and *neither . . . nor . . .*
- signal expectations with adverbs like *presumably* and *ironically*.
- use *can't / couldn't possibly* to say what is impossible.

Lesson A *How private is "private"?*

1 Grammar in context

A How private do you consider these things to be? What else do you consider as private?

- your cell phone number
- your marital status
- favorite websites
- your date of birth
- your mailing address
- your photographs

B 🔊 CD 1.12 **Listen to a seminar. What invasions of privacy do the students mention?**

Professor: In the college debate next week, the subject to be discussed is changing attitudes toward privacy. Do you think privacy has a different meaning nowadays?

Gert: Yes, definitely. I mean, people put pictures online and share intimate details with hundreds of so-called friends on social networks. You can watch videos of absolutely anything, you know, people brushing their teeth – all kinds of things that were once considered private.

Ricard: Right. And every few minutes, they post updates saying what they're doing. "The cat just bit me," or "Gonna wash my hair." We don't need to know things like that.

Lorraine: True. You can get to know more about people on the other side of the world than about someone next door or the guy upstairs. But I guess it's pretty harmless.

Gert: Maybe, but what about real invasions of privacy? Like online stores bombard you with ads offering personal recommendations because they know what you've searched for. And applications programmed to monitor your email, then on your screen you get those pop-up ads based on what you've just written? They're the ones I find creepy.

Lorraine: Well, you can just ignore ads. What worries me is the information demanded from you if you just want a username for a website – sometimes they want your mailing address, cell phone number, date of birth . . . everything. There must be a lot of people happy to give away all this information, but they have no idea of how it'll be used. They get taken in by websites eager to make money by selling their databases to other companies.

Professor: Privacy is not an easy concept to define. So, let's see if we can come up with a definition of privacy.

C Pair work **Discuss the questions.**

1. What do you think Gert means by "so-called friends"?
2. What is Lorraine referring to when she says "But I guess it's pretty harmless"?
3. Why do you think Gert uses the word *bombard*?
4. Why are some websites a cause for concern, in Lorraine's opinion?
5. Which of the students' views do you agree with?

2 Grammar Adding information to nouns

Figure
it out

A Write how the students say these things without relative clauses. Then read the chart.

1. the guy who lives upstairs
2. websites that are eager to make money
3. ads that offer personal recommendations
4. pop-up ads that are based on what you've just written

> ### Noun phrases
>
> *Grammar extra*
> *See page 146.*
>
> You can add information to nouns with different types of expressions instead of using a relative clause.
>
> | | |
> |---|---|
> | An adverb or adverbial phrase | *the guy **upstairs** (= who lives upstairs), someone **next door*** |
> | A prepositional phrase | *people **on the other side of the world*** |
> | An adjective phrase | *people **happy to give away this information*** |
> | An active infinitive | *an easy concept **to define*** |
> | A passive infinitive has a future meaning | *the subject **to be discussed*** |
> | A present participle (-*ing* form) | *ads **offering personal recommendations*** |
> | A past participle has a passive meaning | *applications **programmed to monitor your messages*** |

B ◀») CD 1.13 Rewrite the comments. Replace the underlined words with the type of phrase given. Do you agree with the comments? Discuss with a partner.

1. The invasion of privacy is an important matter <u>that we should discuss</u>. (active infinitive) I mean, how to protect our privacy is an issue <u>that should be taken seriously</u>. (passive infinitive) And anyone <u>who is willing to part with personal information</u> is just taking a risk. (adjective phrase)
2. I hate it when online stores monitor the items <u>that you have put in your basket</u> and then bombard you with emails <u>that offer you discounts on those same things</u>. (prepositional phrase, present participle) I delete all emails <u>that are sent by shopping websites</u> on principle. (past participle)
3. It's useful that they send advertisements <u>that they target at you personally</u>. (past participle) Sometimes you get discount coupons <u>that are for things you really need</u>. (prepositional phrase)
4. Giving your phone number in stores to get a refund is nothing <u>that we should worry about</u>. (active infinitive) The thing <u>we should watch</u> is when they want your fingerprints. (active infinitive)
5. Friends <u>who share your personal details with strangers</u> – that's one of the potential dangers <u>that exist in social networking</u>. (present participle, prepositional phrase) For example, I know far too much about the person in the apartment <u>that is downstairs</u>. (adverb)

3 Listening and speaking Privacy or convenience?

A When do people have to give their fingerprints? Is it a reasonable request?

B ◀») CD 1.14 Listen to Mark tell Mary about a trip to a theme park. Are the sentences true (T) or false (F)? Correct the false information.

1. Mark knew beforehand that he would have to give his fingerprint. _____
2. The man behind Mark in the line agreed with Mark's point of view. _____
3. Mary thinks the theme park knows that people will object. _____
4. Mary would rather be inconvenienced than give her personal information. _____
5. Mark's wife thought it was a convenient way of opening the lockers. _____

About
you

C Pair work What do you think of Mark's story? What would you have done in his position?

*Speaking
naturally*

See page 138.

Lesson B *A smarter home*

1 Vocabulary in context

A What items of technology do most people have in their homes? Make a list.

B ◀))) CD 1.15 Read the article. Are any of the items of technology from your list mentioned?

Who's smarter, YOU or the BUILDING?

In many parts of the world, **labor-saving** appliances such as dishwashers and vacuum cleaners are regarded neither as remarkable objects nor as luxuries. In others, both **solar-powered** and **wind-powered** energy supplement the regular electricity supply, so people can enjoy **energy-efficient** or even **carbon-neutral, air-conditioned** comfort. Many homes boast not only **high-speed** Internet connections but also **high-tech** streaming entertainment systems. It might seem as if there is nothing left to invent nor any domestic task that cannot be automated. Homes are getting smarter, and in the not-too-distant future, the so-called ultra-modern home will be available to all. Here's how your day might look very soon.

7:00 a.m. Your bedside alarm decides when to wake you by checking the schedule downloaded from your computer. It plays either easy-listening music or bird song (or any sound of your choice), getting louder as the lights fade up to just the right level. The blinds open to reveal sparkling **self-cleaning** windows. Meanwhile, in

your state-of-the-art kitchen, a **custom-built** robot is preparing your breakfast as you head for the **climate-controlled** shower room. A touch-screen panel in the mirror either reads your messages to you or gives you the traffic and weather reports you'll need for the day.

6:30 p.m. You say, "I'm home" as you get back from work. The hallway lights go on, and the aroma of a **home-cooked** meal wafts out of the kitchen. You enter the kitchen; the lights go on, and off in the hallway. The lifelike robot greets you with a **human-like** "Hello" and serves dinner.

10:30 p.m. The **computer-controlled** system takes over. It not only powers down the lights and the heating, but it also locks down the house and activates the security system. Everything is going well until you make a **last-minute** decision to go out to a late movie. Now . . . what was that top-secret, voice-activated code for overriding the whole smart operating system to unlock the front door?

About you

C Pair work Discuss the questions.

1. Which items of technology in the article would you like to have? Why?
2. Which items do you think will become common in the next 10 to 15 years?
3. Are there any items that you think are frivolous or not particularly useful?

Word sort

D Find compound adjectives in the article to complete the chart. Add seven more from the article. Then use the adjectives to describe technology that you use or know about.

climate -controlled	custom-	1.	5.
-efficient	home-	2.	6.
-like	high-	3.	7.
-powered	labor-	4.	
air-	last-		
carbon-	self-		

"We have a climate-controlled section in the refrigerator for fresh produce."

Vocabulary notebook

See page 29.

② Grammar Combining ideas

Figure
it out

A **Use the article to help you rewrite these sentences. Then read the grammar chart.**

1. Solar-powered and wind-powered energy supplement the regular electricity supply.
2. Dishwashers are not regarded as remarkable objects or luxuries.
3. It gradually powers down the lights, and it activates the security system.

---

either . . . or, both . . . and, neither . . . nor, not only . . . but also

Grammar extra
See page 147

You can use these conjunctions to combine two phrases or clauses in one clause or one sentence.

Use *either . . . or . . .* to list two alternatives.	*It plays **either** easy-listening music **or** birdsong.* *It **either** reads your messages **or** gives you a traffic report.*
Use *both . . . and . . .* to combine two phrases or clauses in an affirmative context.	***Both** solar-powered **and** wind-powered energy supplement the regular electricity supply.*
Use *neither . . . nor . . .* to combine two phrases or clauses in a negative context.	*Dishwashers and vacuum cleaners are regarded **neither** as remarkable objects **nor** as luxuries.*
Use *not only . . . but also . . .* to combine two phrases or clauses in a more emphatic way.	*Many homes boast **not only** high-speed Internet connections **but also** high-tech entertainment systems.*

B **Rewrite the comments using the conjunctions given. You may have to change the form or order of the words, or leave some words out. Then practice with a partner.**

> **Common errors**
>
> Use *both . . . and . . .* to emphasize that there are two people or things.
> Use *either . . . or . . .* when there is a choice of alternatives.
> *Technology improves **both** our efficiency **and** our quality of life.*
> (NOT . . . ~~improves either . . . or . . .~~)

1. *A* You know what I don't like? High-tech gadgets with all those functions that you don't want or use. (neither . . . nor) Like my alarm clock tells the time and gives the temperature outside. (not only . . . but also)
   B It's like my cell phone. I don't open the calendar, and I don't use the voice-activated calling. (neither . . . nor)

2. *A* You know, chores were much harder for our grandparents' generation. I mean, my grandmother washed everything by hand, and she hung it out to dry. (not only . . . but also)
   B Well, they didn't have the luxury or the convenience of all our labor-saving devices. (neither . . . nor)

3. *A* Imagine running your home from your laptop. You could control the heating system, the lights. (both . . . and) Well, everything, really. Then if you forgot to turn off the stove or the coffee pot, you could just do it when you got to work. (either . . . or)
   B It'd be handy, too, on vacation. I mean, you could check on your house and you could water your plants. (not only . . . but also)

4. *A* I'd love a robot that can cook or clean. (either . . . or) I think chores are boring and a waste of time. (both . . . and)
   B Me too. My friend bought one of those robot vacuum cleaners. It saved her time and did a better job than she did. (not only . . . but also)

About
you

C **Pair work** **What do you think about the views above? Discuss your ideas. Do you agree?**

Lesson C *Invariably, it's more efficient.*

1 Conversation strategy Signaling expectations

A Do you think you're good at multitasking? What two things can you do at the same time?

B 🔊 CD 1.16 Listen. What does the research that Lucia read say about multitasking?

Rashad	All these people with headphones on – working, emailing, messaging . . . I couldn't possibly do that.
Lucia	Me neither.
Rashad	I mean, multitasking is supposedly an essential skill these days, and theoretically, you can pack 12 hours into an 8-hour day, but I'm skeptical. You can't possibly concentrate on more than one thing.
Lucia	Well, I was reading about this recently, and evidently, if you're multitasking, you're either doing things badly or not at all.
Rashad	So there's been research on this, presumably?
Lucia	Yeah. Apparently, they gave people these tasks to do and found that "high multitaskers" weren't just slower; they had poor memories and couldn't switch tasks easily, either. So being able to multitask is really a myth and might even be harmful.
Rashad	Sounds like there's a lot to be said for doing one thing at a time.
Lucia	Well, it's almost invariably more efficient. And ironically, the people who said they were bad at multitasking performed better than those who said they were good at it, and vice versa.
Rashad	Maybe I'd be better at it than I thought, then.

C **Notice** how Rashad and Lucia use adverbs to signal what they predict, expect, or assume to be true. Find the examples they use in the conversation.

> **Adverbs can express what you . . .**
> predict: *predictably, inevitably, invariably*
> expect: *presumably, supposedly;* don't expect: *ironically*
> assume to be true: *evidently, apparently, supposedly*
> think is possible (in theory): *potentially, theoretically*
> think is ideal: *ideally*

D Rewrite the sentences, replacing the underlined words with the adverb form of the word in bold. Then discuss the information with a partner. Do you agree?

Mothers supposedly spend a lot more time . . .

1. Mothers <u>are **supposed**</u> to spend a lot more time multitasking than fathers, <u>or so people say</u>. The **invariable** <u>belief is that</u> they're making dinner and helping the kids with homework.
2. <u>There is the</u> **potential** <u>that</u> multitasking for a period of time can overload the brain and cause stress. <u>It **appears** that</u> it's harmful to the brain.
3. <u>There is</u> **evidence** <u>that</u> workers distracted by phone calls and email suffer a drop in IQ. <u>The</u> **ideal** <u>thing is</u> you should avoid distractions. <u>The</u> **potential** <u>is</u> it's like losing a night's sleep.
4. Some people think multitasking makes them more productive, <u>which is</u> **ironic**. You have to <u>**presume** that</u> they haven't read the research about its effect on your brain.
5. <u>In</u> **theory**, it's possible for multitasking to be addictive. The **invariable** <u>habit of high multitaskers is to</u> place a high value on new information. They switch from emails to texts to calls because it's exciting to them, <u>which is</u> **inevitable**.

② Strategy plus *can't possibly . . .*

◀)) CD 1.17 You can use *can't possibly* or *couldn't possibly* to emphasize that something is impossible.

You **can't possibly** concentrate on more than one thing.

A ◀)) CD 1.18 **Listen. Five people talk about multitasking. Number the summaries of their views 1–5.**

☐ All young people do it. ☐ It's dangerous while driving. ☐ It's actually pretty easy.
☐ You get less work done. ☐ It affects your concentration.

B ◀)) CD 1.19 **Read the responses below. Then listen again and number the responses 1–5.**

_____ Right. You couldn't possibly say that multitasking is a good skill to have, then.
_____ Yeah, it can't possibly be that hard to do two simple everyday tasks at the same time.
_____ Right. You can't possibly concentrate on driving if you're on the phone.
_____ I know. I mean, you can't possibly expect them to do anything different.
_____ Exactly. But you can't possibly avoid phone calls and things, even if you work at home.

About you

C ◀)) CD 1.20 **Listen again. Write your own responses. Then compare with a partner.**

③ Listening and strategies How do you multitask?

A ◀)) CD 1.21 **Listen to three conversations. Write answers for each item below.**

1. Write the job each multitasker has.
2. Write three tasks each multitasker does at the same time.
3. Write the mistake each multitasker admits to.

B ◀)) CD 1.22 **Listen again to some of the things the speakers say. Complete the comments below with expressions from the box. There are two extra expressions.**

| can't possibly   couldn't possibly   inevitably   invariably   ironically   potentially   presumably |

1. You _____ expect people to do three or four things at the same time and do each thing properly.
2. _____, I end up making mistakes when I try to do more than one thing at once. It's usually better to take your time.
3. That's what drives me crazy – trying to have a conversation with someone and they're checking messages on their phone. _____, I just make an excuse and leave.
4. I don't know about you, but I _____ just sit and watch a TV show. I have to do other stuff at the same time.
5. I can see you can listen to music and study – it helps you concentrate, _____. I mean, that kind of multitasking seems fine.

MY WIFE DOESN'T THINK I'M VERY GOOD AT MULTITASKING.

About you

C **Pair work** **Do you agree with the comments above? Discuss with a partner.**

A Actually, I agree. You can't possibly expect people to do three or four things at the same time and do each thing properly.
B Oh, I totally agree. I mean, invariably you end up making a mistake with something.

Lesson D *Technology adoptions*

1 Reading

A **Prepare** When new gadgets come onto the market, how many people in the class: **a. buy them immediately? b. wait and see what other people say about them? c. never buy them?** Take a class vote.

B **Read for main ideas** Read the article to see if your class fits the model in the diagram. Complete the labels in the diagram with terms and percentages in the article to help you find out.

As technology changes, so do adoption lifecycles

1 For decades now, conventional marketing wisdom about product adoption cycles has been based on a model first described in the 1950s. The Adoption Process model (also known as the Diffusion of Innovation) illustrates how consumers purchase new products and services (see Rogers, 2003*). It categorizes consumers according to their behavior as early adopters at one end of the cycle and laggards at the other.

2 Until recently, cutting-edge technologies were mainly used by a minority group of "innovators," who accounted for approximately 2 percent of consumers. These were the enthusiasts that tried out every new gadget on the market. They were also the ones who found any bugs or problems in the products, gave honest feedback, and became loyal users. The next group of customers were the more cautious "early adopters," who represented 13.5 percent of consumers. Then came the majority of mainstream consumers, who are described as "early majority" and "late majority" consumers, each group representing 34 percent of the total market. They viewed new technology with more caution. Typically, they waited until a new piece of technology was truly tried and tested and until the price had been considerably reduced. It invariably took several years for this to happen, and at this point, when the majority of consumers had purchased a product, it was said that it had truly penetrated the market and become a mainstream "must-have" item. The remaining 16 percent of consumers are labeled "laggards" – that is, those who are either very late adopters or who never buy high-tech products.

3 However, some researchers are beginning to find that these typical adoption patterns are becoming less relevant in today's marketplace and that mainstream consumers are *all* becoming early adopters. The length of time it takes for a new technology to enter the mainstream market is also shortening. When tablets hit the market in 2010, it was the fastest uptake of any device ever. It was faster than the spread of laptops and faster than the penetration of smart phones. Over 15 million tablets were sold in the first nine months after the initial release – a phenomenal rate by any standards.

4 Furthermore, in the past, advanced technologies often first appeared in the workplace and then migrated into the

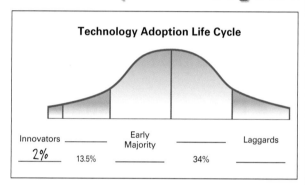

Technology Adoption Life Cycle

Innovators _____   Early Majority _____   Laggards _____
__2%__   13.5%   _____   34%   _____

domestic setting as recreational products. That is no longer the case, and it is increasingly the general domestic consumer who is driving what is used in the workplace, as employees show up at work with their new "toys" and expect to be able to use them. Authors of one study point out that the average family is now instrumental in driving recent technology adoptions. Having the latest technology is one way to catalog your children growing up and share it with other family members. Over 85 percent of families with children have cell phones, and they are more likely to have both music and video playback features on their phones.

5 Perhaps part of the reason for the change in how technologies are adopted is that the millennial generation is now a much larger segment of the consumer population. Millennials, that is, children born in the 1980s, grew up with media and digital technologies. Generation Z kids born in the 1990s are even more connected and net-savvy and are often known as "digital-natives." In the near future, they will become the majority of the consumer population, and the only logical assumption is that the technology lifecycle as described in traditional models may well be obsolete and in need of radical revision.

*Rogers, E.M. 2003. *Diffusion of Innovations* (5th Edition). New York: Free Press.

Reading tip

Writers sometimes explain a term using *that is, or,* parentheses ( ), or a dash – . *Millennials, **that is,** children born in the 1980s ,* . . .

C Check your understanding Find words in the article with a similar meaning to the words in bold below. Use those words to answer the questions.

1. What does the product adoption cycle **show**? (para. 1) *It illustrates . . .*
2. The model **groups** or **classifies** consumers into five types. What are they? (para. 1)
3. When did the majority of consumers typically **buy** a product? (para. 1)
4. What percentage of consumers does the "early adopter" group **represent**? (para. 2)
5. What product **got into** the market more quickly than any other? (para. 2)
6. What trends are marketers now noticing after the **first launch** of a product? (para. 3)
7. What is driving technology adoptions: the workplace or **home** use? (para. 4)
8. What influence are younger people having as a **section** of the consumer population? (para. 5)

D React Pair work Ask and answer the questions in Exercise C. Do you recognize the trends described in the article?

2 Focus on vocabulary Suffixes

A In this summary of the article, complete the second sentences with a form of the bold words in the first sentences. The words can all be found in the article

Study tip

Learn suffixes like *-al* / *-ical* for adjectives and *-tion* / *-sion* for nouns. In reading, they can help you understand new words. In writing, using different word forms helps you avoid repetition.

1. Technology companies love to **innovate** and hope that consumers will **adopt** their products quickly. However, consumers vary in their approach to *innovation* and their _____ of new technology.
2. Consumers used to be more **cautious**. Their _____ was due to the high price of gadgets.
3. Tablets immediately **penetrated** the market and became a **phenomenon**. Such a rapid _____ of the market was truly _____.
4. New gadgets used to be for work, not **recreation**. Once they became _____, the market grew.
5. The children who reached adulthood at the **millennium** are now consumers. This _____ generation is less conservative and more net-savvy than older generations.
6. We can no longer **assume** that Bourne's model is still relevant. Our _____ have to change.
7. The market has changed **radically**, and experts are **revising** their theories. Bourne's model therefore needs a _____ _____.

B Pair work Take turns using the words in Exercise A to discuss your observations about how people buy and use technology.

3 Viewpoint What type of consumer are you?

Group work Discuss the questions.

- How would you describe yourself as a technology consumer? Are you an early adopter? A laggard?
- How about other types of purchases? Do you have the same approach?
- What new technologies have recently been released into the market? Which ones interest you?
- Describe someone you know – anyone who's a different consumer type from you with regard to technology. What do you think of that approach?
- What differences, if any, do you see between the generations and their approach to buying technology?

In conversation . . .

If you need time to think, you can say *Let's see* or *Let me think*.

"Well, let's see, I suppose you could say that I'm in the late majority of consumers. I tend to wait . . ."

Writing *The bar graph illustrates . . .*

In this lesson, you . . .
- describe graphs, charts, and tables.
- describe and compare statistics.
- avoid errors with *as can be seen,* etc.

Task Write a report about Internet use.

Write a report for a business class or your employer about Internet use. Use graphs, charts, or tables in your report.

A Look at a model Look at the graph and complete the paragraph.

The bar graph illustrates the percentage of the population who were Internet users in each geographic region in _____. As can be seen in the graph, North America accounted for the highest percentage of Internet users in comparison with other regions, at _____ %, followed by _____ at 67.8%. In comparison, the region with the lowest percentage was _____, which represents _____ % of Internet users.

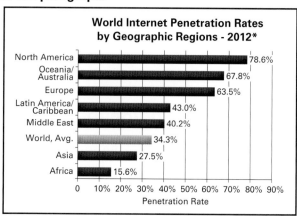

B Focus on language Read the chart. Then underline the expressions for describing and comparing in the paragraph in Exercise A.

Describing and comparing information in graphs

The graph shows / illustrates . . . **As can be seen** in the graph . . . *. . . as shown* in the table.
In 2012, Internet users **accounted for / represented** 32.7 percent of the world population.
North America had a high percentage of users **in comparison to / compared** to Africa.
In comparison / contrast, Africa had the lowest percentage of Internet users.

Common errors

Do not add *it* to the expressions *as can be seen, as is shown.*
As can be seen in the pie chart, most Internet users live in Asia.
(NOT As ~~it~~ can be seen in the pie chart, . . .)

C Write and check Write a report on Internet use, using the information from the graph in Exercise A and the pie chart below. Then check for errors.

> The pie chart shows the percentage of Internet users by world region. As can be seen in the chart, the highest percentage of users are in Asia. They account for 44.8% of the world's users. . . .

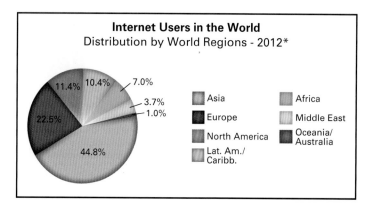

*Source: Adapted from Internet World Stats - www.internetworldstats.com/stats.htm. Penetration Rates are based on a world population of 7,012,519,841 and 2,405,510,175 estimated Internet users on June 30, 2012. Copyright © 2012, Miniwatts Marketing Group

Vocabulary notebook *High-tech gadgets*

Learning tip *Adjective + noun collocations*

When you learn a new compound adjective, find out what nouns you can use after it. Then use the expression to say something true about your life.

not-too-distant future; self-cleaning windows, oven
  I hope to graduate in the not-too-distant future.
  I'd love a self-cleaning oven and self-cleaning windows.

Dictionary tip

When you look up a compound word in an online dictionary, look at the other items in the drop-down menu as you type. You can often find other useful compounds.

high-p| 🔍
high-pitched
high-powered

A **Complete each comment with one adjective from the box. Then make the sentences true for you.**

air-conditioned	custom-built	high-speed	labor-saving	last-minute

1. We've had _high-speed_ Internet connections in this country for years. _High-speed_ trains, too.

2. I don't live in _____ comfort. It gets hot in the summer, so I'd love an _____ bedroom.

3. I'm always making _____ decisions. I'm always making _____ changes to plans, too.

4. We don't have too many _____ appliances or gadgets, apart from a washing machine.

5. I'd rather have a _____ kitchen than a _____ robot in the house.

B **Find each adjective in Box A in the article on page 22 and write the noun it describes. Then find at least two other nouns in Box B that you can use it with.**

A				B	
energy-efficient	_____	_____	_____	airline	face
carbon-neutral	_____	_____	_____	appliances	food
climate-controlled	_____	_____	_____	car	house
home-cooked	_____	_____	_____	dinner	mall
human-like	_____	_____	_____	environment	sculptures
solar-powered	_____	_____	_____	equipment	travel

C **Word builder Complete the compound adjectives in each group with the same word.**

1. wind-_____; battery-_____; high-_____
2. energy-_____; cost-_____; fuel-_____
3. _____-tech; _____- level; _____-class
4. ____-sufficient; ____-explanatory; ____-conscious

D **(Focus on vocabulary) Complete the chart of these words from Exercise 2A on page 27.**

Verb	Noun	Adjective
	adoption	
		cautious
	assumption	
innovate		
	phenomenon	
	revision	

Self, self, self!

The top adjectives with *self* include:
self-sufficient, self-serving, self-conscious, self-explanatory, self-employed, self-taught, self-centered, self-reliant, self-evident

3

Society

In Unit 3, you . . .

- talk about different social pressures.
- use participle clauses to link ideas.
- add emphasis with *only, even, so . . . that,* and *such . . . that.*
- change your view as you speak.
- use *even so* and *even then* to introduce contrasting ideas.

Lesson A *Social pressures*

1 Grammar in context

A What kinds of pressure do people have in their lives? Make a list.

B 🔊 CD 1.23 Listen. What pressures does each person talk about? Are any on your list?

WE ASKED PEOPLE,

"What are some of the social pressures you've resisted?"

1. CHELSEA, 30 Toronto, Canada, designer

Growing up, I was always branded a rebel, which is a little unfair. I guess, though, that I've never really conformed to social norms, being single and not having had any children at the ripe old age of 30! I just never met anyone, working as hard as I do. But having built up a successful career, I'm happy with my life choices. People say, "Oh, you'll regret it when you're old and lonely." But looking around, I see plenty of elderly people with families who are still lonely.

2. VICTOR, 36 Cancún, Mexico, ex-PR consultant and restaurant owner

I recently decided to get out of the rat race, having been in it most of my adult life. I'd been thinking about doing something different, but then I got laid off and was offered a generous severance package. So, presented with a golden opportunity to change my life, I bought a small restaurant here. Working in the PR industry, people are under enormous pressure, you know, to look good, have the right clothes, and be "perfect," which is really stressful. Not to mention the work hours. I got out. I'm earning less now, running this place, but I just know I'll be a lot happier going forward.

3. CHIN-SUN, 23 Seoul, South Korea, businesswoman

Thinking about it, this is probably going to sound silly, but I feel tremendous pressure to have an active social life. I don't have that many friends compared to my co-workers, or so it seems. I dread Fridays, when they ask if I'm going out with friends on the weekend. And speaking of friends, with social networking, you're supposed to have hundreds of them, and I don't. I mean, not wanting to be rude or anything, I can't see how you can have that many friends, really.

About you | **C** **Pair work** Which of the pressures above are common in your society?

"I don't think there's a lot of pressure to have kids, but I do think people feel pressure to . . ."

2 Grammar Linking events

Figure it out

A How do the people in the article on page 30 express the ideas below? Rewrite the clauses in bold. Then read the grammar chart.

1. **When I look around**, I see plenty of elderly people with families who are still lonely.
2. I've never really conformed to social norms **because I'm single and haven't had any children**.

Participle clauses 🔽

Grammar extra
See page 148.

You can use participle clauses to link events and add information about time or reason.
The subject of the participle clause and the main clause is usually the same.

Present participle	***Growing up***, I was always branded a rebel. (= When I was growing up) I never met anyone, ***working as hard as I do***. (= because I work hard)
Perfect participle	***Having built up a successful career***, I'm happy with my life choices. I've never conformed to social norms, ***not having had any children***.

B Complete the things the people say about pressures in life. Write participle clauses, using the verbs given. Sometimes there is more than one answer.

> **In conversation . . .**
>
> Expressions like *generally speaking, thinking about it, bearing in mind, speaking of,* and *talking of* are participle clauses, but they often have a different subject from the main clause.
>
> *Bearing in mind the economy, it's no wonder people feel pressured.*

1. _____ (be) a woman, I feel a certain pressure to dress well. I mean, _____ (not want) to sound sexist, but unlike my male colleagues, I feel I have to wear something different every day to the office. I think most women do, generally _____ (speak).

2. _____ (grow up) in a family where money was tight, I felt a lot of pressure – especially as a teenager. I used to feel really bad, _____ (not be) able to afford brand-name sneakers or the latest cell phone. So now, _____ (experience) that, and you know, _____ (bear) in mind that kids just want to fit in, I always try to buy my boys the things their friends have.

3. Well, _____ (come) from an academic family, I was to supposed go to a top school. But when I was 18, _____ (work) hard to get the grades I needed, I decided I really wanted to pursue a career as an artist. So, _____ (make up) my mind to do that, I kind of dropped out of formal education altogether. _____ (look back), it was the best decision I ever made.

4. _____ (stay) home and _____ (raise) a family, I've sometimes felt pressure from my friends who work outside the home. They probably think that, _____ (not have) a proper career, I haven't really "done" anything, which is really unfair. I mean, _____ (think) about it, I'd say raising kids is the most important job there is.

> BEING A COLLEGE STUDENT, I FEEL PRESSURE TO RISE TO EXPECTATIONS. JUST NOT THIS EARLY IN THE MORNING.

About you

C **Pair work** Write your view about each comment in Exercise 2B. Then discuss your comments with a partner. What other social pressures are there? Where do these pressures come from?

"Being a student, I don't really feel any pressure about how to dress. Not having had any fashion sense my entire life, I tend not to worry about these things."

Lesson B *New experiences*

1 Vocabulary in context

A ◀))) CD 1.24 **What challenges might students face before starting college? Make a list. Then read the web page. How many of your ideas are mentioned?**

So you've graduated from high school and you're ready to take the next step in your academic career. You'll probably be so excited that you can only think of the fun ahead. However, going to college can be such an overwhelming experience that some 35 percent of freshmen drop out in the first year and many leave before the end of the first semester. But don't worry! There are **steps** you can **take** to help you face the challenges and make your first semester both successful and enjoyable.

If, in the first few weeks, you feel so anxious that you only want to **take refuge** in your room, don't. That will only make things even worse. It's only natural to feel like this, and you won't be the only one, so talk to someone about it.

> "It takes time to adjust to college life. It may even take most of the first year." —RORY

On the social side, **take advantage of** what college life has to offer. For example, **take part in** extra-curricular activities; take up a new sport or hobby – it's such a great way to meet

people that it's worth the effort. However, don't let your social life **take precedence over** your studies. You are there to get a degree, after all.

> "Remember to take care of yourself by getting enough sleep. The consequences of sleeping only four hours a night are so huge that you don't even realize till it's too late." —CAITLIN

Academically, it's up to you to **take responsibility for** your studies, and you should **take into account** the fact that you may struggle with new academic challenges. **Take the initiative** and talk to a professor about any problems you have.

> "If you don't understand something, ask. **Take charge.**" —ERKAN

In class, learn how to take criticism without taking offense or taking it personally. If you're shy, **take note of** how successful students interact, and use their strategies for participating. If you get a bad grade, **take heart**: it's only one bad grade and is unlikely to throw your studies off course. Even the best students don't always get straight A's.

After the first few weeks, time will go by so fast that your first semester will be over before you know it. Look back and **take stock of** all you've achieved. Then **take credit for** surviving your first semester of college. Good job!

Word sort

B **Find expressions in bold with these meanings, and write them below. Then find other expressions with *take* on the web page. What do they mean? Compare with a partner.**

hide (in) _take refuge (in)_	take priority (over) _____
have courage or confidence _____	reflect and assess _____
participate, be involved (in) _____	notice _____
take control (of) (2 expressions) _____	accept praise for _____
_____	make use of _____
do something positive _____	do something before others do it _____
think about, consider _____	_____

About you

C **Pair work** **Do you agree with the advice given on the web page? What other advice could you give to someone starting college?**

Vocabulary notebook

See page 39.

② Grammar Adding emphasis

Figure
it out

A Add one word to each sentence and cross out the underlined words to keep the same meaning. Use the web page to help you. Then read the grammar chart.

1. You may get anxious, <u>and the result will be</u> that you'll take refuge in your room.
2. Taking up a new sport is a good way to make friends, <u>and the result will be</u> that you won't regret it.
3. Adjusting to college may take a year, <u>which is surprising</u>.
4. Before you go to college, you may think about the fun ahead <u>and nothing else</u>.

---

so . . . that, such (a / an) . . . (that), even, and only ⬇️

Grammar extra
See page 149.

You can use *so . . .* or *such . . .* (*that*) to emphasize the results or effects of something.
Use *so . . .* + adjective / adverb (*that*) . . . or *such . . .* (*a / an*) + (adjective) noun (*that*) . . .
You'll be **so excited that** you can only think of the fun ahead. Time goes **so fast** you won't notice.
It's **such an** overwhelming **experience that** many students drop out.

Even can add emphasis or signal that something is surprising. *Only* means "no one else" or "nothing else." Use them before the phrase or part of the sentence you want to emphasize.

You don't **even** realize. (NOT . . . ~~even don't~~ . .)	You **only** want to take refuge in your room.
It may **even** take a year to adjust to college life.	It will **only** make things worse.
That will make things **even** worse.	It's **only** natural to feel anxious.
Even the best students don't always get A's.	**Only** you can take charge of your situation.

About
you

B Complete the conversations with *so . . . that, such (a / an) . . . that, only,* or *even*. If none fit, write a dash (–). Then practice with a partner. Do you agree with the answers? Share your ideas.

1. **What problems do people face when they move to a new city?**
   A My friend said he ____–____ didn't _____ anticipate how difficult it would be until he moved last year. He said finding an apartment was _____ hard work _____ he ended up taking refuge on a friend's couch. He _____ got a place a month ago. I'd have been _____ depressed _____ I would've given up! It took him _____ long to settle _____ he almost moved back. But he has _____ positive outlook _____ things always work out for him.
   B There are probably things you _____ don't _____ take into account – like changing your address on your driver's license. You're usually _____ busy when you move _____ you _____ don't _____ have time to stop and think.

2. **What's it like starting a new job?**
   A You know, my first day at this job was _____ big deal _____ I couldn't eat. I _____ felt nervous the week before I started. But you can _____ do your best to fit in. I worked _____ hard my first week _____ it was over before I knew it.
   B Well, I'm pretty outgoing, but _____ I get nervous in new job situations. But it _____ lasts a few days. I'd say you should take the initiative to get to know people. Then you'll get _____ involved _____ you'll forget you were _____ nervous. In the end, _____ you can take responsibility for how things turn out.

③ Viewpoint Take the initiative

Pair work Discuss four challenges that people may face in new situations. What advice would you give? Prepare one idea to put on a self-help website.

"Starting a new job is so stressful for people that they quickly burn out."

Lesson C *Having said that . . .*

1 Conversation strategy Changing views

A What kinds of peer pressure do young people experience? Make a list.

B ◀)) CD 1.25 **Listen. What do Carol and Ashley say are the main pressures on young people today?**

Carol	I do think life was a lot easier when I was your age – for young people, I mean.
Ashley	You do? In what way?
Carol	Well, there wasn't all this peer pressure to have the latest fashions and cell phones and that sort of thing. But having said that, there were other pressures.
Ashley	Like what?
Carol	Oh, back in the day, women were expected to stay home and raise a family. I mean, some women worked, but even so, their options were limited.
Ashley	Well, I guess that's changed, which is good. But then again, they say women still do more of the household chores.
Carol	True.
Ashley	I think the worst thing now is like pressure to get good grades. You can study and study, but even then, you're not guaranteed a good job at the end of it.
Carol	Yes, there's so much competition for jobs nowadays. But then, I suppose there always was.

C **Notice** how Carol and Ashley change their view and express a contrasting view with expressions like these. Find examples in the conversation.

> *Having said that, (though), . . .*
> *But then, . . .*
> *(But) then again, . . .*

D Link each comment (1–6) with a contrasting view (a–f). Use an expression from Exercise C.

1. There are so many social problems today.
2. You're not cool if you don't have a car.
3. Getting a good job is a real problem.
4. Looks are important, as is keeping up with the latest trends.
5. And you have to have the latest gadgets.
6. There's so much pressure to do well in school.

a. _____, it's hard to live without a cell phone.

b. _____, fashion's always been a big thing for a lot of people.

c. _____, education was the only way for my parents' generation to get ahead, too.

d. _____, you had to have a motorbike to be cool at one time.

e. _Having said that, though_, there have always been issues to fix in society.

f. _____, I don't know anyone who's unemployed.

About you

E **Pair work** **Take turns starting conversations using the full comments above. Continue each conversation with your own views.**

2 Strategy plus *even so, even then*

CD 1.26 You can use **even so** to introduce a contrasting idea. It means, "despite what was just said."

A similar expression is **even then**, which means "despite the situation that was just described."

. . . *some* women worked, but **even so**, their options were limited.

You can study and study, but **even then**, you're not guaranteed a job.

A CD 1.27 Read the comments below. Then listen to people talking about various issues. Predict which comment each person makes next. Number the comments 1–4. There is one extra.

_____ But even so, they all still want to fit in with their friends.

_____ Even then, I'm sure he got lower grades than he could have – deliberately.

_____ And even then, they're not guaranteed to get a place in college.

_____ Even so, the major problem is that too many kids skip school.

_____ But even so, we still see some cases of this kind of behavior.

About you

B CD 1.28 Pair work Listen and check your answers. Then discuss the issues with a partner. Do you see these types of problems and peer pressures in your society?

3 Listening and strategies *It's an issue . . .*

A CD 1.29 Discuss the sentences below. Do you agree? Then listen to a conversation. Which sentence best summarizes the main topic of the discussion? Check (✓) the box.

☐ 1. Parents are just not aware of the issues young people face.

☐ 2. Parents face challenges as their children grow up and become more independent.

☐ 3. Parents and children never used to have conflicts about how children should behave.

B CD 1.30 Listen again. Complete the contrasting views the speakers give next.

1. Troy: You shouldn't let kids drive till they're 21.
   Even then, you can't be sure they'll be safe.

2. Troy: Yeah. They're legally old enough at 16 or 17.

   _____

3. Lucy: You even hear of kids texting at the wheel.

   _____

4. Troy: A lot of my friends have stories about their kids growing up too fast. _____

5. Lucy: I think I was an easy kid to raise.

   _____

About you

C Pair work Discuss the opinions in Exercise B. Do you agree? How else do kids pressure parents? What would you do to resist pressure if you were a parent?

"Actually, I agree that young people should wait before learning to drive. Though having said that, I guess some kids need to drive at 16, like if they've started working. Even so, it might be better . . ."

Speaking naturally

See page 139

Lesson D *Language and society*

1 Reading

A Prepare When you study a language, what kinds of things do you learn? Make a list.

B ⬇ Read for main ideas Read the course outlines. Write the title of each course in the space provided. There are two extra titles.

Language and Social Roles   Accent and Dialect   Right or wrong? Can technology help?

Language and Education   Language Change   What is bilingualism?

Spring semester courses in LANGUAGE and SOCIETY

HOME   PEOPLE   RESEARCH   STUDY   COURSES   RESOURCES

Participants should gain an understanding of how language reflects social structure and social change.

Course 101: _____

1 Language is constantly in development, and this course looks at one aspect of this: neologisms, i.e., new words. New words enter the language, sometimes pushing old words out of use. New words are very seldom completely new and are typically made up of existing words or segments of them. Scientific terms such as *nanotechnology* and *psychotherapy* combine classical Latin and Greek roots in new ways. Computer and Internet terminology reuses familiar everyday words, giving them novel meanings (*mouse, friend, memory stick, paste*), and new words are formed from the initial letters of existing words (*RAM, USB*). Sometimes names such as trade names form new words (*to Google*), or words change word class (*a big ask, a must-have*). On other occasions, English simply borrows from other languages (*pizza, sushi*). Such developments reveal a great deal about changes in society.

Course 102: _____

2 The purpose of this course is to examine styles of speaking and their social and professional consequences. Everyone speaks with an accent. When we say someone "has no accent," we usually mean the person is using the one associated with people of high social status or education. The term *non-standard accent* refers to geographical / regional varieties of speech, none of which is either inherently superior or inferior to any other. Even so, research shows that people do evaluate regional accents as being more, or less, friendly and pleasant, even judging whether people are suitable for certain types of jobs on the basis of their accent. Additionally, geographical regions and social groups frequently possess their own distinct grammar and vocabulary. However, accents and dialects are increasingly coming under pressure from mass media and centralization, threatening their very existence.

Course 103: _____

3 Correct grammar is usually seen as the grammar employed by educated people of higher social status, such as great writers, or those in power. In this course, we use a corpus (a large computer database of recorded conversations and written texts) and dedicated software to investigate thousands of examples of people from every social and educational background speaking and writing. We find there is consensus in that people generally follow the same rules of grammar. Nevertheless, we can also observe numerous cases where everyone seems to "break the rules" without comment. When everyone ignores a grammatical convention, is the rule still valid – or should we rethink it?

Course 104: _____

4 Many languages utilize different forms, titles, and names to address people who are friends and intimates, as compared to strangers, superiors, or people with whom a more formal relationship is appropriate. In this course, we examine how English creates, reflects, and maintains social relations. We ask: What is politeness? What is the status of titles and forms of address such as *Professor, Sir, Ma'am*? How do changes in English mirror shifts in social perceptions and relationships? For instance, using gender-marked vocabulary such as *fireman, waitress, chairman* is now regarded as outdated and even offensive by many, and neutral alternatives such as *firefighter, server*, and *chair(person)* are considered more acceptable. What kinds of social structures, therefore, does contemporary English reflect?

C Read for detail Which course covers these questions? Write the course number. Then discuss the questions with a partner.

1. Does television affect the way people adapt or change the language they use? _____
2. How can examples of actual language be studied? _____
3. Is it possible to avoid sexist language? _____
4. Does the way you speak affect your career prospects? _____
5. What words from foreign languages have been introduced? _____
6. Do native speakers make mistakes? Is this acceptable? _____

2 Focus on vocabulary Synonyms

Find synonyms in the course outlines to replace the words in bold. Then discuss the questions with a partner about your language. Give examples, if possible.

frequently

1. Are new words **often** invented in your language? What are some examples? (101)
2. Which words are **rarely** used anymore? (102)
3. What do you think your **way of speaking** can **show** about you? (102 / 101)
4. Are some accents **seen** as **essentially** good, even **better than** others? (104 / 102 / 102)
5. Are some accents seen as **less good**? (102)
6. Which accents, if any, do people **assess** as being more "friendly"? (102)
   Is there general **agreement** on that? (103)
7. Are there **rules** for addressing people of different social status, gender, or age? (103)
8. Do people of higher social status use language that is **different**? (102)

3 Listening and speaking Language and gender

A ◀))) CD 1.31 **Read the outline below. Can you predict the missing words? Then listen and complete each sentence with one, two, or three words.**

Course 105 Language and Gender

A controversial and _____ area, this course analyzes language and gender on the basis of facts or _____. Questions include: Do men _____ more than women? Are women less assertive or less _____? Researching such questions, we find _____ difference between the sexes, so should we instead consider who is dominant? Put simply, people of a _____ talk more. We also look at "sexist" language and whether communication between the sexes is _____. Finally, we ask: Do comparisons imply that one type of talk is _____ another?

B ◀))) CD 1.32 **Listen again and answer the questions. Write notes.**

1. Why does the professor advise the students to read only the books on the reading list?
2. In Lecture 1, what question will be considered in addition to the ones in the outline?
3. Lecture 2 will cover studies that found that men talk more. Why is that?
4. In Lecture 3, what is one of the examples given of possibly "sexist" language?
5. Lecture 4 is about Tannen's work. Why does she say men and women's language is different?
6. In Lecture 5, what does the professor say should be studied instead of male–female differences?

C Pair work Discuss which lecture you think sounds most interesting. What views do you have on men and women's language? Are there issues of sexist language in your language?

"Actually the Language and Gender course sounds really interesting. Not having studied it before, I think I'd learn a lot about how men and women communicate."

Writing *I recommend it.*

In this lesson, you . . .
- plan and write an evaluative report.
- express results in writing.
- avoid errors with *therefore.*

Task | **Write a report on a course.**

Write an evaluation of an international summer course you attended, taking into account other students' positive and negative views. Make a recommendation for future students.

A **Look at a model** Look at some students' comments on a course. Check (✓) the comments that are included in the report. Would you put the other points in paragraph 2 or 3? Write the number.

STUDENTS' COMMENTS

☐ Good food, accommodations
☐ We enjoyed the group work
☐ Some lectures were too long
☐ One professor talked too fast
☐ Too much reading
☐ Campus too far from city
☐ Good social program and good to meet other students
☐ Difficult assignments

The purpose of this report is to evaluate the residential Business Management Program, which I attended in July. As requested, I will report on both the positive and negative aspects.

On the positive side, the course was extremely well designed, giving all students an opportunity to take part. Group work was an integral part of the program. As a result, the classes were lively and varied. In terms of the social program, everyone enjoyed meeting people from other countries, making many new friends in the process.

On the negative side, some students complained that there was too much reading, leaving little time for evening activities. A further complaint was that one professor spoke so quickly that some students could not understand her.

In conclusion, the course was both useful and enjoyable. Having said that, there are some aspects which should be changed, such as the amount of reading. Even so, it was an excellent course, and I would therefore recommend it to other students.

B **Focus on language** Read the chart. Then underline the examples of results in Exercise A.

Expressing results in writing

You can express a result in writing with present participle clauses, *so / such . . . that . . .,* or *so.*
*There was too much reading, **leaving little time for evening activities.***
*She spoke **so** quickly **that** students could not understand her.* OR *She spoke quickly, **so** students . . .*

You can also use *as a result, consequently,* or *therefore.*
*Group work was part of the course. **As a result, / Consequently,** the classes were lively.*
*It was an excellent course, and I would **therefore** recommend it.*

Writing vs. Conversation

■ Conversation
■ Academic writing

as a result

therefore

consequently

C **Rewrite the sentences, using the structures given.**

1. The teacher spoke too fast. This made it difficult for students to follow. (participle)
2. The campus was too far from the city. We were only able to go there once. (*so . . . that* or *so*)
3. Some lectures were too long. This left no time for questions. (participle)
4. There was a good mix of nationalities. English was widely used. (*Consequently* or *As a result*)
5. The accommodations were excellent. We recommend staying on campus. (*therefore*)

D **Write and check** Write an evaluation of a course that you have taken. Use Exercises A and C to help you. Then check for errors.

Common errors

Do not use *therefore* by itself to join two clauses.
*It was excellent. **Therefore,** I would recommend it.* OR
*It was excellent, **and therefore,** I would recommend it.*
(NOT ~~It was excellent therefore I would recommend it.~~)

Vocabulary notebook *Take credit!*

Learning tip   Paraphrase

When you learn an expression, write it in a sentence that paraphrases the meaning. It will help you remember the meaning of the expression.

take the initiative
  I need to take the initiative on a project at work, and start it without waiting for my co-workers.

A Complete the sentences with the correct expressions from the box. Use the underlined paraphrases to help you.

take advantage of	take credit for	take into account	take part in	take responsibility for

1. It's good to _____ events that your friends organize and join in what they are doing.
2. I should _____ being single and make the most of the fact that I have few responsibilities.
3. When you see some teens behaving badly, you should _____ how easily they can be influenced and consider the peer pressure they are under.
4. If I do something wrong, I have to _____ it and take the blame for it.
5. You should _____ the good things you do in your community because it's important to know how to accept praise and be recognized.

B Use each expression in a sentence and paraphrase its meaning.

1. take heart _____
2. take precedence _____
3. take refuge in _____
4. take steps _____
5. take stock of _____
6. take note of _____

C Word builder Find the meanings of these expressions. Write each one in a sentence, and write a paraphrase of its meaning.

take action	take place	take for granted
take exception to	take effect	take issue (with)
take into consideration		

What we take!

The top collocations of *take* include:
take care, advantage, place, seriously, step(s), precedence, for granted, account, action.

D **Focus on vocabulary** Look at the course outlines on page 36. Find words for the paraphrases in bold. Then write sentences using the words and giving examples. Refer to Exercise 2 on page 37 to help you.

Give an example of . . .
1. something you **don't often** do and something you **often** do.
2. an issue on which there is **agreement** in your group of friends.
3. something you **think of** as very important in life.
4. something you do that **shows or makes evident** your personality.
5. a **way that something is usually done** in society that you don't agree with.
6. how people **judge** you by your **way of speaking** or how you dress.
7. an area in your country that has very **different** pronunciation.
8. something that you feel is **essentially** dangerous.
9. a thing you own that is **better than** a friend's and something that is **not as good**.

Checkpoint 1 *Units 1–3*

1 Peer pressure

A Circle the correct auxiliary verb. Then complete the sentences with an appropriate adverb from the box. Sometimes there is more than one answer.

evidently	inevitably	ironically	presumably
ideally	invariably	potentially	supposedly

1. *A* My friend says she feels a lot of pressure from her parents, as I **am / do**, really. You know, to take all these extra classes, play an instrument, do a sport. I mean, do you?
   B Oh, yeah. _____, our parents never did all this stuff._____, they just want us to have more opportunities than they **did / are**. Well, I know my mom **is / does**.

2. *A* There's _____ all this bullying in schools. But you know, I've never experienced it. And I know my friends **haven't / have**, either. Have you?
   B Well, _____, a lot of it happens online. So _____, you don't see a lot of it. And our school has a strict policy on bullying, which a lot of schools **does / do**, I suppose.

3. *A* I don't really feel any strong peer pressure, though my best friend **does / is**. Do you?
   B Well, there's _____ some. My friends are all pretty confident, but I **do / am**, too.
   A That's good. I mean, _____, you want supportive friends. Well, I **have / do**. Some people are always worrying about what others think – as my friend **is / are**. And _____, that's bad for you.

About you **B** Pair work **Ask and answer the questions in Exercise A. Use *even so* and *even then*.**

"Actually, my parents don't pressure me at all. But even so, I still want to do well so I don't disappoint them. So yeah, I try to get good grades and everything."

2 Using technology

A Complete the comments using *to, not to, one,* or *ones*. Complete the underlined idioms.

1. There's software on my computer that I don't know how to use. And I'll probably never be able _____. I mean, I'd like _____, but . . . it's _____ me.
2. You know, my phone has all these useless functions. Like the most useless _____ for most people is the stock market report. I don't see _____ it.
3. I can't use the remote to record anything. Well, I could, but I prefer _____. I can't make heads _____ it. And I always mess up the satellite channels when I try _____.
4. We want to get one of those things that cleans your floors. Well, we were going _____. Oh, what are they called? It's on the tip _____ – those, um, robot things.
5. We never had calculators in my day. Not like the _____ they have now. You had to learn all your math tables by _____. You just had to come _____ with it all.
6. A gadget I can't live without? I don't know off the top _____. Nothing comes _____. I'd like to get a scooter, but I'll never be able _____. The _____ I want is so expensive.

About you **B** Pair work **Discuss the comments above. Are any true for you? Express a contrasting view with expressions like *Having said that, But then,* and *(But) then again*.**

"I have no idea how to use spreadsheets, but I'd like to. Having said that, I'm not sure I need to."

③ Bookworms

A Complete the *take* expressions in both interviews. Then in 1, write participle clauses using the verbs given. In 2, write *both . . . and, either . . . or, neither . . . nor,* or *not only . . . but also.*

1. _____ (grow up), I was always a bookworm. Reading always **took** _____ **over** everything else. If I **take** _____ of all my successes in life, it's probably due to reading. My mom has to **take** _____ **for** teaching us to read. _____ (not have) a career, she stayed home and **took** _____ **for** our education. She used to **take** _____ of how much we read every day. And _____ (live) near a library, we always **took** _____ of it. By the age of 10, I had a wide vocabulary, _____ (read) as much as I did. I often won the local spelling bees when I **took** _____ **in** them. Also, _____ (read) all the classics, I was good at general-knowledge quizzes, too. These days, _____ (work) as much as I do, I still like to **take** _____ **in** a book. It's a great way to escape from life!

2. I haven't read _____ a book _____ a magazine in months. Well, unless you **take into** _____ the books I read to my kids. They want me _____ to read every night _____ to tell them stories about when I was a kid. So I read and tell stories every single night. Sometimes I have _____ the time _____ the energy after a day's work. But even if you are busy, you can **take** _____ to help your kids read. Like now they have electronic readers for kids, which are great. They're _____ fun _____ educational. Kids can _____ read _____ listen at the same time. If they don't know how to say a word, they can _____ ask me _____ point to it and hear it. It's a great way to get kids to **take the** _____ and read.

About you

B **Pair work** Discuss the ideas above. Use expressions like *I do think* to add emphasis.

"I do think it's good for parents to read to their kids."

④ Solar power

A How many compound adjectives do you remember? Make a list. Then use them to discuss different technologies with a partner. Use *can't possibly* and *couldn't possibly.*

"I bet a lot of people couldn't possibly live without their labor-saving devices."

B Circle the correct options to complete the information from a website selling solar-power panels.

Worried about heating costs? **If so, / If not**, why not install solar panels in your home to reduce your energy bills? They are now **such / so** affordable that everyone can benefit from them. And what's just as important, **if not / if so** more important, is that it's **such / so** a clean source of power that you'll be helping to reduce pollution, too. With some systems, you can **even / so** get paid for the energy you produce. The panels **such / only** take a day to install. Your heating bills will fall **so / such** rapidly that you'll be pleased that you've made **so / such** a great investment.

C Rewrite the comments using the phrases in parentheses.

1. I know there are a lot of people for solar energy. (happy to pay)
2. Solar power is not a cheap technology, or so I heard. (to install)
3. The people have it, and they said it cost a fortune. (next door)
4. Solar panels change the look of your home. (on the roof)
5. It's definitely something because it saves money. (to be considered)
6. People will be disappointed. (hoping to get their money back quickly)
7. I also heard that some homes can't have it. (built before a certain date)

Amazing world

In Unit 4, you . . .

- talk about the natural world.
- use the future perfect and future perfect continuous.
- use prepositional expressions like *due to* and *far from*.
- add ideas with expressions like *what's more* and *not to mention*.
- use *in any case* to state conclusions or add information.

Lesson A *Animal behavior*

1 Vocabulary in context

A Which creatures (animals, birds, insects) do you find interesting? Lovable? Scary?

B 🔊 CD 2.02 **Listen and read the excerpts from a nature documentary. Complete the photo captions with these words: a. breeding, b. hibernation, c. migration.**

Animal Behavior

Every September, the arctic tern leaves its **breeding grounds** in the Arctic and heads south to the Antarctic. When it arrives back in the Northern Hemisphere the next summer, it will have flown on average 70,000 kilometers (almost 44,000 miles), which means by the end of its thirty-year lifespan, the arctic tern will have flown the equivalent of three round trips to the moon.

The longest _____

In order to **survive the winter months**, many small mammals **store food** before they **go into hibernation**. Groundhogs, however, **build up** their fat reserves and then **dig a burrow**, where they **hibernate** until spring. By the time the groundhog is in its deep sleep, its heartbeat will have dropped from 80 to 4 beats per minute and its body temperature will have fallen to only a few degrees above the outside temperature. By the time spring arrives, if it has not been **attacked** by **predators**, the groundhog will have been hibernating for almost six months.

Groundhog

After **mating**, a female emperor penguin **lays** a single **egg** before returning to the ocean, where she **feeds** and spends the winter. Penguins don't **build nests**. Instead, the male emperor balances the **egg** on his feet, huddling together with other males in the **colony** to **keep warm**. By the time the females return, these male penguins will have been protecting the eggs for 65 days. They won't have eaten for 115 days and will have lost nearly half of their body weight. Once the **eggs hatch**, the females **feed** and **raise the young**, while the males head to the ocean to feed.

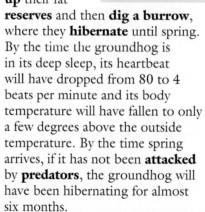

The _____ habits of emperor penguins

Word sort

C **Copy the chart and write the bold words and collocations in the documentary. Add others you want to learn. Which facts did you know? Which didn't you know? Tell a partner.**

survival (food and sleep)	having young	homes and groups
feed	lay an egg	

Vocabulary notebook

See page 51.

"I knew that penguins lay eggs, but I didn't know that they only lay single eggs."

② Grammar Talking about the past in the future

A Circle the correct verb form in the sentences. Use the documentary to help you. Then read the grammar chart.

1. By the time a penguin egg hatches, the emperor male **will have lost / will lose** half his body weight.
2. By the time spring arrives, the groundhog **will be hibernating / will have been hibernating** for six months.

Future perfect and future perfect continuous 🔽

Grammar extra
See page 150.

You can use future perfect forms for events that are in the past when you view them from the future.

Use the simple form to suggest that an event will be complete before a certain time.	*How far **will** the tern **have flown**?* *It **will have flown** 70,000 kilometers by the time it arrives back in the Arctic.*
Use the continuous form to suggest that an event will be in progress at a particular time in the future.	*How long **will** it **have been hibernating**?* *By then, it **will have been hibernating** for six months.*

Common errors

Do not use the future perfect in *if* or time clauses.
*When it **arrives** back, it will have flown 70,000 kilometers. If it **has not been attacked** . . .*
(NOT ~~When it will have arrived back . . .~~)
(NOT ~~If it will not have been attacked . . .~~)

B Complete these excerpts from the documentary. Use a future perfect form of the verbs given. Sometimes there is more than one correct answer.

1. It's winter in Canada and too cold for the monarch butterfly to feed and survive. So it starts its journey south, and by the time it arrives in Mexico, it __will have flown__ (fly) more than 4,000 kilometers (2,485 miles).
2. Giant pandas almost exclusively eat bamboo. At the end of the day, when it finishes feeding, it _____ (eat) 40 pounds of bamboo and it _____ (forage) for 16 hours.
3. These gray whales are leaving their feeding grounds in the cooler north to breed in the warmer south. When they reach Mexican waters, they _____ (swim) 160 kilometers (about 100 miles) a day for 8 to 10 weeks.
4. After mating at sea, female leatherback turtles come ashore. It's here that they dig a hole, and by the end of the night, they _____ (lay) 80 or more eggs.
5. Some bald eagle nests weigh more than a ton. But by the time they reach this weight, the bald eagles _____ (add) sticks to the nest for several years.
6. This female elephant is heavily pregnant. By the time she is ready to give birth, she _____ (carry) the baby for over 22 months.

C Pair work Take turns asking and answering questions about the facts in Exercise B. How much can you remember?

③ Viewpoint A wildlife presentation

Pair work Choose a creature that interests you, and prepare a presentation. Take turns giving your presentations to the class. What new facts do you learn?

"By the time this penguin reaches the open sea, it will have traveled more than 50 miles across the frozen ice."

Lesson B *Desert landscapes*

1 Grammar in context

A **What do you know about deserts? Make a class list.**

> The largest hot desert in the world is the Sahara.

B 🔊 CD 2.03 **Listen to extracts from a geography lecture about deserts. Which three slides does the professor refer to? Number the slides 1–3. There is one extra slide.**

1 "Deserts are, for lack of a better description, among some of the most fascinating and diverse landscapes on earth. They cover approximately one-third of the earth's land surface and stretch across all continents. But what is a desert? Most people think of them as hot, sandy places thanks to photographs of sand dunes in the Sahara desert. But in fact, only about 10 percent of the world's deserts are covered with sand dunes, including the Sahara. In line with USGS* definitions, a desert is an area that has less than 250 millimeters (10 inches) of rain per year. So Antarctica is a desert, apart from being one of the coldest places on earth. And in addition to cold deserts, there are also mountainous deserts.". . .

2 "Deserts are also commonly believed to be wastelands, on account of their harsh living conditions for wildlife and plants. But far from being barren, deserts are often very rich in plant life. Death Valley in the United States has over 1,000 plant species in spite of the fact that it has some of the most extreme conditions. And many species of animals can also survive in a desert climate by virtue of having adapted to the environment. Some, like the camel, can go up to eight days without drinking. As for smaller mammals, many have adapted by means of living underground or by hunting only at night.". . .

3 "One problem with deserts is that they expand and encroach on arable land. In fact, there is great concern in many parts of the world about this process, known as "desertification." Take for example the Gobi desert, which has spread, in part due to the fact that agricultural practices have changed from those in use prior to the 1950s. China was faced with increasing areas of arid land in place of its valuable grasslands. And, as a result of experiencing increasingly severe dust storms, China has started planting trees with the aim of halting desertification. By the end of the planned 70-year project, they will have planted more than 4,500 kilometers (approximately 2,800 miles) of trees."

*United States Geological Survey

C **Complete the sentences with information from the lecture. Then replace the underlined words with an expression from the lecture. In some, more than one expression can be used.**

1. Most people think of deserts as _____ places <u>because of</u> photographs of the Sahara.
2. <u>According to</u> USGS definitions, a desert is an area that _____.
3. <u>As well as</u> cold deserts, there are also _____ deserts.
4. Deserts are <u>not at all</u> barren and can be _____.
5. Many animals can _____ in a desert climate <u>through</u> their adaptation to the environment.
6. <u>As well as</u> larger animals like _____, there are many small mammals that live in the desert.
7. The Gobi desert has spread <u>because of</u> farming practices that didn't exist <u>before</u> _____.

2 Grammar Combining ideas

Figure
it out

A How does the professor express the ideas below in her lecture? Rewrite the sentences.

1. Deserts are believed to be wastelands because they have harsh living conditions.
2. Antarctica is a desert although it is one of the coldest places on earth.
3. Death Valley has over 1,000 plant species even though it has some of the most extreme conditions.

Prepositions 🔽

Grammar extra
See page 151.

Prepositions can be a word or a phrase. They can be followed by a noun phrase or an *-ing* form.
In line with *USGS definitions, a desert has less than 250 millimeters of rain **per** year.*
*A camel can go up to eight days **without drinking**.*

If a preposition starts an *-ing* clause, the verb has the same subject as the verb in the main clause.
As a result of *experiencing severe dust storms, China started planting trees.*

Some prepositions can be followed by *the fact that* + a clause. Use *the fact that* if the subject changes.
*Antarctica is a desert, apart from **the fact that it is** one of the coldest places on earth.*
*The Gobi desert has spread due **to the fact** that agricultural practices have changed.*

B Rewrite the sentences. Replace the underlined ideas with the expressions given, and make any other necessary changes. Some have more than one correct answer.

1. <u>It is not true that</u> deserts are unpopulated – they are home to almost one-sixth of the world's population. (Far from) Far from being unpopulated, deserts are home to . . .
2. Many animals burrow underground to avoid the harsh sun, <u>and</u> they are nocturnal. (In addition to)
3. Plants such as cacti <u>not only</u> have long roots, <u>but they</u> can store their own water. (Apart from)
4. Some desert plants survive for hundreds of years <u>because of</u> these kinds of adaptations. (thanks to)
5. Many desert areas are expanding <u>because</u> humans graze animals in semi-arid areas. (on account of)
6. Environmentalists are concerned <u>that</u> these farming practices have caused desertification. (about)

3 Listening The Antarctic

A 🔊 CD 2.04 Listen to Part 1 of an exclusive interview with an expert on the Antarctic. Complete the interviewer's notes. What else do you learn about the climate there?

Temperatures in degrees centigrade	Lowest ever	Summer	Winter	
	Minus _____	_____	_____	

B 🔊 CD 2.05 Guess which sentences are true. Then listen to Part 2 and circle T (True) or F (False).

1. Antarctica is different from everywhere else on the planet – even the Arctic. **T / F**
2. Antarctica has been cold for over 30 million years. **T / F**
3. Scientists study Antarctica to see if there could be life on other planets. **T / F**
4. Some fish and animals survive in Antarctica thanks to antifreezes in their bloodstream. **T / F**
5. On one of the expert's visits to Antarctica, 18 people shared one tomato. **T / F**

APART FROM THE FACT WE HAVE NO FOOD, WATER, OR SHELTER, THIS IS A GOOD WAY TO GET AWAY FROM IT ALL.

Lesson C *What's more . . .*

1 Conversation strategy Adding ideas

A Match words from a conversation with definitions. Guess the topic of the conversation.

1. overfishing _____
2. species _____
3. apathetic _____
4. subsidies _____

a. not interested and unconcerned
b. exploiting fish to the extent that they can't replace themselves
c. government money used to help projects that are beneficial to the public
d. a class or group of individuals that are related to one another

B ◀))CD 2.06 Listen to a seminar discussion. What factors contributed to the problem of overfishing?

Overfishing

Julio	Well, the biggest issue seems to have been overfishing. Something like three-quarters of the world's fish species have been completely exploited. It's only a matter of time before the fishing industry collapses completely.
Maria	Not to mention all the other industries that depend on it. So who or what's responsible for it all?
Julio	Well, the international community has been increasing fishing capacity, for one thing . . .
Ulma	And additionally, governments give subsidies, so large-scale fishing operations took over. And big commercial fleets are much more efficient at finding fish as well.
Maria	And on top of that, I guess consumers got used to having a wide variety of fish available, so the demand was there. Also, fish became much more affordable.
Ulma	What's more, the public has, to a large extent, been pretty apathetic. And then industry has been slow to respond to concerns. In any case, apathy has contributed to the problem.

C **Notice** how the students use expressions like these to add and focus on a new idea. Find the ones they use.

Also, . . .	*Additionally, . . .*
And then . . .	*In addition, . . .*
. . . as well	*What's more, . . .*
. . . not to mention . . .	*On top of that, . . .*

D ◀))CD 2.07 Listen to more of the discussion. Write the missing expressions. Then practice.

Julio True. And of course another problem is all the pollution that runs into the oceans.

Maria Yeah, _____ the amount of trash that's dumped in them. Apparently, there's a huge trash pile in the middle of the Pacific that you can see from space. _____, whales and dolphins can eat that stuff.

Ulma And _____, it's irresponsible, dumping waste where we get our food.

Maria _____, all that pollution is changing the chemistry of the ocean, which affects the lifecycle of fish. _____, it has an impact on shellfish. Coral _____.

Ulma _____ there's the issue of meltwater from the ice caps caused by rising temperatures.

Julio There's a lot of debate about that, but in any event, it's impacting the ocean.

2 Strategy plus *In any case, in any event*

CD 2.08 You can use *in any case* to add more information to make an argument stronger or clearer.

You can also use *in any case* or *in any event* when you reach a conclusion that you think is the only possible one.

In any case, apathy has contributed to the problem.

In any event, it's impacting the ocean.

In conversation . . .

In any case is more frequent.

| In any case | ■ ■ ■ ■ |
| In any event | ■ |

CD 2.09 **Find two appropriate conclusions for each conversation. Write the letters a–f. Then listen and check your answers. Practice with a partner.**

1. **A** It seems like global warming is still a controversial issue. But don't scientists all agree that temperatures are rising? And what's more, that it affects the oceans with sea levels rising?

   B I suppose the controversy is about what's *causing* the increase in temperatures. _____ _____

2. **A** You know what's interesting to me? We really don't know that much about the oceans.

   B Yeah, though they're making new discoveries all the time.

   A Yeah, no. They definitely know more now than, say, 20 years ago. _____ _____

3. **A** There are some amazing creatures in the ocean, like jellyfish that glow in the dark.

   B I know. Not to mention the ones that can kill you, like the box jellyfish.

   A Actually, there are a lot of poisonous creatures in the ocean. Like, well, I can't think. _____ _____

---

a. In any event, there's definitely evidence that the atmosphere is getting warmer.
b. But in any event, there are lots of species we haven't discovered yet.
c. But in any event, there are a lot of deadly things in there.
d. In any case, you have to be careful in some places when you go swimming.
e. In any case, there's no doubt that the climate is changing.
f. Though we haven't made it to the bottom. In any event, we're a long way from fully exploring it.

---

3 Strategies The human impact on nature

About you

A Add an idea to each comment below. Include an expression from Exercise 1C.

1. I think humans do a lot to protect nature and wildlife. For example, if we didn't have zoos, we probably wouldn't be able to preserve some species. *What's more, . . .*

2. Well, one of the ways we impact nature is by building homes on sensitive areas, like wetlands. That forces the wildlife out of their natural habitats.

3. I think in many ways we've forgotten how to live with nature. You know, by the time they graduate from high school, one in three kids won't have been on a hike or seen a forest.

B Pair work Discuss the ideas in Exercise A. Add more ideas to each conversation, and draw conclusions using *in any case* or *in any event*.

A *I'm not so sure it's good to keep animals in zoos.*

B *Yeah, but zoos have programs to help endangered species. And on top of that, . . .*

Speaking naturally

See page 139.

Lesson D *Biomimicry*

1 Reading

A **Prepare** Look at the title of the article and the photos. What do you think *biomimicry* is?

B ⬇ **Read for main ideas** Read the article. What inventions has nature inspired?

How NATURE *inspires* SCIENCE —a look at some notable inventions

By the end of this century, as one looks back on the multitude of achievements, one may be surprised to find that a number of technological and scientific advances will be based upon observations in nature, as opposed to accidental discovery or a result of trial and error in a laboratory.

A relatively new field of research, called biomimicry, is providing significant insights and solutions for scientists and inventors in areas from medicine and technology to transportation and construction.

Using nature to solve design problems is not new. The Wright brothers observed the flight of birds while building their plane. However, in recent years, biomimicry has become an established discipline among scientists, and one that is generating some remarkable inventions. Here are some that in the not-too-distant future will have had a considerable impact on our lives.

1. SHARKSKIN A University of Florida engineering professor noticed that sharkskin remains amazingly clean and that plants and sea animals have difficulty adhering to it. He created a pattern that mimics the shark's tiny scales. Apart from the fact that it was up to 85 percent cleaner than smooth surfaces, it also prevented harmful bacteria from sticking to it.

The result was a material that can be used for hospital tray tables and bed rails, as well as other areas where there is a high risk of passing on infections. In several years, it is likely that Professor Brennan's invention will have had demonstrable benefits in terms of reducing hospital-acquired infections, and it will undoubtedly have saved thousands of lives.

2. TERMITE MOUNDS A Zimbabwean architect was faced with the difficult task of finding a workable solution to the problem of designing a new building that would stay cool even without air conditioning. Looking for an affordable alternative, he found his inspiration in African termite mounds. He noticed that the mounds termites build catch air at the base and circulate it up through their mud home. As a result of replicating the system in his building, he reduced energy costs by a measurable amount. His building uses one-tenth of the energy of similar buildings and shows that there is a viable alternative to using air-conditioning systems.

3. GECKO FEET For human beings, walking up walls is the stuff of movies – unimaginable in real life. Or is it? Inspired by the millions of tiny hairs on gecko feet, scientists are working hard to produce a "gecko tape" to use on the soles of footwear. The tape mimics the hairs on the gecko's feet and is a powerful and dependable adhesive. Scientists hope to have a product for space stations and underwater applications in the near future. And who knows? By the end of the century, they may have created a boot that enables us all to climb buildings like Spiderman. Imagine how profitable that would be!

C React Pair work **Look back at the article. Discuss the questions with a partner.**

- What do you think about biomimicry as a science?
- Which of the inventions in the article do you think is most exciting? Most valuable? Why?
- What other applications can you think of for the sharkskin material? How about for the gecko tape?

❷ Focus on vocabulary Suffixes with *-able*

A **Read the article again. Circle the words that end in *-able*. Then replace the words in bold with a word from the article ending in *-able* that has a similar meaning.**

remarkable

1. Studying nature has led human beings to some **amazing** scientific inventions. ____
2. A **large** number of inventions initially failed. ____
3. People using biomimicry in the past is **hard to imagine**. ____
4. When it comes to preventing harmful bacteria from sticking to it, the sharkskin material is very **reliable**. ____
5. The sharkskin material has had a **clear** effect on hospital infection rates. (2 words) ____
6. One of the most **noteworthy** inventions is a fabric that mimics a butterfly's shiny wings. ____
7. The architect came up with a **practical** plan for keeping buildings cool. (2 words) ____
8. The gecko tape is not likely to be a **feasible** or **money-making** invention. (2 words) ____
9. Many of the inventions are not **expensive to produce**. ____

B **Do the statements above agree with the information in the article? Write Y (Yes), N (No), or NG (Information not given).**

C Pair work **Share what you learned about biomimicry using the *-able* words in Exercise A.**

❸ Listening and speaking The genius of the natural world

A 🔊 CD 2.10 **Listen to a presentation about the applications of biomimicry. Match the examples from nature that the presenter talks about to the real-world problems below. Number the pictures 1–4.**

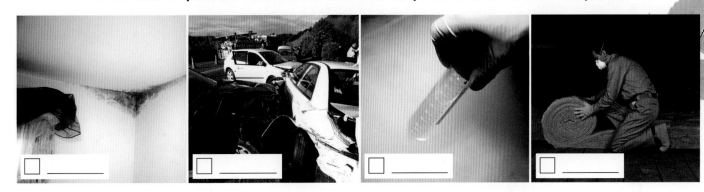

B 🔊 CD 2.11 **Listen again. Have the problems already been solved? Write Y (Yes) or N (No) on each picture above.**

About you

C Group work **Look back at the examples in the lesson. How else could the ideas be applied to real-world problems? What other amazing things are in nature? What problems could they solve?**

"Maybe in the future scientists will have developed a material that cleans itself, like that flower. If they used it on cars, you would never have to clean your car."

Writing *Does it matter?*

In this lesson, you . . .
- write a persuasive essay.
- use academic prepositions and *one*.
- avoid errors with *upon*.

Task   **Write an essay.**
The World Animal Foundation estimates that by 2025 as many as one-fifth of all animal species may well have become extinct. Does this matter?

A **Look at a model** Read the introductions to two essays that answer the question above. What view does each one take? What arguments does each one make?

1. The estimate that 20 percent of animal species may disappear within a short time is alarming. The loss of any species matters because it can upset the balance of nature. Each organism depends upon another to survive, and the disappearance of one species may have unknown consequences for another. The earth maintains a delicate balance, which relies upon the complex interaction of plant and animal species. We do not always see what is happening beneath the surface. The loss of species may be a warning that we are destroying our planet and therefore our very existence.

2. The claim that a large proportion of animal species is at risk of dying out is a subject of great debate within the academic community and amongst scientists in particular. One might think that this is a major problem and that one's worst fears for the earth will materialize. However, one can equally argue that species have become extinct throughout the history of this planet. In terms of our survival, however, this has not proved critical. Therefore, the extinction of species, far from being a disaster, can simply be considered part of the normal evolutionary process.

Question-based essays

Show you understand the question by restating it in your own words. Give your opinion in your introduction and conclusion.

B **Focus on language** Read the chart. Then underline the examples of formal prepositions and circle examples of *one* for general statements in Exercise A.

Prepositions in academic writing; *one* for general statements

Some prepositions and prepositional expressions can make your writing sound more formal, e.g., *amongst, beneath, throughout, upon, within, in terms of.*
Each organism depends **upon** *another.*
It is a subject of debate **within** *the academic community and* **amongst** *scientists. . . .*
In terms of *our survival, this has not proved critical.*

One / one's can refer to "people in general" or "you / your." You can use it to give opinions.
One *might think this is a major problem and that* **one's** *worst fears will materialize.*

C Complete the sentences with prepositions. Then rewrite them using *one / one's.*

1. A healthy environment is dependent _____ how well people manage their resources.
2. We should do everything _____ our power to protect these species.
3. There are complex systems _____ the earth's surface that people do not fully understand.
4. I wonder how the leopard and rhino, which are _____ the most threatened species, can survive.
5. The effects _____ tourism will be so huge _____ the world that we cannot imagine them.

D **Write and check** Write an essay to answer the question in the task above. Then check for errors.

Common errors

Do not overuse *upon*. Use it after *depend, rely, agree. Look upon* means "to think about in a certain way," not "look at."
Let us look at this subject in more detail. (NOT. . . ~~look upon~~ . . .)

Vocabulary notebook *Golden eggs*

hibernate
Animals hibernate or sleep in the winter.
Computers hibernate when they're running but are not being used.

A   Complete each sentence with a word in the box. Sometimes you'll use a word twice.

breed	colony	grounds	lays	migration	predator
burrow	feed and raise	~~hatch~~	mate	nest	young

1. 🦌   When eggs hatch ____, baby birds, fish, or insects come out.
   🚶   If you plan something in secret, you hatch ____ **a plan**.

2. 🦌   Animals that _____ for life stay together forever.
   🚶   A presidential candidate chooses **a running** _____, who becomes vice president if elected.

3. 🦌   In academic writing, the offspring, or babies, of animals are called their _____.
   🚶   You can also use the expression **the** _____ to mean all young people.

4. 🦌   A _____ is a group of birds or animals.
   🚶   It can also be a country that is governed by a more powerful country.

5. 🦌   A _____ is a place where most birds have their young.
   🚶   **A** _____ **egg** is a sum of money you save for a special purpose.

6. 🦌   When animals _____, they have young. A specific type of animal is also called a _____.
   🚶   If you say someone or something is part of **a dying** _____, it means there aren't many left.

7. 🦌   Breeding, feeding, fishing, or hunting _____ are places where these activities take place.
   🚶   To have _____ for something means to have reasons for it, such as _____ **for divorce**.

8. 🦌   To _____ means to dig into something and a _____ can be the hole where an animal lives.
   🚶   A person can also _____ into something. It means he or she investigates it.

9. 🦌   The movement of birds, animals, or people is called _____.
   🚶   From that word, we get other words like *immigrant, emigrate*, etc.

10. 🦌   A bird, a fish, or an insect _____ an egg.
    🚶   Someone that makes a lot of money for others is called **the goose that** _____ **the golden egg**.

11. 🦌   In biology, a _____ is an animal that attacks and eats other animals.
    🚶   In business, it's a company that tries to buy or take over other companies.

12. 🦌🚶   Both animals and humans have to _____ their families.

B   Word builder   Here are some more idioms with animals. Find out their meaning.

be a guinea pig	beat a dead horse	clam up	have ants in your pants
be in the doghouse	be a fish out of water	get off your high horse	have butterflies in your stomach

C   🔍 Focus on vocabulary   Can you think of a thing or person for each expression? See Exercise 2A, page 49.

1. a **remarkable** animal that has **considerable** intelligence _____
2. a **dependable** source of information or a **notable** authority on the natural world _____
3. something you've learned about nature that previously was **unimaginable** to you _____
4. a **viable** or workable alternative to fossil fuels _____
5. an **affordable** way to experience nature _____
6. a **profitable** product with **measurable** results that resulted from replicating nature _____

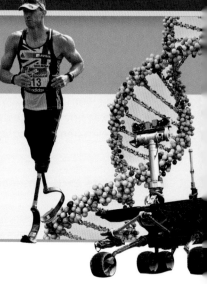

Progress

In Unit 5, you . . .

- talk about inventions, progress, and human achievements.
- use adverbs with continuous and perfect passives.
- use modal verbs with passive forms.
- make a point with expressions like *I look at it this way*.
- use expressions like *absolutely not* to make responses stronger.

Lesson A *Out with the old*

1 Vocabulary in context

A What are some common gadgets people use these days? Why are they useful? Make a list.

B ◀)) CD 2.12 Read the article from a hiker's blog. Which items in the photos are mentioned?

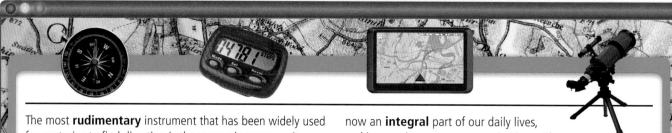

The most **rudimentary** instrument that has been widely used for centuries to find direction is the magnetic compass. It was probably invented by the Chinese and was based on the metal lodestone, which had long been admired for its ability to point toward north. **Countless** lives have undoubtedly been saved over the centuries on land and at sea thanks to the compass, which functions equally well in daylight, darkness, or thick fog. Even in our electronic age, magnetic compasses are still being made, and their basic design has not changed for centuries. They are **compact**, **functional**, and **portable**.

Toward the end of the twentieth century, alternatives to the compass were being intensively developed, and **significant** advances were made – thanks to satellite technology. GPS* is

now an **integral** part of our daily lives, making moving maps, communicating with smartphones, and offering handheld location devices. It had originally been developed for military purposes, but it soon became part of everyday technology, and **innovative** ways to use GPS – from tracking migrating birds to helping golfers judge their shots – are continually being found through ongoing research. The system has already been incorporated into aircraft and ship design as **standard**, and many other technologies also derive considerable benefit from it.

But what about the **humble** compass? Is it **obsolete** now? Has it been completely forgotten? We'd like to hear your views.

*Global Positioning System

C Find more formal adjectives in the blog with similar meanings to the words in the chart.

Vocabulary notebook
See page 61.

easy-to-carry	portable	creative		useful	
important		out-of-date		usual	
modest		basic		"a lot of"	
necessary		small			

About you

D Pair work Take turns using the adjectives you found to talk about everyday objects you own.

"My cell phone is becoming a bit obsolete. It's one of those older flip-phones, but it's functional."

2 Grammar Information focus 1

Figure
it out

A **Write these sentences in the passive. Find similar sentences in the blog to help you, and underline them. Then read the grammar chart.**

1. They are continually finding new applications for GPS.
2. All serious hikers were still using the compass until very recently.
3. Has GPS completely replaced the compass?
4. The Chinese had originally developed the compass.

Adverbs within continuous and perfect passive verbs ⬇

Grammar extra
See page 152.

The most common position for adverbs is after the first auxiliary verb (*am / is / are / was / were; has / have / had*). Time and attitude adverbs, e.g., *already, always, continually, currently, finally, just, long, since, still; fortunately, sadly*, etc., and the adverbs *also, probably, apparently, reportedly* are usually in this position.
*Compasses **are still being made**. They **were continually being improved** in the last century.
GPS **has already been incorporated** into aircraft. It **had originally been developed** for military use.*

Adverbs that say "how" and "how much" or that describe the participle often go before the participle, e.g., *badly, intensively, seriously, largely, greatly, widely, completely*.
*Alternatives to the compass **were being intensively developed**. It **has been widely used**.*

Some adverbs can go in both positions, e.g., *increasingly, previously, largely, originally, initially, continually, generally*.
*GPS **is increasingly being used** . . . OR GPS **is being increasingly used** . . .
It **has previously been used** . . . OR It **has been previously used** . . .*

B **Look at these examples of progress. Rewrite the underlined parts of the sentences in the passive. Add the adverbs given — sometimes there are two — and use *by* if necessary.**

1. Do you know how memory foam was developed? Well, NASA had developed the material (originally) to improve the safety of aircraft cushions. And now, of course, they are incorporating memory foam (generally) into a whole range of everyday products, like memory-foam beds, which they are using (increasingly) in hospitals. They have saved countless lives (apparently) because foam beds reduce pressure sores when patients are bedridden for long periods of time. And they have improved the lives of these patients (fortunately, greatly).

2. It's interesting when you think about a lot of the things we use in everyday life. Inventors had devised many of them (initially) for other purposes. While they were developing these products (still), no one really thought about spin-offs. Take, for example, smoke detectors. They had produced them (apparently) in the 1970s to help detect toxic gases in the space station. Now they are installing them (increasingly) as standard in newly built homes all over the world.

3. The abacus is a tool that we have used (long) for counting and in fact even today, they are using abacuses (currently) in many parts of the world. People think that the Chinese had invented them (originally). And I guess the ones that we are familiar with today were. But they had constructed similar counting boards (already) in Roman times, and they had used them (reportedly, widely) across Europe. Although calculators have overtaken the abacus (largely), it's interesting that they have not made it obsolete (completely).

About
you

C **Pair work** **Read the information again. Then take turns retelling the information. What other examples of progress can you think of?**

Lesson B *What drives us?*

1 Grammar in context

A One kind of progress is when people push the limits of what the human body can do. Why do you think people take on challenges like running marathons or walking across deserts?

"I guess people like to test their limits." "Well, people also do these things to raise funds for charity."

B 🔊 CD 2.13 Listen. What dangers did Beaumont face on his expedition?

AN AMAZING ACHIEVEMENT

In 2008, a 25-year-old Scottish man, Mark Beaumont, set a new record by cycling around the world in 195 days. Although it was an incredible feat, things did not always go smoothly. Pedaling across difficult terrain was often extremely painful. On top of that, his wallet and camera were stolen, and at one point he could easily have been killed in the United States when a motorist drove through a red light. In fact, the whole trip might well have been cut short at several points, owing to sickness, flooded roads, and mechanical problems. Sometimes, when traveling through particularly dangerous regions, he was made to sleep in grim police cells for his own protection.

Beaumont was lucky. He put his life in danger and survived. Others who pursued incredible feats, like climbing Mt. Everest, have died in their attempts. Indeed, the majority of people who have died on Everest were young people with families and partners, so what drove them? They must have known the dangers, so why did they consciously choose to put themselves in harm's way? Some would argue that

adventurers like these should not have been permitted to attempt such dangerous expeditions. After all, there are easier – and safer – ways to challenge yourself, raise money for charity, or break world records. Did Mark Beaumont feel that he might not have been given another opportunity to make his mark on the world and pursue his ambition if he hadn't taken this chance?

About you

C Pair work **Answer the questions.**

1. What drives people like Mark Beaumont?
2. What do you think of people who attempt feats like this? Are they adventurous, or reckless and irresponsible?
3. What does *make your mark on the world* mean? How do other people make their marks on the world?
4. If you had an opportunity to follow a dream, what would you do?
5. Would you ever follow a dream that put you in harm's way?

2 Grammar Information focus 2

Figure it out

A Rewrite the sentences in the passive, starting with the words given. Use similar sentences in the article to help you. Then read the grammar chart.

1. Something might well have injured Beaumont. *Beaumont . . .*
2. Something could easily have cut the trip short. *The trip . . .*
3. They shouldn't have allowed him to do it. *He . . .*

Grammar extra
See page 153.

Past modals and the passive; the verb *make* in the passive ⬇

Active sentences	Passive sentences
A motorist **could** easily **have killed** him.	He **could** easily **have been killed** (**by** a motorist).
Sickness **might** well **have cut short** the trip.	The trip might well **have been cut short** (**by** sickness).
They **shouldn't have permitted** him to do it.	He **shouldn't have been permitted** to do it.
They **ought (not) to have allowed** it.	It **ought (not) to have been allowed**.

The verb *make* has a different pattern in the active and passive when it is followed by a verb.
Active: *They made him **sleep** in police cells.*   **Passive:** *He was made **to sleep** in police cells.*

B Look at more feats and things people might have said *beforehand*. Rewrite the sentences as what people might have thought *afterward*. Add the adverbs, where given.

1. **Kristen Ulmer, an extreme skier, skied down the face of Grand Teton, U.S., in 1997.**
   a. An avalanche could bury her alive. *She could easily have been buried alive by an avalanche*. (easily)
   b. They might postpone her attempt due to bad weather. *Her attempt* _____. (well)
   c. They shouldn't encourage her to do it. *She* _____.
2. **Philippe Petit walked a tightrope between the twin towers in New York City in 1974.**
   a. The wind could blow him off. *He* _____. (easily)
   b. They should make him wear a safety harness. *He* _____. (also)
   c. They should never allow him to do it. *He* _____.
3. **Alain Robert got arrested in 2010 after climbing the Lumiere skyscraper in Sydney.**
   a. They shouldn't arrest him, and they shouldn't throw him in jail, either. *He* _____.
   b. He could kill someone if he falls. *Someone* _____. (well)
   c. A company might sponsor him for advertising. They shouldn't give his stunt so much press.
      He _____. *His stunt* _____.

C Pair work Discuss the feats in this lesson. What else might have happened to the people?

3 Listening *Kristen Ulmer on extreme skiing*

A ◀ඖ CD 2.14 Listen to a reporter talk about her recent meeting with Kristen Ulmer. Number the topics in the order the speaker mentions them (1–5). There is one topic the interviewer doesn't mention.

☐ childhood   ☐ college   ☐ giving up extreme skiing   ☐ marriage   ☐ travel   ☐ film career

B ◀ඖ CD 2.15 Listen again. Circle a, b, or c to complete the sentences.

1. Kristen started doing dangerous skiing   a) as a child.   b) in college.   c) for movies.
2. As a child, she   a) was made to ski.   b) was an expert skier.   c) enjoyed skiing.
3. Her rule in Asia was   a) never discuss skiing.   b) tell everyone about skiing.   c) look good.
4. In Asia, she might have   a) gotten sick.   b) lost her life.   c) killed someone by accident.
5. While she was filming, she was   a) not well known.   b) almost killed.   c) badly paid.
6. Now she wants to   a) transform her performance.   b) keep filming.   c) coach other athletes.

About you

C Pair work Would you ever do the kinds of things Kristen has done?

Lesson C *Just think . . .*

1 Conversation strategy Making a point

A How has humanity progressed in the last 100 years? Share ideas with the class.

B 🔊 CD 2.16 Listen. What does Alba think about space exploration? How about Jack?

Alba	I see another rocket's just been launched. All this money that's being wasted on going into space. Just think what could have been done with those billions of dollars!
Jack	Yes, . . . but one way to look at it is that all kinds of things have been discovered through space exploration.
Alba	Like what?
Jack	Well, satellite technology, more accurate weather forecasting – they've both come from space programs. And you can't say that we don't need those things.
Alba	Absolutely not. But I look at it this way: there are other things we could spend the money on. Don't you think it would have been better spent on things like schools?
Jack	Not necessarily. But anyway, things like the space program encourage kids to go into science and engineering. It makes it exciting. I mean, life would be very limited if we never looked beyond our immediate environment.
Alba	Well, let me put it another way: maybe we *should* explore space but not till we've made our own world a better place.
Jack	Maybe. Maybe not.

C **Notice** how Alba and Jack use expressions like these to make their points. Find the expressions they use in the conversation.

(Let's) put it this way: . . .	**One way to look at it is (that) . . .**
To put it another way: . . .	
Let me put it another way: . . .	**Just think.**
(I) look at it this way: . . .	**(Just) think about it.**

D 🔊 CD 2.17 Listen to the rest of Alba and Jack's conversation. Write the expressions you hear.

Alba Well, _____ what could have been done to research alternative fuels, for example, if we'd had all those billions of dollars. _____: there are better things to spend money on.

Jack Yeah, possibly. But _____: Plenty of countries don't have space programs, but they don't necessarily spend their money on better things.

Alba I'm not sure that's entirely true. I mean, some countries are way ahead in terms of using alternative energies. I mean, _____: that in itself does more for the planet.

Jack Well, _____ not only have better technologies been developed, but also new medicines are being discovered. _____ – all that research that's done in space.

About you **E** **Pair work** Practice the whole conversation. Whose opinions do you agree with?

2 Strategy plus *Absolutely (not), not necessarily*

CD 2.18 You can use **Absolutely (not)** or **Definitely (not)** to make a *yes* (or *no*) response stronger.

Use **Probably (not)** and **Maybe (not)** if you do not want to commit strongly to a response.

If you want to say something is not completely or always true, you can say **Not necessarily**.

> You can't say we don't need those things.

> Absolutely not.

About you

Match the statements with the responses. Write the letters a–e. Then practice with a partner. Practice again, giving your own responses.

1. Space exploration is certainly not a waste of money or a waste of time, as some people say. _____
2. Do you think we'll ever discover life on other planets? _____
3. Don't you think we should send humans to Mars, no matter how much it costs? _____
4. Another thing about space programs is they promote international cooperation, which is good. _____
5. Life wouldn't be as exciting if we didn't explore space. _____

a. Probably not. Though there are still plenty of things to explore on earth.
b. Absolutely not. For every dollar spent on space, $8 of economic benefit has reportedly been generated.
c. Definitely. I mean, they've successfully landed a spacecraft there, so why not a human.
d. Not necessarily. I mean, if you want to keep your technology a secret, then it's not good.
e. Maybe. Maybe not. But imagine if we did find other life forms. There'd be a lot of issues to consider.

3 Listening and strategies *What's the point of research?*

A **CD 2.19** **Listen to a conversation. What applications of research do they mention? Check (✓) the topics. There are two extra topics.**

☐ education ☐ social studies ☐ agriculture ☐ climate ☐ medicine

B **CD 2.20** **Listen again. What specific research do the speakers mention? Complete the chart.**

Research questions:	Research question:
How far can crickets _____ ?	How do snails _____ ?
How much _____ do they do?	**Possible applications of research:**
Possible application of research:	To improve _____
To ensure _____	To help people after _____

About you

C **Pair work** **Discuss these questions. Give examples or reasons to support your ideas.**

- What research has contributed most to society in the last 10 years?
- Which areas deserve more research? What outcomes would you like to see?
- What subjects do you feel should not be researched? Why?
- Who should pay for research?

Speaking naturally

See page 140.

> DO YOU THINK I COULD BE THE FIRST PERSON TO DISCOVER AN ALIEN LIFE FORM?

> ABSOLUTELY. WHY DON'T YOU START BY LOOKING IN YOUR ROOM?

Lesson D *Smart ideas*

1 Reading

A **Prepare** Scan the article. What is the focus of the article? Check (✓) one topic.

☐ How to become an inventor   ☐ How different inventions come about
☐ How to market a new invention   ☐ Why some inventions fail

B ⬇ **Read for main ideas** Read the article. Where do these sentences fit in the article? Write the correct letters in the spaces.

   a. There is seemingly no end to the number of inventions we can look forward to in the future.
   b. Necessity is the mother of invention – or so the saying goes.
   c. The smartphone app is another good example.
   d. It is generally believed that inventions are the result of focused effort by inventors seeking specific solutions to specific problems.
   e. Clearly, many inventions have come about from a mix of astute observation and inspired thinking.
   f. In reality, most people probably will never invent something as world-changing as the steam engine.

INVENTION: INSPIRED THINKING OR ACCIDENTAL DISCOVERY?

❶ "To invent, you need a good imagination and a pile of junk," or so Thomas Edison, one of the world's most famous inventors, is quoted as saying. Yet how do successful inventions come about? How have inventions been achieved in the past? What makes something a brilliant invention?

❷ _____ Brilliance, however, is not enough, and obviously, hard work and persistence need to follow. James Dyson noticed his vacuum cleaner would frequently clog up and stop picking up dirt. On a visit to a local factory, he observed how dust was removed from the air by large industrial cyclones, and it inspired him to try the same principles on a smaller scale in a vacuum cleaner. He developed over 5,000 prototype designs before finally succeeding with his invention: the first cyclonic bagless vacuum cleaner.

❸ _____ Surprisingly, many innovations that have enhanced the efficiency, comfort, and convenience of everyday life have often been discovered by accident. The steam engine, superglue, artificial sweeteners, and synthetic dyes, to name but a few, all came about when their inventors' minds were being applied to quite different problems. If Dr. Percy Spencer had not noticed that a candy bar had melted in his pocket as he was testing microwave radiation for use in radar, the microwave oven may never have been invented.

❹ _____ No invention is more true of this proverb than the ice-cream cone. When an ice-cream seller ran out of plates on which to serve his ice cream, he used a rolled-up waffle instead. The ice-cream cone had inadvertently been created, and with great success.

❺ _____ Few will have the skills to engineer something like a vacuum cleaner or microwave oven. Even so, when you consider some of the everyday things that have been developed, it's clear that inventions do not have to be complex or life-changing to be hugely successful and incredibly marketable. Tags that label your electrical cords, silly bands for kids, or suitcases with wheels are all examples of inventions that gained huge popularity and left people wondering, "Why didn't I think of that?"

❻ _____ By 2011, there were already more than half a million of them, many of which were incredibly simple and straightforward, and many of which had actually been invented by ordinary people and even children. One, nine-year-old Ding Wen from Singapore, invented a drawing app that allows users to draw with their fingers across a touch screen and then shake the device to clear the screen. Another was 14-year-old Robert Nay, an eighth grader from Utah, whose Bubble Ball physics game had reportedly been downloaded more than two million times within two weeks of its launch. What these apps had in common was originality, simplicity, ease of use, and wide demographic appeal.

❼ Nevertheless, no matter how inventions come about, whether by sheer brilliance or by a stroke of luck, one thing is clear. _____ What's more, our willingness to adopt them, whether for their effectiveness or simply for our own amusement, means that there will be always be a ready market.

Reading tip
Writers sometimes use a quotation from a famous person or a saying to start and set the theme of an article.

2 Focus on vocabulary Adjectives into nouns

A Complete the sentences below with the noun form of the words given. Use the article to help you. Then match the pictures with the sentences. Write the letters a–d.

Tip

Words with the suffixes *-ance*, *-ence*, *-ency*, *-ity*, *-ness*, and *-ment* are often nouns.

a. a bladeless fan

b. a doodling app

c. mop slippers

d. sticky notes

☐ 1. With the _____ (willing) of millions to download these, their _____ (popular) is clear. What apps have you downloaded? How useful are they?

☐ 2. The _____ (convenient) of this invention is evident, and it certainly wins a prize for _____ (original). It also provides plenty of _____ (amuse). But would you really buy something like this?

☐ 3. The sheer _____ (brilliant) of this invention is clear, and the _____ (simple) of its design is appealing. It also improves the _____ (comfortable) of our everyday lives. What other inventions have made life better?

☐ 4. This simple invention certainly improved the _____ (efficient) of many people's working lives. It's _____ of use (easy) and _____ (effective) are part of its winning formula. What other inventions have contributed to a better workplace?

B Pair work Discuss the questions above. Think of as many ideas as you can.

3 Viewpoint The best ideas . . .

Pair work Think of ideas for each description below and see if you agree on any of them. Discuss why you made your choices and how the inventions have impacted people's lives.

Think of . . .

- an invention that improves efficiency in travel.
- an invention that has changed the world.
- an app that is really convenient to have.
- a device that you couldn't live without.
- a simple invention that you wish you had thought of.
- an invention that you'd like to see.
- an app that you would like to develop.

"I guess high-speed rail has really improved the efficiency in travel. The convenience of jumping on a train rather than going to the airport is one reason high-speed trains are so widely used."

In conversation . . .

You can use *I guess*, *I think*, or *I suppose* to sound less direct or assertive.

Writing *It is often said . . .*

In this lesson, you . . .
- compare and contrast arguments.
- use *it* clauses + passive.
- avoid errors with *affect* and *effect*.

Task Write an opinion essay.
Some people argue that technological progress is always positive. Others dispute this. What is your view and why?

A Look at a model Look at the introduction to an essay responding to the question above. Underline the thesis statement. Circle the topics that the student will discuss in the essay.

It is often said that technological progress is important and can only have positive or beneficial effects on our lives. Progress, it is argued, especially in the fields of medicine, communications, and infrastructure, has improved the quality of life for human beings. In contrast, others disagree, saying that progress mostly has a negative impact, in particular on the environment. While progress can have both positive and negative effects, I would argue that the positive effects of progress outweigh the negative.

To compare opinions, include:

Introduction – outline the issues and give your view

Opinion 1 with reasons and examples

Opinion 2 with reasons and examples

Conclusion – summarize the arguments and restate your view

B Focus on language Read the chart. Then rewrite the underlined parts of the sentences below using *it* clauses and the adverbs given.

it clauses with the passive in academic writing ⬇

You can use *it* clauses with the passive to introduce what people say or think. Adverbs like *often, generally, well, widely* emphasize what is commonly said.
It is often said that technological progress is important.
It is generally accepted . . . / ***widely recognized*** . . . / ***well known*** . . .
It has also been reported / shown / suggested that . . .

Useful expressions

while / whereas
although
However, . . .
In contrast, . . .
Nevertheless, . . .
On the one / other hand, . . .

1. <u>People accept</u> that progress is inevitable, but we should examine this carefully. (generally)
2. <u>People recognize</u> that progress in industry can cause pollution. (widely) On the other hand, people <u>understand</u> that some industries are making efforts to become "greener." (also)
3. <u>Scientists have shown</u> that life expectancy is increasing as a result of medical advances, although <u>some people suggest</u> that this is only the case in wealthier societies. (also)
4. <u>People know</u> that progress in communications leads to a better-functioning society. (well) Nevertheless, <u>they recognize</u> that privacy and security issues are a growing problem. (widely)
5. <u>People have suggested</u> that technological progress often comes out of military programs. However, <u>people believe</u> that developments like the Internet benefit everyone. (generally)
6. <u>People have reported</u> that so-called industrial progress adversely affects the poor. In contrast, <u>people say</u> that the wealthy become wealthier. (often)

C Write and check Now write your own opinion essay for the question. Then check for errors. Read a classmate's essay. Do you share the same views?

Common errors

Do not confuse *affect* and *effect*. *Affect* is a verb; *effect* is a noun.
*Progress **affects** everyone.* (NOT ~~Progress effects everyone.~~)
*Progress has several positive **effects**.* (NOT . . . ~~several positive affects.~~)

Vocabulary notebook *Old or ancient?*

Building synonyms

It's useful to learn more than one way to express
basic concepts like *big, small, many, important,
good, bad,* etc., especially for formal writing.

bad= inferior, poor
   With recent advances in GPS, older versions now seem inferior.
   You can be fired for poor performance at work.

Dictionary tip

Your word-processing software
probably has a thesaurus to
help you find synonyms, but
check them in a dictionary
before you use them.

A **Choose a synonym from the box for these words. Then complete the
example sentences.**

compact	countless	functional	integral	obsolete	✓ portable

1. easy to carry = portable   We have a portable   grill that we barbecue on.
2. useful = _____   Kitchen appliances should be both _____ and attractive.
3. small = _____   With gas prices so high, people are now buying _____ cars.
4. essential = _____   Having ideas is an _____ part of making progress.
5. many, a lot of = _____   There have been _____ inventions that didn't work.
6. out of date = _____   The typewriter has more or less become _____.

B **Write synonyms for these adjectives. Then write a sentence that uses the synonym you came up with.**

1. modest, ordinary = _____   _____
2. creative, new = _____   _____
3. simple, basic = _____   _____
4. important, big = _____   _____
5. usual, not special = _____   _____

C **Word builder These words are all synonyms of one or more words in Exercises A and B. Find their
meanings. Then write them next to their synonyms above.**

archaic	elementary	everyday	groundbreaking	major	practical

D **Focus on vocabulary Look back at the article on page 58. Look for the words there and in Exercise 2A
on page 59 to help you complete the chart below.**

Adjective	Noun
willing	willingness
popular	
	convenience
original	
amusing	
	brilliance
simple	
	comfort
efficient	
easy	
	effectiveness

Business studies

In Unit 6, you . . .

- talk about business, retail, and threats to companies.
- use relative clauses that begin with pronouns and prepositions.
- use determiners and pronouns like *some, any, other(s), another.*
- persuade people of your views using negative and tag questions.
- say *granted* when someone makes a good point.

Lesson A *A case study*

1 Grammar in context

A How do people get discounts when they shop? Make a list.

B ◀))CD 2.21 Read the case study for an online coupon company. How does the business work?

A CASE STUDY – Online coupons

For decades savvy shoppers have been clipping coupons from newspapers and magazines, with which they can save money on everything from groceries to spa treatments. The emergence of the Internet provided a new opportunity to coupon businesses, many of which have been very successful. Then came *Groupon*.

BACKGROUND

Like many start-up companies, *Groupon* was founded by a forward-thinking entrepreneur, in this case, Andrew Mason. As with many such entrepreneurs, some of whom have become overnight multimillionaires, Mason had a deceptively simple idea: attract subscribers to whom you email special deals. These daily promotions give subscribers steep discounts, some of which may exceed 50 percent, on a range of goods and services. The success of any deal depends on the extent to which people sign up. If the number of people who sign up falls short of the target, the deal doesn't go through.

GOALS AND GROWTH

Some of the main goals for the company were to grow their subscriber base in key cities around the world; sell daily deals, which was revolutionary in the coupon business; and create awareness of the brand in national and international markets.

In just three years, it had more than 85 million global customers, all of whom "opt in" to the site. The company also had more than 55,000 merchants from whom deals were sought.

A SUCCESS STORY

Over 90 percent of participating companies, most of which are small businesses, said the *Groupon* promotion attracted new customers, and 87 percent reported increased awareness of their product or service in the community. *Groupon* may not be suitable for every enterprise, but for plenty of small business owners, many of whom struggle to grow, it can be a lifesaver, especially in an uncertain economy. One such small business, a bakery in New York, offered half-price cupcakes. More than 9,000 coupons were purchased, new customers came in, and business spread by word of mouth, all of which has to be good for the bottom line!

C **Pair work** **Discuss these questions about the article.**

1. What does the writer mean by "savvy" shoppers?
2. Why does the writer refer to the idea behind *Groupon* as "deceptively simple"?
3. Why was *Groupon* "revolutionary" in the coupon business? What did it do?
4. What kinds of successes do small businesses report after using *Groupon*?
5. Why is *Groupon* a "life saver" for some businesses? Why is it good for the "bottom line"?

2 Grammar Adding and modifying information

Figure it out

A How does the writer of the case study express the ideas below? Rewrite each pair of sentences as one sentence. Then read the grammar chart.

1. The emergence of the Internet provided a new opportunity to coupon businesses. Many of these coupon businesses have been very successful.

2. The company also had more than 55,000 merchants. Deals were sought from these merchants.

Pronouns and prepositions in relative clauses ⬇

Grammar extra
See page 154.

You can add pronouns + *of,* e.g., *all of, some of, most of, many of,* etc., or prepositions to relative clauses. Use *whom* for people and *which* for things.

*In three years, the company had more than 85 million customers, **all of whom** "opt in" to the site.*
*The Internet provided a new opportunity to coupon businesses, **many of which** have been successful.*
*Over 90 percent of companies, **most of which** are small businesses, said the promotion attracted customers.*
*Mason had an idea: Attract subscribers **to whom** you email special deals.*
*Shoppers clip coupons from newspapers, **with which** they can save money.*

Conversation vs. Writing

Relative clauses with pronoun + *of whom* / *of which* are approximately 10 times more common in academic writing than in conversation.

B Complete the relative clauses from another case study.

1. An entrepreneur needed capital with *which* he was hoping to start his own business.

2. He'd had several ideas, some _____ had potential, but they needed a lot of capital up front.

3. He applied for loans to several banks, all _____ turned down his applications.

4. The friends to _____ he turned for financial help were unable to lend him any money.

5. He talked to several advisors, most _____ advised him not to borrow without a business plan.

6. He finally decided to start a business for _____ he needed very little money – auto detailing. There were several places in his area, most _____ charged very high prices.

7. He sent out flyers for an introductory special offer, to _____ over 100 people replied.

8. Within three weeks, he had serviced cars for 40 customers, many _____ became regular clients.

C Pair work Take turns retelling details from Exercise B. How much can you remember?

---

3 Listening and speaking Too good to be true?

A ◀))) CD 2.22 Listen to four consumer experts talk about special promotions. Draw lines to match the goods with the promotions they talk about. There is one extra promotion.

Goods or services	Promotions
1. electronics	a. "buy one, get one free"
2. restaurants	b. a mail-in rebate promotion
3. clothes	c. "buy one, get one for 50% off"
4. neck massage	d. kids eat free
	e. try it for free

B ◀))) CD 2.23 Listen again. What problems does each expert mention? Take notes.

About you

C Pair work Which of the promotions in Exercise A do you think work best? Why? Which promotions have you used? What did you buy?

Speaking naturally
See page 140.

Lesson B *Bringing in the customers*

1 Vocabulary in context

A How many ways do you shop? What's your favorite way to shop? Take a class vote.

online from a major retailer	online from smaller companies	online at auction sites
in store from a superstore	in store from locally owned stores	other ways?

B ◀))) CD 2.24 **Listen to the podcast. What changes in retail does the speaker predict?**

PODCAST   LISTEN   READ   WATCH   👍 👎 🖨 ✉ Share

STATIONS

ABOUT

SUPPORT

LOG IN

SIGN UP

How do you **lure** people into a retail store? Lower prices will **tempt** some people, and some will be **attracted** by special offers, but others know they can probably get what they want cheaper online. In most developed economies, online shopping has grown steadily by about 20 percent a year, while in-store shopping has more or less remained stagnant. To compete, retail stores need to find other ways to **persuade** customers to leave their computers, and **convince** them that there's a better shopping experience in store.

But **coaxing** people to come in and buy is not so easy. Some retailers have found that an effective way of **wooing** customers is to create a store that combines conventional décor and layout with high-tech facilities. Such an environment may look very traditional but also offers facilities like self-service checkouts. Another store might have terminals with self-service ordering for home delivery. Yet another might **entice** customers by creating a social space – a so-called "third place" between work and home – where people can enjoy coffee or read in a relaxed setting without feeling **pressured into** buying things they don't need. Any store that makes people feel at ease will probably generate more business. No store wants to **scare** people **off** or **discourage** them from buying products by creating a cold, unfriendly atmosphere. Some evidence points to the fact that in-store music relaxes customers. Other evidence suggests it can actually irritate people. Equally, no store wants to be so overwhelming that it **puts** people **off** or even **alienates** them. There's a fine balance between **deterring** customers and **drawing** them **in**.

The atmosphere needs to **appeal** to *you*, be like your *home* – not some other unfamiliar place. And since most people don't live in homes the size of aircraft hangars, a store with a small footprint will be less likely to **intimidate.** The superstores of the late twentieth century may well have had their day. Such places were good for browsing a vast range of goods, but we can now browse the whole shopping world online. So in retail, small may prove to be beautiful after all.

Word sort

C **Make a chart of verbs in the podcast for attracting people and deterring them. Then use at least six new verbs to tell a partner what attracts you to stores and what deters you.**

Attract	Deter
lure	

Vocabulary notebook

See page 71.

② Grammar Referring to people and things

Figure it out

A Find words in the podcast to replace the ideas in bold. There may be more than one correct answer. Then read the grammar chart.

1. Cheaper prices will attract **certain** people, and **certain people** will find special offers appealing.
2. **Every (and it doesn't matter which)** store that creates a good atmosphere will do well.
3. Lowering prices is one way to attract customers, but stores need to find **additional** ways, too.
4. One store might have nice music. **A different store** might have a restaurant.

Grammar extra
See page 155.

some, any, other, others, another

Some and *any* have "strong" forms. You can use the strong form of *some* to talk about "certain but not all" people or things. The strong form of *any* means "it doesn't matter which."
*Lower prices will tempt **some people**, and **some** will be attracted by special offers.*
***Any** store that makes people feel at ease will probably generate more business.*

Use *other* before a plural or uncountable noun, after *the, your, this, some*, etc.
*Stores need to find **other** ways to attract customers.*
***Other** evidence suggests music can actually irritate people.*
*It needs to be like your home, not **some other** unfamiliar place.*

Common errors

Don't use *another* with a plural noun.
*Retail stores need to find **other ways** to attract customers. (NOT ~~another ways~~)*

Others is a pronoun. Don't use it before a noun.
*. . . but **others** know they can probably get what they want cheaper online. (OR **other people**)*

Use *another* before a singular count noun or as a pronoun to replace a singular count noun.
***Another** store might offer self-service ordering. Yet **another** might create a "third place."*

B Complete the sentences with *some, any, other, others, some other,* and *another*. There may be more than one answer. Then discuss the ideas in pairs. Would they entice you to shop in store?

1. _____ retailers are staying open 24/7 to draw customers in to compete with online stores.
2. _____ retail experts say stores need to attract customers by becoming "idea centers." For example, there are _____ customers who want to see kitchen appliances in a kitchen layout. _____ want to touch products before buying. _____ store that doesn't create an experience may not last.
3. One way stores can compete is to give excellent customer service. _____ way is for stores to provide services you *can't* get online. _____ stores entice people with home-baked cookies that _____ customer can take. _____ stores offer special deals only to in-store customers.
4. There are so many choices for consumers online. Stores could offer a limited selection, but there needs to be _____ choice. _____ suggestion is for retailers to offer shopping advice. Once a retailer has _____ customer in the store, it needs to keep them so they don't go to _____ store.

③ Viewpoint *Online or in store?*

Pair work Discuss the questions.

- What are the advantages of shopping online? Are there any disadvantages?
- In what other ways can regular stores compete with online stores?
- What kinds of services do you think shoppers will demand in the future?
- What other changes do you think there will be in the retail business?

In conversation . . .

You can ask *You know what I mean*? to check that others agree with or understand you.

Lesson C *Don't you think . . . ?*

1 Conversation strategy Persuading

A Do people you know ever boycott, or refuse to patronize a company on principle? Is corporate social responsibility, the idea that companies should be charitable, popular?

B 🔊 CD 2.25 Listen. What is "buycotting"? Do Erkan and Dion agree that it works?

Erkan Have you heard that expression "to buycott"?

Dion Not sure. What is it?

Erkan It's when you buy a company's products because you support its corporate policies. Like if they support a cause you believe in or if they do business ethically. It's like the opposite of *boycott*.

Dion Oh, right. Does it work? I mean, consumers don't have that much influence, do they?

Erkan But don't you think companies *should* listen to their customers?

Dion Well, to some extent, maybe.

Erkan I think people want businesses to give something back to the community and to have ethical practices. It makes sense for any corporation to do that, doesn't it?

Dion Well, granted the notion of corporate social responsibility is very popular. It's fine in theory. In practice it's more complex than that, isn't it? And in any event, don't companies only do what's good for their bottom line?

C **Notice** how Erkan and Dion use negative questions and tag questions to persuade each other that their opinions are right. Find examples in the conversation.

> *Don't you think companies* **should** *listen to their customers?*
> *It makes sense for any corporation, doesn't it?*

D Read more excerpts from the conversation. Rewrite each first question as a negative question, and add a tag question to each response. Then practice with a partner.

1. *Erkan* But do you believe corporate social responsibility is a good thing?
   Dion Yes. But it's not what drives a company, _____ ?

2. *Dion* And is a company's responsibility to its shareholders, rather than doing good?
   Erkan Well, it's not just a case of either-or. Any business can do both, _____ ?

3. *Erkan* Do workers feel better when their company stands for something they believe in?
   Dion Perhaps. But many companies are just struggling to survive, _____?

4. *Dion* Are companies having a hard time as it is, without moral pressure from interest groups?
   Erkan Well, it depends. They should still do business ethically, _____?

About you **E** **Pair work** Do you agree with any of the opinions in the conversation and Exercise D? Discuss the ideas. Use negative and tag questions to persuade your partner.

A Don't you believe corporate social responsibility is a good thing? I mean, I do.
B Actually, I do, too. More companies should do business ethically, shouldn't they?

2 Strategy plus *Granted*

🔊 CD 2.26 You can use *granted* when someone makes a point that is good, but it doesn't change your opinion.

Well, **granted** the notion is very popular . . .

In conversation . . .

Granted often comes near the beginning of what people say, but it can also come in other places.

A 🔊 CD 2.27 **Match the statements with the responses. Write the letters a–e. Then listen and check.**

1. Don't you think companies often forget that it's their employees that make them successful? _____
2. Manufacturers need to make sure that they're environmentally friendly, don't you think? _____
3. Doesn't the research show that people prefer to buy from socially responsible businesses? _____
4. Don't you believe companies should give a percentage of their profits to charity? _____
5. It's interesting to see the gender and racial balance of people on a company's website. _____

> a. They can tell you a lot, granted, but it doesn't mean that they reflect who the company actually employs.
> b. Well, granted it's nice to give something back to the community. But you can't make it law, can you?
> c. Well, they should, granted. But there's the cost, isn't there? The cost of going green can be prohibitive.
> d. People should come first. Granted. But it's often the staff that gets laid off when times are tough.
> e. Um, they might *say* that, granted, but when it comes down to it, they probably buy what's cheap.

About you **B** Pair work **Discuss the statements above. Do you think any are particularly controversial?**

3 Strategies Big business vs. small business

About you **A** Rewrite the conversations below. Write A's comments using a negative question or a tag question. Add *granted* to B's responses and then complete the idea.

1. *A* It's better to support small, local businesses. We should all support our neighborhood stores.
   B Well, yeah, it's nice to buy things at small stores and everything. But . . .
2. *A* Big companies typically employ a lot of people. That's a good thing.
   B Yeah, I guess. I mean, they *do* provide a lot of jobs, but . . .
3. *A* The trouble with those big-box stores, you know, the huge superstores, is that they've driven out small-business owners.
   B Well, that can happen. But . . .
4. *A* Small clothing stores tend to give you better personal service. I mean, they have more time for you.
   B Well, it's true. But . . .
5. *A* The biggest advantage of small stores, like small shoe stores, is you can find things that are different. You can also usually find better-quality things.
   B Well, the quality of the products is usually good at small stores. But . . .

THE PROBLEM WITH MY SMALL BUSINESS IS IT KEEPS GETTING BIGGER AND BIGGER.

Lemonade 10¢

B Pair work **What are the advantages of big businesses versus small businesses? Prepare a debate to present to the class.**

A Don't you think that generally it's better to support small, local businesses?
B Not necessarily. I mean, granted, small business is good for a community, but . . .

Lesson D *Organizational threats*

1 Reading

A Prepare How might a company "leak" or lose electronic data (information)? Make a list.

B 📥 **Read for main ideas** Read the article. How many of your ideas are mentioned? What types of data leakage can you find? What are the reasons for it?

Data leakage - are you protected?

1 Like any company, your business is no doubt one in which technology is widely used. Online banking, sales, networked collaboration, and communication are central to your operation, and your IT professionals carefully safeguard your electronic data. But how secure is that data? You might well have software that protects you from the external threats of hacking and industrial espionage, but are you overlooking another threat that's closer to home?

2 You probably encourage your staff to take work home. With laptops, portable storage devices, and smartphones, it's easy for employees to finish off that report at night or reply to email on the train to work. Thanks to technology, you have a productive workforce that works for you during off hours. However, this means your confidential company data is out "in the open," outside of your premises. It's less secure and is vulnerable to misuse and theft. And you don't need reminding that the loss or leaking of sensitive financial data, strategic plans, and intellectual property could not only cost your company its competitive edge but could ruin it completely.

THE ENEMY WITHIN?

3 Research* commissioned by Cisco® and carried out by InsightExpress in 10 countries estimated that within a two-year period, over 250 million confidential records were either lost or stolen. The research also revealed the extent to which employee behavior, both innocent and malicious, can put company data at risk. While insiders were responsible for 21 percent of electronic crimes – as opposed to 58 percent for outsiders – the companies surveyed estimated that 33 percent of insider crimes were costly or damaging.

REASONS FOR DATA LEAKAGE

4 Yet, even without crime, there are many more mundane reasons for data leakage. The report paints a worrisome picture of employee behaviors, among which is using company computers to access personal email. Even though many employers do not allow this, almost 80 percent of employees do it, over 60 percent of whom do it at least once a day. Unauthorized applications for email,

online banking, or shopping can put your computers at risk from theft or viruses from malicious sites.

5 Other common behaviors are when employees knowingly bypass or change security settings to access sites for personal use and also when they fail to use passwords or log off correctly. According to the report, one-third of employees leave their computers on without logging off when they leave their desks, including overnight, and a fifth leave logon information in insecure places, often next to their computers.

6 Remote working also causes problems if employees transfer or copy data from company computers to home computers, to which others may have access and many of which may not have the same level of security. Computers and storage devices can be lost or stolen when used in public, and the practice of discussing sensitive company information in public, where others can overhear, is widespread. Incredibly, 25 percent of employees admit to sharing such information with friends, family, and strangers.

WHAT'S TO BE DONE?

7 The practices described above may not even be considered problematic by employees, many of whom would see their actions as entirely legitimate. Training and insistence upon the observance of security protocol is one way to handle it.

Continued on the next page …

* http://www.cisco.com/en/US/solutions/collateral/ns170/ns896/
ns895/white_paper_c11-499060.html

C Understanding inference Answer the questions about the article. Then compare with a partner.

1. Who is the article written for? What is it trying to do? Why does the title ask that question?
2. What does the writer mean by ". . . another threat that's closer to home"?
3. What do 60 percent of employees do every day?
4. What point is the writer trying to make by quoting the percentages of insider crime?
5. What does the writer think about employees sharing information outside the company?
6. Why might employees think their use of a company computer is "legitimate"?

About you | **D** React What did you read in the article that surprised you about data leakage? Will the information make you change any of your behaviors in the future?

2 Focus on vocabulary Adjectives

A Find the words below in the article. Can you figure out their meanings? Then match them to the words in the second column with a similar meaning. Write the letters a–g.

1. secure (para. 1) and insecure (para. 5) _____
2. confidential and sensitive (para. 2) _____
3. vulnerable (para. 2) _____
4. malicious (para. 3) _____
5. mundane (para. 4) _____
6. widespread (para. 6) _____
7. legitimate (para. 7) _

a. open to attack
b. harmful
c. everyday, unexciting
d. acceptable
e. common, affecting many people or places
f. private and not to be discussed openly
g. safe and unsafe

About you | **B** Pair work Use the adjectives above to rephrase the questions. Then discuss with a partner.

• What are acceptable uses of an employer's computer? What's not acceptable?
• How common do you think hacking is these days?
• Are you personally open to attack by harmful software?
• How do you keep your private information safe, especially online?
• Do you ever feel that really private information about you is unsafe online?

3 Listening and speaking The top threats

A ◀))CD 2.28 Look at these threats to organizations. Guess the top five threats companies fear. Then listen to an interview and check your guesses. Number the threats 1–5.

☐ unplanned IT and telecom outages   ☐ adverse weather
☐ industrial disputes   ☐ loss of personnel talent
☐ malicious software and other cyber attacks   ☐ loss or theft of confidential information
☐ interruption to utility supplies   ☐ new laws or regulations

B ◀))CD 2.29 Listen again. In what specific way can each threat impact a business? Write notes on a separate piece of paper.

C Pair work How could the other threats described in Exercise A disrupt business? What other threats might organizations face?

Writing *It can occur in any company.*

In this lesson, you ...
- write about causes of and solutions to a problem.
- use modals to avoid being too assertive.
- avoid errors with *can* and *could*.

Task **Write a report on data security.**
Write a report for your boss, describing the possible causes of data leakage. Propose some potential solutions in your workplace.

A **Look at a model** Brainstorm some ideas about the causes of and solutions to data leakage for a report. Then look at the extracts from a report below. Does it include any of your ideas?

Leakage of sensitive data is a serious problem, which can occur in any company for a number of reasons. One reason may be the fact that employees take work outside of the office on portable devices. Some of these devices might be shared with other people or may not be as secure as company computers. Second, employees can access their personal email and other websites from work computers and they may fail to observe security procedures when doing so. This could allow malicious software to attack company servers. Another cause of data leakage is thought to be . . .

All of the above factors can cause data leakage, which could potentially damage the company's profits and image. To prevent data leakage, a number of security measures should be employed, many of which are simple to implement.
1. As a company, we need to control what data leaves the building. It would be advisable not to allow employees to take work home.
2. We could also enforce the rules on using private computers.

. . .

B **Focus on language** Read the chart and underline the modal verbs in Exercise A.

Using modal verbs in writing ⬇

You can use modals to avoid being too assertive in describing situations.
*These factors **can** cause data leakage.* (= they can and do)
*Some devices **might / may / could** be shared with others.* (it is possible)

You can also use modals to make polite recommendations.
*It **would** be advisable not to allow employees to take work home.*
*We **could** also enforce the rules on using private computers.*

Describing cause

One reason for this might be . . .
A possible cause could be . . .
This may be a result of . . .
It can be caused by . . .

C **Rewrite the underlined parts of each sentence below using the modal verbs given.**

1. Security is improved if procedures are in place. Data leakage is a result of poor security. (can, may)
2. A possible cause of data leakage is that employees don't realize that they should not discuss work with friends and family. One reason for this is a lack of training. (could, may, might)
3. Data leakage is also caused by employees' use of instant-messaging programs. (might)
4. Certain Internet sites are infected by viruses, so it is advisable to limit access to them. (may, would)
5. Employees' laptops infect company computers, which causes data loss. (might, may)
6. One possible solution is to check employees' devices on a regular basis for malware. (could)

D **Write and check** Write the report on data leakage in the task above. Then check for errors.

Common errors

Do not use *could* for things which in fact do happen.
Employees can access their personal email. = They do this, we know.
(NOT *Employees could access* . . ., except in sentences like this:
Employees could access their email if we allowed it. = It would be possible.)

Vocabulary notebook *It's tempting.*

Verb	Noun	Adjective		Mostly as verb
tempt	temptation	tempting		coax

A   Complete the charts with verbs from the podcast on page 64. Then add nouns and adjectives from the same word family to the chart on the left.

Verb	Noun	Adjective(s)		Mostly used as verbs
	conviction (= a belief)			put off
deter				scare off
		discouraging / discouraged		woo
persuade				
	pressure			

B   Make a chart with these verbs.

alienate   appeal   attract   coax   draw in   entice   intimidate   lure

C   Word builder Find the meaning of these verbs. Are they verbs that mean "attract" or verbs that mean "deter"?

dissuade   induce   prompt   unnerve   urge

D Focus on vocabulary   Which of the adjectives below have other forms in the same family with the same meaning? What are they? Write them in the chart. Use Exercise 2A on page 69 to help you.

	Adjectives	Nouns	Adverbs
1.	secure / insecure		
2.	confidential		
3.	sensitive		
4.	vulnerable		
5.	malicious		
6.	mundane		
7.	widespread		
8.	legitimate		

Checkpoint 2 *Units 4–6*

1 Breaking records – an ongoing achievement

A Complete the passive verbs, adding the adverbs given. There may be more than one word order. Then replace the words in bold with synonyms, changing *a* to *an* if necessary.

significant

In 1954, Roger Bannister achieved a **big** milestone: he ran a mile in under four minutes. This was something that had _____ (see, previously) as almost impossible, though **a lot of** people had tried. The four-minute barrier has _____ (break, since) numerous times and is now the **normal** time for most medium-distance runners. In fact, records in track are _____ (achieve, still) today, largely thanks to **creative, new** technology. Technology has _____ (use, widely) to enhance performance in the sport. Running shoes are _____ (improve, continually) and are far different from the **basic** rubber-soled shoes of the 1950s, which are now **out of date**. Clothing is much more **useful**, too. Even the **ordinary** T-shirt has _____ (redesign, completely) so that it removes sweat from an athlete's body. In addition, **easy-to-carry** and **small** devices, such as GPS watches, can monitor heart rate, etc., and are now a **necessary** part of tracking a runner's performance. Further advances in sports technology are _____ (make, currently). It's a **continuing** process, and it may only be a matter of time before we see the headline, "The three-minute-mile barrier has _____ (shatter, finally)."

B Pair work Discuss each of the topics below about sports and athletics today. Use *In any case* to make your argument stronger and *In any event* to reach your final conclusion.

- use of performance-enhancing drugs
- high salaries that some athletes receive
- training children from an early age to compete
- use of technology to improve performance

2 They could easily have become extinct.

A Unscramble the underlined verb phrases. Then complete the relative clauses.

1. In the last few years, the tiger <u>been have could wiped off easily</u> the planet by poachers. But the extinction of tigers <u>prevented may been have well</u> by innovative programs, some _____ focus on preserving tiger habitats. How else can we protect endangered species?

2. When some endangered species were first brought into captivity, there were critics, many _____ believed that breeding endangered animals in captivity <u>have not been should permitted</u>. Although some programs <u>failed well might have</u>, many didn't. What is your view on keeping animals in captivity?

3. News reports have detailed specific cases of wild animals attacking their trainers, all _____ suffered severe injuries, which <u>killed have could easily</u> them. Other reports highlight how wild animals, many _____ are losing their habitats, encroach into neighborhoods and are shot. In other cases, animals <u>have been to perform made</u> in jobs and entertainment. What is your response to this treatment of animals? How can people protest, and to_____ should they send their complaints?

B Pair work Discuss the questions above. Use expressions like *Apart from anything else, What's more*, etc., to add and focus on new ideas. Use *granted* if your partner makes a good point that doesn't change your opinion.

"Well, it's important to educate people about tigers in addition to preserving their habitats."

3 That's the business!

A Read the headline. Then write as many words as you can to replace *woo* and *deterred*.

> Stores use smart tactics to **woo** customers.
> Don't be **deterred**! But be careful.

attract   intimidate

B Complete the sentences. Use a form of the future perfect of the verbs given, if possible, or the simple present if not. More than one form may be correct. Then add the words from the box.

another	another	any	other	others	some	some	some

"Black Friday" is the start of the holiday shopping season. By the time Black Friday _____ (arrive), retailers need to be ready. Most stores _____ (prepare) for the sales for weeks. They _____ (stock) their shelves with goods at low prices. When the doors _____ (open), _____ store that is not ready may end up not making a profit for the whole year. Stores _____ (advertise) their deals for days. _____ reduce prices by 50 percent. _____ take up to 75 percent off. By the time the doors open, _____ customers _____ (wait) in line for several hours. _____ shoppers _____ (camp out) for more than 24 hours to get the best deals. However, not all are genuine. _____ stores advertise deals, but there's only one item at this price. _____ tactic is to sell old goods. _____ is to sell products made just for the sale. By the time stores close, they _____ (serve) millions of customers. They _____ (take in) millions of dollars in revenue, and no doubt some customers _____ (spend) more than they intended to.

C Rewrite each comment in two ways: (1) as a negative question; (2) by adding a tag question. Then discuss the ideas with a partner. Use strong responses and expressions like *Just think* and *Let's put it this way* to make your point.

1. It's crazy to camp out all night until a store opens.
2. It makes sense for stores to offer big discounts.
3. People buy things just because they're on sale.
4. Sales are just a clever marketing tool.

A Don't you think it's crazy to camp out all night until a store opens?
B Oh, absolutely not! Just think: you can get some really great deals.

4 Surviving it all

Complete the prepositional phrases. Then choose the correct words to complete the article.

Bald eagles are not actually bald, which may not be in _____ with most people's expectations. _____ from being the national symbol of the United States, it is a protected species. Northern eagles migrate but return to the same breeding **ground / young** year after year and **mate / hibernate** for life. They often build their **nests / burrows** near water on _____ of the fact that they feed mostly on fish. They **dig / lay** between one and three eggs, which **mate / hatch** after 35 days. The eagles sit on the nest to **keep / store** the eggs warm and also to prevent them being attacked by **predators / reserves** such as squirrels. The parents initially **hatch / raise** the young in the nest, but once the chicks have feathers, the parents stop **feeding / breeding** them and they may go up _____ several days without eating. Far _____ being neglectful, the parents are simply encouraging the chicks to leave the nest and learn to fly. Once out of their nests, the chicks are fed by the parents to build up their fat **reserves / habits** and are taught to hunt so they can **survive / migrate** the winter months. Bald eagles don't **store / build up** food or **hibernate / breed**, and they often hunt other birds. Their presence in an area can be unwelcome _____ to the fact that they can destroy other birds' **colonies / grounds**.

Relationships

In Unit 7, you . . .

- talk about relationships, marriage, and family life.
- express the idea of *if* in different ways.
- use *wh-* clauses as subjects and objects to focus information.
- finish a point with expressions like *in the end*.
- say *then* and *in that case* in responses to draw a conclusion.

Lesson A *Parenting*

1 Grammar in context

A What's the best age to become a parent? Tell the class your views.

B ◀》CD 3.02 Listen to the podcast. What's the speaker's main proposal about parenting?

STATIONS • ABOUT • SUPPORT • LOG IN • SIGN UP

PODCAST [LISTEN LIVE 🎧]   👍 | 👎 | 🖨 | 🖼 | SHARE

Our Family Season continues with Rachel Birken's take on the topic of parenting.

A friend of mine struggling with sleepless nights after the birth of her daughter recently said to me, quote, "Had I known having a baby would be this hard, I might have waited a few more years. Why aren't parenting classes mandatory, especially in high school?" Which got me thinking: Why *aren't* they?

Ask any new parent this question: "Would you have benefited from parenting classes?" and you'll probably get the answer, "Absolutely!" Most parents experience problems with sleepless nights, anxiety about their baby's health, and as their children grow, issues with behavior and setting boundaries. Should you think your experience will be any different, think again. Parenting is a skill to be learned.

Some school districts have recognized this and introduced programs where students take care of a computerized baby doll that behaves like a real baby. It cries in the night and needs to be changed and comforted. It helps young people understand what is involved in starting a family.

One college senior I know who did this told me it was a cool experience and that had he not taken that class, he wouldn't have realized what hard work a baby is.

Were I in charge of education, I would make all students from the age of 12 do this for a whole weekend every year.

Should you need further evidence that parenting classes are a good idea, school and city districts all over the country are expanding programs that offer workshops in parenting skills – not to students – but to *parents* of their students. Clearly, there is a need out there.

So let's make parenting classes mandatory. Otherwise, we run the risk of creating a generation of parents who are unprepared to tackle the most important job of their lives.

C Pair work Discuss the questions.

- What reasons does the speaker give or imply for her proposal? What are they?
- What gave her the idea in the first place?
- How does the baby doll program work? What is its goal?
- Why do you think parenting classes are offered by city and school districts?

② Grammar Hypothesizing

Figure
it out

A **Rewrite these phrases without *If*. Use the podcast to help you. Then read the grammar chart.**

1. If you ask any new parent this question, . . .
2. If I had known having a baby would be this hard, . . .
3. If you need further evidence that parenting classes are needed, . . .
4. If we don't do this, we run the risk . . .

Conditional sentences without *if* ⬇

Grammar extra
See page 156.

You can use these structures to introduce a hypothetical idea without using the word *if*.

Imperative . . . *and* . . .	***Ask*** any new parent the question, ***and*** you'll get the answer, "Absolutely!"
Inversions *Were* + subject (+ infinitive) *Had* + subject + past participle *Should* + subject + verb	***Were I*** in charge of education, I would make this class mandatory. ***Were she*** to have another baby, she would be better prepared. ***Had I known*** it would be this hard, I would have waited. ***Should you think*** your experience will be any different, think again.
Otherwise	Let's make them mandatory. ***Otherwise***, parents will be unprepared.

Writing vs. Conversation

Inversions are much more common in writing and formal speaking than in conversation.

B **Change the *if* clauses, using the words or structure given.**

Had I had
1. ~~If I had~~ the chance to take care of a doll in school, I would have said, "No way." (*Had*)
2. If I were to become a school principal, I would make parenting classes mandatory. (*Were*)
3. If you make parenting classes mandatory, students will hate them. (imperative)
4. If I were to become a parent in the next year, I'd be very happy. (*Were*)
5. If you ask most kids what it's like to have children, they'll say, "It's easy." (imperative)
6. Teaching kids about relationships is a good idea. If we don't, how do they learn? (*Otherwise*)
7. I'd want my kids to take other "life" classes like personal finance, if that were possible. (*should*)
8. If I had known more about life when I left school, things would have been easier. (*Had*)

About
you

C **Pair work Do you agree with the sentences above? Change them to express your own views.**

"Had I had the chance to take care of a doll in high school, I would have done it."

③ Listening and speaking Bringing up baby?

A 🔊 CD 3.03 **Listen. What was Brandon's class? Was it a positive experience?**

B 🔊 CD 3.04 **Listen again. Are the sentences true or false? Write T or F. Then correct the false sentences.**

1. It was a mandatory class. _____
2. He knew before he did it how hard it would be. _____
3. He found changing diapers the worst part. _____
4. It taught him how much time a baby needs. _____
5. His friends said how annoying it was to do. _____
6. He's not sure if it's a good idea for his age group. _____

About
you

C **Pair work Agree on four classes you would make mandatory to help students prepare for life.**

Lesson B *Questions to ask*

① Vocabulary in context

A 🔊 CD 3.05 **What issues do you think couples should discuss and agree on before they get married? Make a list. Then read the article. Which of your ideas are mentioned?**

Getting married? *Don't just wait and see what happens.*

So you've met the man or woman of your dreams and decided to become **husband and wife**. You're probably **sick and tired** of reading the divorce statistics, but they're not encouraging. In many Western countries, around 40 percent of marriages end in divorce. Why divorce rates are so high is not clear. But what many couples fail to do is to discuss the important issues before the wedding. So, **stop and think** now – you'll save yourself **time and energy** and maybe avoid a lot of **pain and suffering**.

MONEY

Is how you spend money a problem right now? When you're married, it will likely become a problem **sooner or later**. Agree now on how much you will spend – for example, on rent, vacations, entertainment, etc. – and what your financial goals are. Do you know if you'll keep separate bank accounts?

WORK

How many hours a week you work can be an issue. Tell each other now if you intend to work **above and beyond** a normal workweek; otherwise, **slowly but surely** those long hours will cause resentment. Discuss whether or not you would both move to another city because of work. How would you feel were your partner to work away from home and commute **back and forth** on weekends?

CONFLICTS

Every relationship has its **ups and downs**, but **in this day and age**, marriage is all about **give-and-take**. How you resolve differences can be critical and may predict the **success or failure** of a marriage. Can you agree without arguing how often your in-laws can visit?

You can't always **pick and choose** where you **live and work**, but can you compromise should you have different views?   [MORE...]

About you **B** **Complete the expressions with words from the article. Then discuss the comments with a partner. Do you agree with the views given?**

1. I know that divorce causes a lot of pain _____, but it takes a lot of time _____ to discuss these questions, too. I think you should just get married if you want to and then wait _____ what happens.
2. I don't think people stop _____ before getting married. There are a lot more things to agree on above _____ the ideas in the article.
3. Sooner _____ everyone argues. You can't avoid it as husband _____.
4. All couples have their ups _____. You can't agree on everything, so pick _____ what you argue about.
5. I agree marriage is about give _____, but I like to get my own way, and slowly _____ I usually do.
6. In this day _____, we don't need advice about marriage. I'm sick _____ of reading articles like this.
7. It's not a problem to live _____ in two places. It'd be fun to travel back _____.

Word sort **C** **Make a chart of the expressions in bold in the article. Add more ideas.**

and	but	or
wait and see		

Vocabulary notebook
See page 83.

2 Grammar Information focus

Figure it out

A Underline the sentences in the article with these meanings.

1. How do you spend money? Is it a problem right now?
2. Why are divorce rates high? It's not clear.
3. Will you keep separate bank accounts? Do you know?
4. Where do you live and work? You can't always pick and choose.

Wh– clauses as subjects and objects

Grammar extra
See page 157.

A *wh–* clause can be the subject or object of a verb. Using a *wh–* clause as the subject gives extra emphasis to it. Notice the statement word order in the *wh–* clause.

Subjects
Is **how you spend money** a problem right now?
What many couples fail to do is (to) discuss the important issues.
How you resolve differences can be critical.

Objects
Can you agree **how often your partner's family can visit** without arguing?
Tell each other now **whether / if you intend to work long hours**.
Agree now on **what your financial goals are**.

In conversation . . .
You can also say *whether or not* when there is a choice of two options.
Discuss **whether or not** you would both move to another city.

B Rewrite the two sentences as one sentence. Keep the clauses in the same order.

1. Should you tell your husband or wife this? Which of his or her friends don't you like?
   Should you tell your husband or wife which of his or her friends you don't like?
2. Why do couples divorce? It's usually obvious, don't you think?
3. How many hours a week do you work? It can easily become a problem, can't it?
4. It's important to discuss this. Do you both want children?
5. You should also decide this. How many children do you both want to have?
6. You need to find this out. Does your partner have different religious or political views?
7. Who does the chores? This will become an issue sooner or later.
8. Is it important to decide this? How often will you go out separately with your own friends?

About you

C Pair work Discuss the questions and statements above. Do you have the same views?

3 Viewpoint A manifesto for marriage

Pair work Discuss the 10 most important issues you need to agree on before you get married. Use these ideas and add your own.

chores	money	visiting in-laws
leisure time	raising children	work

A *How you spend money is the first thing to discuss, I would say.*
B *Yes. It seems to me you should agree on what you spend money on.*

In conversation . . .
You can soften opinions with *I would say, I would think, I would imagine*, and *It seems to me*.

Speaking naturally
See page 141

OF COURSE I'LL MARRY YOU! HERE'S A LIST OF CHANGES I'LL NEED YOU TO MAKE FIRST.

Lesson C *In the end*

1 Conversation strategy Finishing a point

A ◀))CD 3.06 **What are the advantages and disadvantages of Internet dating sites? Make a list. Then listen. What do Tara and Carmen think about them?**

Tara	Did I tell you I'm going out on a date tonight?
Carmen	No. Who with?
Tara	This guy I met on an Internet dating site.
Carmen	Is that . . . all right?
Tara	Oh, yeah. Talk to anybody these days, and you'll probably find they're using dating sites.
Carmen	So you think it's OK, then?
Tara	I do. Really and truly. It's just like being at a party. You see somebody you like, you arrange to meet and –
Carmen	But you don't *really* know who they are. I mean, when all's said and done, surely it's better to get to know them a little first.
Tara	Well, you do. You email or call. It's so convenient. And in the end, you don't waste time on people you're not interested in.
Carmen	I guess.
Tara	You know, all the time I spend working, I'll never meet anybody otherwise.
Carmen	Well, in that case, do you have time to date? I mean, at the end of the day, if you're always working, you probably don't have time for a boyfriend.

B **Notice** how Carmen and Tara summarize and finish their points with expressions like these. Find examples in the conversation.

> **at the end of the day**   **in a word**
> **in the end**   **in a nutshell**
> **when all's said and done**

In conversation . . .

The most common expressions are *in the end* and *at the end of the day*. In writing, you can use *in a word* and *in a nutshell* or the more formal *in the final analysis*.

About you

C ◀))CD 3.07 **Listen. Complete Tara's comments with the expressions you hear. Then discuss the views with a partner. Do you agree with her?**

1. People don't go out to meet people – it takes time. _____, we're all too busy.
2. I read an academic article about Internet dating that said, "Online daters are just like face-to-face daters. _____, there is no difference between them."
3. You can email and call or video chat before you first meet. So really, _____, you're already friends.
4. You don't need to go out and spend money on movies or restaurants. _____, it's a lot cheaper.
5. And because you do it from home, you don't get into difficult situations. _____, it's safer, too.
6. There are lots of people that you can get to know online. _____, you don't have to choose just one.

2 Strategy plus . . ., *then*

🔊 CD 3.08 You can end a response with ***then*** to draw a conclusion from what someone just said.

So you think it's OK, **then**?

You can also say ***In that case***, which means "because of what was just said."

In conversation . . .

In that case usually comes near the beginning of what people say.

A Match the comments with the responses. Write the letters a–f. Then practice in pairs.

1. Some research shows that 94 percent of online daters go out more than once. _____
2. Apparently, only 5 percent of people who use online dating actually establish a relationship. _____
3. Online daters prefer instant messaging to email because it's more like a real conversation. _____
4. They tend not to use their webcams, though. _____
5. What a lot of people do is to email or chat for weeks before they actually meet. _____
6. Look at the people using Internet dating sites, and you'll find mostly middle-aged people. _____

a. That's interesting. Email isn't considered a good way to get to know somebody, then.
b. Well, in that case, you've got a good chance of getting at least a couple of dates.
c. OK, so in that case, what do they have to talk about when they get together?
d. So it's not just young people, then?
e. Well, in that case, it doesn't have a very high success rate, then, does it?
f. So in that case, you don't need to look your best when you're dating online.

About you | **B** Pair work Take turns reading the comments. Use your own responses with *then* or *in that case*.

3 Strategies

A Circle the best options to complete the rest of Carmen and Tara's conversation. Sometimes both are correct. Then practice in pairs.

Carmen: So if there are hundreds of people on the site, how do you choose one, **then / in a word**?

Tara: Well, you fill out a long questionnaire about yourself and the site gives you a short list. **In that case / At the end of the day,** they do all the hard work and match potential dates.

Carmen: So **in that case / in a word,** the computer chooses someone?

Tara: No. Well, kind of. I mean, it gives you a selection to choose from based on your questionnaire. I mean, **in that case / when all's said and done,** it's pretty efficient.

Carmen: That's one way of putting it. But I suppose it's just like regular dating. I guess **in the end / in that case,** it's really no different from meeting a stranger at a party.

About you | **B** Pair work What are the best ways to meet people? Discuss the ideas below and add your own.

online dating   through friends   at work / school   through parents   at clubs

Lesson D *Smart families*

1 Reading

A Prepare Look at the title of the article and the photo. Brainstorm ideas, words, and expressions that you expect the writer to include. What arguments do you expect to read?

B ⬇ **Read for main ideas** Read the article. How many of your ideas were included?

TECHNOLOGY –
is it driving families apart?

1 Look inside any family home in the evening, and you might see a typical enough scene: Mom and Dad, each on their own laptop or tablet, streaming movies, catching up on work, or maybe answering email on their smartphones. Meanwhile, one child is chatting online with one school friend while texting another. The other is playing a video game with a friend on the other side of the city at the same time as playing chess against an uncle in another state. Each member of the family is totally absorbed in his or her own piece of technology. How you interpret such a scene might depend on your attitude toward technology. Do you see a close family that is enjoying "quality time" together? Or do you perceive this family unit as "together" only in a physical sense, as a dysfunctional family whose members are isolated from one another, inhabiting parallel virtual worlds?

2 For some, the effect of technology on human relationships is worrisome. It appears to be the case that many people would much rather spend time with their gadgets than with one another. Technology, they claim, becomes a substitute for face-to-face human relationships, which is a cause for concern.

3 According to some experts, technology is changing how people interact with each another, and for the worse. Some teachers say it is difficult to get students' attention and they have to compete with texting and surfing the Web to such an extent that many schools now require students to leave mobile devices in their lockers. In the same way, young people try to get their parents' attention but have to contend with smartphones, tablets, and other technology.

4 However, a report from the Pew Internet and American Life Project offers a more hopeful and encouraging view, suggesting that far from replacing human contact, new technology can actually enhance family relationships.

Just over half of the 2,253 people surveyed agreed that technology had enabled them to increase their contact with distant family members and 47 percent said it had improved the interactions with the people they live with.

5 Thanks to more sophisticated, lighter, and more portable tablet, smartphone, and computer technology, family members who might otherwise have sat in separate rooms can now be in the same one while still occupying a different mental space. Look back at our typical family scene above. Is it any different from four people reading their own books? Does the fact that each person is immersed in a screen rather than a paper page make their activity any less sociable?

6 Moreover, even the closest of families and couples need time away from each other at some point to pursue their own interests. Technology allows people to be both present and absent simultaneously.

7 Where technology will lead us remains to be seen. How it affects the quality of our family relationships is up to all of us.

> **Reading tip**
> Writers sometimes give their own views in a question. *Is it any different from four people reading their own books?*

C **Read for inference** Do you think the writer would answer "yes" or "no" to these questions? Give reasons for your answers.

- Is technology driving families apart?
- Is reading books better for family relationships?
- Should families spend as much of their free time together as possible?
- Do we know where technology will lead us?
- Is it the responsibility of families to decide what impact technology has on their relationships?

D **Read for detail** Are the sentences true (T), false (F), or is the information not given (NG)? Find evidence in the article for your answers. Then compare with a partner.

1. The writer believes the family in the example is dysfunctional. _____
2. Some people believe that we prefer the company of our computers to being with other people. _____
3. Teachers who can't get their students' attention resort to using technology. _____
4. The Pew study says that technology makes family relationships more distant. _____
5. Technology allows people to do their own thing in the same part of the house. _____
6. Reading is better for family life than using computers. _____

② Focus on vocabulary Building synonyms

A Replace the words in bold with expressions from the article. You may have to change the form.

1. When you read the first paragraph, how did you **understand** the family scene? (para. 1)
   Did you **see** a **family that doesn't get along**? (2 expressions, para. 1)
2. Do you think technology is **replacing** face-to-face relationships? (para. 2)
   Is this **something that you worry about**? (2 expressions, para. 2)
3. When have you had to **compete** with technology to get someone's attention? (para. 3)
4. Can technology **improve** family relationships, in your opinion? (para. 4)
5. Is it rude to be **absorbed** in a screen when you are with other people? (para. 5)
6. How often do you use more than one piece of technology **at the same time**? (para. 6)
7. Do you think it's important for families to **do** different activities? Why? Why not? (para. 6)

About you **B** **Pair work** Ask and answer the questions above. Use all the new expressions in your answers.

③ Listening and speaking Keeping tabs on the family

A 🔊 CD 3.09 Look at the ways of monitoring people. Which family members might use them and why? Then listen to a radio show and check (✓) the devices the expert describes.

	Who might use it?	What does it do?
☐ parental controls on a computer		
☐ a screen-time control device		
☐ a GPS tracking device for the car		
☐ a camera in the living room		
☐ a device that detects body movement		

B 🔊 CD 3.10 Listen again and answer the questions in the chart. Write one example for each item.

About you **C** **Pair work** Do you agree with the expert's views? What do you think about each monitoring device in the chart? Would you ever use one? How would you feel if someone monitored you?

Writing *It just takes a little thought.*

In this lesson, you . . .
- write a magazine article.
- use expressions like *a number of* and *a little*.
- avoid errors with *a number of*, etc.

Task   **Write a magazine article.**

A college magazine has asked you to write an article called *Enhancing friendships –
a how-to guide.*

A **Look at a model** Look at the extract from an article. Which topics does it cover? Write them in
the article. Brainstorm other ideas that the article could include.

| being considerate | communication | remembering birthdays, etc. | spending time together |

Relationships with friends are very important to our well-being. However, many of us often
take the people closest to us for granted, which can result in losing friends. There are **a**
number of factors that lead to improved relationships, including _____, _____,
and support. With just a little thought, you can enhance any friendship. . . .

There are a variety of ways to keep in touch with people. Social networks, texts, and phone
calls enable us to find out what is happening in our friends' lives and update them about events
in our own. They don't take a great deal of effort but do contribute to a feeling of closeness.

Not seeing friends can have a negative impact on your relationship. Therefore, it's
important to spend a certain amount of time with them.

B **Focus on language** Read the chart. Underline examples of the expressions in the article above.

Expressing number and amount in writing ⬇

With plural countable nouns, you can use: *a (large / huge / small) number of, a (wide) variety of,
a (wide) range of, several, many, various; a few* (= some), *few* (= not many).

*There are **a number of / several** factors that lead to improved relationships.*

With uncountable nouns, you can use: *a great deal of, a(n) (large / small)
amount of; a little* (= some), *little* (= not much).

*They don't take **a great deal of** time / effort. It takes **little** time / **a little** thought.*

Expressing effect

*contribute to, create, lead to,
result in, affect, have
an effect / impact on, as a
result, . . .*

Common errors

Use a plural verb with *a number of, several*, etc. + plural noun.
*There **are** a number of factors that **lead to** . . .*   (NOT *There ~~is~~ . . . that ~~leads to~~ . . .*)

C Circle the best expressions to complete the article. Sometimes there are two.

Spending quality time together doesn't need to cost **a huge amount of / a number of / various** money.
It just takes **little / a little / a small amount of** imagination. **Few / A few/ A variety of** friendships can
survive without regular contact, and there are **various / a great deal of / a variety of** ways you can spend
meaningful time together. Here are just **a little / a few / few** ideas: Take a walk. Go to a museum. Exercise.

Sending a message to say "Hi" doesn't take **a great deal of / several / little** time, either, but it can create
a number of / an enormous amount of goodwill. Don't just send messages on birthdays or other special
occasions. A birthday card may have **little / several / a few** effect if you are not in regular contact. You
can find **a range of / various / few** websites that have fun greeting cards to send at any time of year.

D **Write and check** Look at the Task at the top of the page. Write your article. Then check for errors.

Vocabulary notebook *Now or never*

pain and suffering
> *Divorce can cause a lot of pain and suffering, and I feel lucky that my parents never got divorced.*

A   **Use the expressions in the box to complete the sentences.**

above and beyond	live and work	success or failure	back and forth	sick and tired	wait and see

1. I'm not sure how I did on my last exam. I'll just have to _____.
2. People are always throwing trash around in my neighborhood. I'm _____ of it.
3. My dad is so great. If I ever ask a favor, he always goes _____ what I ask for.
4. What determines the _____ of a relationship is your ability to communicate.
5. When I'm working on a project with classmates, we send each other files _____ all day.
6. I'm lucky that I get to _____ in the same city.

B   **Write personalized sentences for these expressions.**

1. time and energy _____
2. stop and think _____
3. ups and downs _____
4. give-and-take _____
5. sooner or later _____
6. slowly but surely _____

C   **Word builder**   **Find the meanings of these expressions. Then use each one in a personalized sentence.**

far and away	now and then	out and about	to and from
last but not least	now or never	over and above	

I think communication is far and away the most important thing in any relationship.

D   **Focus on vocabulary**   **Complete the questions with the words in the box. Then write true answers. Refer to Exercise 2A on page 81 to help you.**

contend	dysfunctional	enhance	immersed	perceive	pursue	simultaneously	substitute	worrisome

1. Why do you think some families are _____? What can _____ their relationships?
2. Is a long email from a friend a good _____ for having a conversation with that person?
3. Do you _____ any differences in the way that older and younger people use technology?
4. Do you find it _____ that people spend so much time on their computers?
5. Do you ever have to _____ with television to get the attention of your family?
6. Do you ever get so _____ in your work that you forget to have dinner?
7. What two things can you do _____?
8. Are there any interests you'd like to _____ when you're older?

In Unit 8, you . . .
- talk about events in history and famous historical figures.
- use the perfect infinitive after verbs like *seem* and *would like*.
- use *it*-cleft sentences to focus on information.
- avoid topics of conversation with expressions like *Let's not go there.*
- say *That's what I'm saying* to focus on your viewpoint.

Lesson A *People in history*

1 Grammar in context

A Who are the most famous figures in your country's history? Why are they famous?

"Atatürk is probably one of the most famous, being the founder of the Republic of Turkey."

B ◀)) CD 3.11 Listen to four people talk about historical figures they wish they could have met. What reasons do they give?

WHICH HISTORICAL FIGURE WOULD YOU LIKE TO HAVE MET AND WHY?

For me it would definitely be Leonardo da Vinci. I'd love to have met him; he was such a creative genius and not just an artist. He seems to have foreseen a number of inventions that only came about hundreds of years later, like flying machines and types of weapons. I'd like to tell him he really did see the future.

Naomi, Chicago

I'd choose Cleopatra – the last pharaoh of ancient Egypt. She is thought to have been very beautiful and is generally considered to have formed some extremely effective political alliances. Not many women were that influential in ancient times. I'd like to have seen how she did it.

Lucinda, Nairobi

I'm Latin American, so I would nominate Simón Bolívar as the person I would like to have known. He's supposed to have been a very charismatic, courageous leader and is acknowledged to have helped achieve independence for several countries in Latin America in the nineteenth century.

Patricio, Caracas

I studied philosophy, so I would like to have spoken face-to-face with the Chinese philosopher Confucius. I'd like to have discussed with him his political philosophy and his ideas about family values. He seems to have had a lot of respect for older people, and even though he lived more than a thousand years ago, his beliefs are still relevant.

Li-yun, Shanghai

About you

C **Pair work** Discuss the questions about the people above. Give reasons for your views.

Which figure do you think . . .
1. attracted admiration and gained the most respect?
2. was the most intelligent and the most talented?
3. had ideas that could be applied nowadays?
4. was particularly clever at political relations?
5. accomplished the most?
6. would make the best role model?

2 Grammar Referring to past time

Figure it out

A Use the interviews to help you complete the answers. Then read the grammar chart.

1. What type of leader was Simón Bolívar? He seems _____.
2. Was Cleopatra good at politics? Yes, she is acknowledged _____.
3. Who does Naomi wish she could have met? She'd like _____.

The perfect infinitive ⬇

Grammar extra
See page 158.

Use the perfect infinitive for events in a period of time that lead up to the present or to a point in the past.
You can use the perfect infinitive after verbs like *seem, appear,* and *happen.*
*He seems **to have had** a lot of respect for older people.*

You can use the perfect infinitive after verbs such as *acknowledge, believe, consider, know, say,* and *think*
when they are in the passive, and after *be supposed to.*
*She is considered **to have formed** some extremely effective political alliances.*

You can use the perfect infinitive after *would like / love / hate,* etc., for events that did not happen.
*I'd love **to have met** Leonardo da Vinci.*
*Li-yun would like **to have spoken** face-to-face with Confucius.*

In conversation . . .

People generally say, e.g., *I would have liked
to do it,* not *I would like to have done it.* Some
also say, *I would have liked to have done it.*

B Complete the sentences using the verbs given and a
perfect infinitive. Some verbs are passive.

What famous person or people would you like to have met?

1. _____ (would love / meet) Mozart. He _____ (seem / be) a brilliant
musician, and he _____ (say / start) composing music at the age of five, which is
amazing. He _____ (think / die) from some kind of fever.
2. I _____ ('d like / travel) with Neil Armstrong, one of the astronauts that landed on
the moon. The moon landing _____ (acknowledge / be) a major event in our
history. My father _____ (happen / meet) one of the astronauts.
3. I _____ ('d like / interview) the captain of the *Mary Celeste.* The disappearance of
everyone on board _____ (consider / be) one of the strangest mysteries of all time.
The entire crew _____ (seem / disappear) from the ship for no reason at all.
4. I _____ ('d love / spend) a day with Catherine the Great of Russia. She became
empress after the death of her husband, Peter III, and _____ (acknowledge / help)
Russia become a great power. She _____ (seem / be) very intelligent.

About you

C Pair work Do you agree with the comments above? What would you have asked each person?

3 Viewpoint *I'd like to have met . . .*

Group work Discuss the questions. Agree on three people that you would all like to have met.

- What famous person from history would you like to have met?
- What contribution is he or she said to have made to history?
- What kind of person is he or she believed to have been?
- What interesting things is he or she supposed to have done?
- What one question would you like to have asked that person?
- How would you like to have spent the day with him or her?

*Speaking naturally
See page 141.*

"I'd love to have met John Lennon. He's generally acknowledged to have been a great songwriter."

Lesson B *Events that changed the world*

1 Vocabulary in context

A **What twentieth-century events do you think most changed the world? Make a list.**

"I think the invention of the Internet changed the world most. We just can't live without it now."

B 🔊 CD 3.12 **Listen to the podcast. What two broad kinds of historical change are mentioned?**

HOME   SUBSCRIBE   EPISODE GUIDE   MEET THE CAST   CONTACT   ▶ **PODCAST**

Many events are said to have been "world-changing," and it's not only headline writers who use this phrase. But what does it mean? In most cases, planet Earth as a whole remains the same, even after a **major** event such as a natural disaster. That said, a catastrophic asteroid impact millions of years ago is believed to have destroyed almost all life – an event that can genuinely be said to have been **universal** and world-changing. However, as a rule, even significant events have mostly **local** effects and only a **superficial** or **temporary** impact on the vast majority of people outside the affected region. Perhaps it is only when we are personally affected that we describe such events as "world-changing."

Occasionally, events do have a **profound** impact, such as the revolution in travel and communications in the twentieth century. For example, it was the invention of the airplane that made it possible to cross continents in a matter of hours, and it was when Internet use became widespread that the world turned into a global village. These innovations brought about **massive** changes, and many would now consider it impossible to live without them.

Equally, change can also be **gradual** or **imperceptible**. It was more than 30 years ago that scientists started alerting us to the fact that the world climate was changing, but the change was neither immediately **apparent** nor **sudden**. Events that may seem **minor** or **insignificant** – for example, **slight** or **minute** changes in average global temperatures over a number of years – can make it difficult to predict **lasting** or **long-term** effects. Generally, it is not the small things that we worry about. We react to **visible** or **rapid** change, and it is the events with **immediate** effects that get the headlines.

C **Pair work** **Answer the questions about the podcast.**

1. Why does the speaker mention an asteroid strike?
2. What do the airplane and the Internet have in common, from the writer's viewpoint?
3. Why is climate change a different kind of event from the invention of the Internet?

Word sort

D **Find adjectives in the podcast that are the opposite of the adjectives below. Can you think of an example of each type of change, effect, or impact?**

lasting effects	temporary	**massive** changes	or
significant events		**gradual** change	or
local effects		**imperceptible** change	or
superficial impact			
major event		**long-term** effects	

"The oil spills in the Gulf of Mexico had lasting effects on the tourist industries."

Vocabulary notebook

See page 93.

2 Grammar Giving ideas extra focus

Figure
it out

A How are these ideas expressed in the podcast? Write sentences. Then read the grammar chart.

1. The invention of the airplane made it possible to cross continents.
2. Headline writers aren't the only ones who use this phrase.
3. The world turned into a global village when Internet use became widespread.

Cleft sentences ⬇

Grammar extra
See page 159.

You can give extra focus to a single noun, phrase, or clause by putting it at the beginning of the sentence, after *it + be*. After nouns, use a relative pronoun – usually *who* or *that*. After other items, use a *that* clause.

Noun   *Scientists started alerting us to the fact that the world climate was changing.*
→ **It was scientists who / that** *started alerting us to the fact that the world climate was changing.*

Phrase   *Generally, we do***n't** *worry about* **the small things.**
→ *Generally,* **it is not the small things that** *we worry about.*

Clause   *We describe events as "world-changing"* **only when we are personally affected.**
→ **It is only when we are personally affected that** *we describe events as "world-changing."*

B Rewrite the numbered sentences as cleft sentences with *it + be* to give extra focus to the underlined words. Then practice telling the information to a partner.

Writing vs. Conversation

It-cleft sentences are about eight times more common in writing.

A. (1) The Internet is a global phenomenon, but <u>a British scientist</u> working in a physics lab in Geneva, Switzerland, invented it. (2) Perhaps <u>the Internet</u> has changed the way people communicate today more than anything else. Tim Berners-Lee devised a new way for scientists to share data by linking documents over the Internet. (3) He took it to the masses <u>only after his bosses rejected his proposal.</u> (4) He posted his idea to an online bulletin board as the "WWW project" <u>at 2:56:20 p.m. on August 6, 1991.</u> (5) He succeeded in creating the World Wide Web <u>because he persisted with his idea.</u> (6) <u>This universal revolution</u> brought us search engines and websites.

B. (1) Two scientists, Francis Crick and James Watson, published an article <u>on April 25, 1953,</u> which answered an age-old question. They had discovered the nature of DNA. (2) <u>This discovery</u> enabled us to understand how parents pass on characteristics, like eye and hair color, to their children. (3) Significant advances in medicine have been possible <u>thanks to their work.</u> In addition, the discovery allowed for the development of criminal forensics. (4) However, DNA wasn't used to convict someone in a criminal case <u>until 1987</u> in Florida, USA.

About
you

C Pair work Think of six people or events that have had the most profound effect on our lives. Make a list. Then compare ideas with another pair. Justify your choices.

"We chose the discovery of penicillin because it was penicillin that changed medicine and led to the discovery of other antibiotics."

Lesson C *Don't get me started.*

1 Conversation strategy Avoiding a topic

A Are you interested in history? Why? Why not? Share your ideas with the class.

B ◀))) CD 3.13 **Listen. What does Tom think about history? How about Celia?**

Tom	You know, I never did like history in school. It just wasn't a subject I enjoyed, remembering all those dates. I didn't see the point.
Celia	Well, I guess it's not just about learning dates. It's about trying to understand why people did things or what society was like through the ages.
Tom	But I mean, so often the facts get distorted, like what happened in the last war. But don't get me started on that.
Celia	Well, yeah. But that doesn't mean we shouldn't try to find out the truth and then learn from it so we don't repeat the same mistakes.
Tom	But that's what I'm saying. We don't learn, do we? I mean, look at what's happening around the world today. We seem to have learned absolutely nothing. It's like history repeating itself. But that's another story.
Celia	Yeah, but even if we still have disputes, maybe we'll deal with them in a different way. I mean, engage in dialog . . . negotiate.
Tom	But most of the time, talks just break down and don't go anywhere. But anyway, let's not get into politics.

C **Notice** how Tom uses expressions like these to avoid talking about certain topics. Find examples in the conversation.

> **Don't get me started (on . . .).**
> **(But) that's another / a whole other story.**
> **Let's not go there.**
> **Let's not get into / talk about politics / that.**
> **I'd rather not talk about it / that.**

In conversation . . .

People say *Don't get me started* about a topic they find annoying, and often before they say more about it. *I'd rather not talk about it* is a more serious way to show you want to avoid a topic.

D ◀))) CD 3.14 **Listen to more of the conversation. Complete the expressions that you hear. Then practice the whole conversation with a partner.**

Celia I know. There've been some terrible events in recent history, as you know.

Tom I know, _____. We probably won't agree on anything, so _____.

Celia OK, but it's amazing how little people know of their own country's history _____.

Tom Yeah, but there'll always be different versions of events, like the latest peace talks. _____.

Celia Yeah. They seem to have collapsed. _____. You know, I wonder how future generations will see us.

Tom Greedy and aggressive, I'd say. You know what I think. _____.

2 Strategy plus *That's what I'm saying.*

🔊 CD 3.15 You can use **That's what I'm saying** in responses to focus on your viewpoint.

But **that's what I'm saying**. We don't learn, do we?

In conversation . . .
People also say *That's what I mean / meant.*

🔊 CD 3.16 **Complete each conversation with two responses from the box. Write a–f. Then listen and practice. Practice again, this time giving your own answers to the questions.**

> a. That's what I meant. There's something in it for everyone.
> b. Yeah. That's what I'm saying. You need to know the context.
> c. That's what I'm saying. And literacy is an important part of that. And now, of course, there's the Internet.
> d. That's what I'm saying. It's such a broad area that it includes anything and everything.
> e. Exactly. That's what I mean. You need to know how it's developed to interpret it.
> f. Right. That's what I'm saying. Beliefs, opinions, philosophy – they all shape our actions.

1. *A* History is an interesting area because you can study the history of anything, can't you?
   B I suppose it involves everything from everyday life to great political events and wars and so on.
   A ☐☐

2. *A* Do you think you need to know the history of art to appreciate it?
   B Well, all art builds on the past, either by developing or rejecting it.
   A ☐☐

3. *A* I guess I'm interested in the history of ideas, like how ideas spread. Isn't that what's important?
   B Yeah. I guess new ideas help us develop and keep history moving.
   A ☐☐

3 Listening and strategies *Tracing family histories*

A 🔊 CD 3.17 **Listen to two friends talk about family histories. Complete the sentences. Circle a or b.**

1. Jennifer's great-grandmother was   a) reluctant to emigrate.   b) 80 when she emigrated.
2. Jennifer's great-grandfather   a) was a baker by profession.   b) enjoyed baking as a hobby.
3. She found out her family history   a) from the Internet.   b) from papers in the attic.
4. Patrick would like to have known   a) who his biological mother was.   b) what his original last name was.
5. He says states should help   a) parents raise adopted children.   b) children find their birth family.

B 🔊 CD 3.18 **Listen again. Answer the questions.**

1. What fact does Patrick mention when he says, "But that's another story"?
2. When Patrick says, "That's what I mean," what is he talking about?
3. Patrick says, "Let's not get into that." What doesn't he want to talk about?

About you

C **Pair work** **Discuss the questions.**

1. Is it important for people to know about their family history? Why? Why not?
2. Have you or any of your friends tried to trace your family history? Was it successful?
3. What do you know of your family history? Are there any interesting stories?
4. Do you think adopted children should be able to contact their biological family? Why? Why not?

Lesson D *Unearthing the past*

1 Reading

A Prepare You are going to read an article about ancient texts. Match the terms on the left with their definitions on the right. Then compare answers with a partner.

1. archaeology _____
2. papyrus _____
3. anthropology _____
4. manuscript _____
5. paleography

a. the study and interpretation of ancient writing
b. a document written by hand rather than printed
c. a kind of paper made from a plant that was common in Ancient Egypt
d. the study of human societies based on material evidence left behind
e. the study of human societies and cultures and how they develop

B 📥 **Read for main ideas** Read the article. What is the Ancient Lives Project? How does it work?

THE ANCIENT LIVES PROJECT

1 They may not have had computers, databases, social networking sites, or spreadsheets, but the ancient Egyptians are known to have kept careful written records, not only of important people and events but also of the minute details of everyday life. In 1896–1897, hundreds of thousands of fragments of papyrus with writing on them were found on the edge of a ruined Egyptian city, in a place which is believed to have been the city's landfill. The fragments, which filled 700 boxes, were taken back to Oxford, England. The manuscripts, written in ancient Greek, now belong to the Egypt Exploration Society – an organization that was established over 125 years ago to carry out archaeological fieldwork and research in Egypt.

2 As a rule, it is archaeologists, anthropologists, and paleographers who sift the evidence of our distant past, feed our hunger for knowledge about our ancestors, bring to life dead languages, and paint a detailed picture of ancient life for us. However, in this case, there were simply not enough experts to read all those tantalizing fragments of ancient Greek, so they mostly remained undisturbed in their boxes. Those pieces that the experts did decipher revealed a fascinating picture of ancient Egyptian life: Literary, religious, and philosophical texts sat alongside bits of gossip, receipts, marriage certificates, personal letters, love potions, wills, sports reports, and other everyday texts.

3 It is not uncommon for archaeologists to involve non-specialists in their work. The two men who discovered the papyrus fragments hired local labor in Egypt. Every year, volunteers take part in archaeological digs, spending hours on their hands and knees, delicately scraping in the sand and soil of lost cities or the remains of our ancestors' homes. It is this slow, painstaking work that helps archaeologists piece together the jigsaw puzzle of the past. It can also be fun: Working with a team at an archaeological site is how many young people choose to spend their vacations.

4 In 2011, a groundbreaking project was rolled out that allowed volunteers all over the world to help reveal the past while sitting at home in front of a computer screen. The Ancient Lives Project grew from a simple idea – log in at its website, look at a papyrus fragment on your screen, check each symbol you see against an on-screen keyboard of ancient Greek letters, click when you think you have a match, and after a few minutes' work, upload the results to the project's paleographers. It is this imaginative use of the collective labor of thousands of volunteers and "armchair archaeologists" that now enables the experts to read and share with us the hundreds of thousands of manuscripts so that we can look into a window on the past. And who knows? We may even see our own reflection.

> **Reading tip**
> Writers sometimes use a pronoun in a way that means you have to read on to find out what it means, as with the first word of the article *(They . . .).*

C **Check your understanding** Are the statements true (T) or false (F) based on the article?

1. The papyrus fragments had been carefully stored away by the Egyptians. _____
2. For a long time, nobody read most of the manuscripts that were found. _____
3. The manuscript fragments were largely official documents. _____
4. Archaeologists often get non-professionals to help with physical work. _____
5. You can earn money by taking part in the Ancient Lives Project. _____
6. You need to be able to understand ancient Greek to participate. _____

D **React** **Pair work** What would the documents you throw away or delete each week reveal to future generations about life today? Discuss.

② Focus on vocabulary Metaphors

A Find metaphors in the article to replace the words in bold.

1. Archaeologists **work carefully through** the evidence of our distant past. (para. 2) sift
2. Paleographers **translate languages that no one speaks anymore**. (para. 2)
3. Archaeologists **satisfy our desire** for knowledge about our ancestors. (para. 2)
4. They **describe in detail** ancient life. (para. 2)
5. Religious and philosophical texts **were found** alongside bits of gossip, receipts, etc. (para. 2)
6. Volunteers help archaeologists to **build a detailed picture** of the past. (para. 3)
7. In 2011, a project **began** that allowed volunteers to help decipher the manuscripts. (para. 4)
8. The translations of the manuscripts will allow people to **observe** the past. (para. 4)

B **Pair work** How important is it to "unearth the past"? Discuss, using the metaphors above.

③ Listening Citizen participation projects

A ◀))CD 3.19 Listen to a talk about citizen participation projects. Check (✓) the ones described.

1.	2.	3.	4.	5.
☐ Ships' records	☐ Whales communicating	☐ Visible stars	☐ The language of apes	☐ The surface of the moon

B ◀))CD 3.20 Listen again. Complete each sentence with three words.

1. The work of volunteers has made _____ to the Ancient Lives Project.
2. The volunteers who sit at their computers doing this kind of work are _____.
3. A project that would have taken 28 years can be done in _____ months with the help of citizen volunteers.
4. In the Old Weather Project, people are looking at _____ from World War I.
5. The data from the Old Weather Project will be used to predict _____.
6. Discovering stories from these ships is also _____.

C **Pair work** Which projects seem most interesting? Would you like to take part in one?

Writing *In the end, . . .*

In this lesson, you . . .
- write a narrative essay.
- order events in the past.
- avoid errors with *in the end* and *at the end*.

Task | **Write a historical narrative.**

You have been asked to write a history of your family, a family member, or someone in the community for a website. Write a short essay.

A **Look at a model** Look at the extracts from a narrative essay. Order the events 1–4.

☐ Annie left her hometown.   ☐ Annie got married.   ☐ The war started.   ☐ Annie's parents died.

> My mother, Annie Mason, left the city where she lived shortly after the war started and went to work on a farm in the country. Prior to leaving home, she had lost both her parents in the war. Shocked and saddened by this tragedy, she decided to leave the city. As the train took her away from her old life, she felt sad and lonely. . . .
>
> On arriving at the country station, she met a young man who offered to carry her bags. This was the man who eventually became my father. It was love at first sight. Finally, she had a chance of happiness.
>
> They moved back to the city once the war had ended. As soon as they found jobs, they married and subsequently had four children, all of whom were successful. In the end, they retired to a small house near the railroad station where they'd first met. . . .

B **Focus on language** Read the chart. Then underline examples of ordering events in Exercise A.

Ordering events in writing 📥

You can use these structures to vary the way you present the order of events.

Time clauses	*After / Once / As soon as* the war ended, they married. *On arriving at the station,* she met my father.
Participle clauses	*Arriving at the station,* she met my father. *Saddened by this tragedy,* she decided to leave the city.
Adverbs and adverbial phrases	*She had **previously** lived in the city.* *They **subsequently / eventually** had four children.* *In the end, / After a while,* they married.

Writing vs. Conversation

Prepositions + *-ing* are more common in writing.

■ Conversation
■ Writing

C Rewrite these sentences, using the word(s) given and making any other changes.

1. ~~After~~ My father met my mother, ~~and then~~ he applied for a job in California. (after)
2. He had ~~previously~~ lived in the U.S., but he moved back to Mexico when his contract came to an end. (previously)
3. ~~As soon as~~ He arrived back in his hometown ~~and~~ he met the woman who became my mother. (as soon as / eventually)
4. After they were married, they moved to San Diego. (once)
5. My mother found out that she was pregnant before their fifth wedding anniversary. (prior to)
6. They had three more children and were happy living in the U.S. (after a while)
7. They moved back to Mexico and left their "American life" behind them. (in the end / participle clause)
8. When he walked into his new home, my father vowed he would never leave again. (on)

D **Write and check** Now write a short essay as described in the Task above. Then check for errors.

Common errors

Use *at the end of* + a noun. ***At the end of the war,*** *they got married.*

In the end refers to the conclusion of all the events. ***In the end,*** *they retired.*

Use *finally* at the end of a series of other events. *She **finally** found happiness.*

Vocabulary notebook *Deep, low, high*

Learning tip | Synonyms and antonyms

When you learn a new word, look up its synonyms (words with similar meanings) and antonyms (words with opposite meanings). Be careful: Different meanings of a word can have different synonyms and antonyms.

a deep conversation = meaningful, profound
≠ trivial, light-hearted
a deep voice = a low voice
≠ a high-pitched voice

A Underline three antonyms to the words in bold below. Circle the synonym.

1. **significant**	meaningless	insignificant	considerable	unimportant
2. **local**	universal	global	foreign	nearby
3. **superficial**	detailed	meaningless	profound	thorough
4. **imperceptible**	unseen	conspicuous	striking	apparent
5. **lasting**	permanent	temporary	brief	fleeting

B Write a synonym and an antonym for each of these words.

	Synonym	Antonym
1. major	_____	_____
2. gradual	_____	_____
3. long-term	_____	_____
4. massive	_____	_____

C Word builder These words are all antonyms of words in Exercises A and B. Find their meanings and add them to the examples above.

abrupt	deep	miniature	obvious	transient

D (Focus on vocabulary) Match the metaphors from the article on page 91 with their meanings.

Metaphor
1. bring something to life _____
2. sift (through), e.g., evidence, facts _____
3. feed a hunger for knowledge _____
4. paint a detailed picture _____
5. sit alongside _____
6. piece together a jigsaw puzzle of something _____
7. roll out (a project) _____
8. look into a window on _____

Meaning
a. satisfy the desire to learn
b. make something interesting or current
c. observe
d. work carefully through
e. explain or describe in detail
f. begin or put into practice
g. figure out a mystery or problem
h. be (together) with

E Now look at these metaphors. Write the metaphor from Exercise D that means the opposite of each.

1. wind something down roll out_____
2. starve someone of something _____
3. kill an idea _____
4. look into a crystal ball _____
5. brush over something _____

THEY SAY PEOPLE WHO DON'T LEARN FROM HISTORY ARE DOOMED TO REPEAT IT.

THEN WE BETTER STUDY. I DON'T WANT TO REPEAT THIS CLASS.

Unit 8: History   93

Engineering wonders

In Unit 9, you . . .

- talk about engineering feats, challenges, and developments.
- use *whoever, whatever*, etc., to talk about unknown people or things.
- start sentences with negative adverbs for extra emphasis.
- give facts using expressions like *considering* and *given* (*that*).
- use *at all* and *whatsoever* to emphasize negative ideas.

Lesson A *Engineers change the world.*

1 Grammar in context

A 🔊 CD 3.21 **Do you know what engineers do? Make a list. Then read the college web page and see how many of your ideas are mentioned.**

Change the world – be an engineer!

Wherever you look, you'll see the work of a talented engineer who has designed, tested, and improved the objects around you. Whatever goes wrong or whenever there is a problem to be solved, however complex, one can rely on engineers to apply their knowledge of math and science – along with some creativity – to come up with a solution. So, what do engineers do? Here's just a sample of their work.

CHEMICAL ENGINEERS Whenever you wash your jeans, remember it was a chemical engineer that developed the fade-resistant dye. Pick up any game console – that scratchproof plastic was made by these engineers. Chemical engineers also help produce medicines and cosmetics, and find solutions to damage caused by harmful chemicals.

CIVIL ENGINEERS These engineers are at the heart of urban planning and transportation design. Wherever you go and whatever you do today, you'll encounter their work. The system of pipes that brings water to your shower, the roads you drive on, the bridges you cross, the buildings you occupy – these are all examples of civil engineering work.

MATERIALS SCIENCE ENGINEERS Engineers in this field work with materials such as ceramics, plastics, and metals. Their work is central to engineering as a whole. Materials science engineers process, design, and test whatever materials are used in all other branches of engineering.

BIOMEDICAL ENGINEERS Bringing together the fields of engineering and medicine, biomedical engineers work on whatever needs to be done to improve health care. They design anything from artificial body parts and lifesaving equipment to drug and gene therapies.

However you look at it, a career in engineering is exciting and rewarding. Whoever you are and whichever field of engineering you choose, you have the potential to design and develop products that will have an enormous impact on society.

B **Pair work** **Discuss the questions.**

1. What skills do engineers need, according to the web page?
2. What types of activities do the different fields have in common?
3. Which field of engineering sounds most interesting? Which is most valuable to society?
4. Does the web page succeed in getting people to consider engineering as a career, in your view?

2 Grammar Talking about unknown people and things

Figure it out

A How does the web page express these ideas? Write the phrases. Then read the grammar chart.

1. It doesn't matter what goes wrong. . . .
2. At any time at all when there is a problem to be solved . . .
3. It doesn't matter how you look at it. . . .

Grammar extra
See page 160.

whatever, whichever, whoever, whenever, wherever, however

The -*ever* words have the meaning "any at all" or "it doesn't matter what, who, where, etc."

Whatever, whichever can be determiners or pronouns.	**Whatever** goes wrong, one can turn to an engineer. These engineers work on **whatever** (task) needs to be done. **Whichever** (field) you choose, you will make an impact.
Whoever is a pronoun.	**Whoever** you are, you have the potential to impact society.
Whenever, wherever, however are adverbs.	**Whenever** there is a problem, an engineer will fix it. **Wherever** you look, you'll see the work of an engineer. **However** you look at it, a career in engineering is exciting.

In conversation . . .

Whatever is the most frequent. It is often used in the vague expressions *or / and whatever.*
We're not all cut out to be engineers **or whatever.**

B 🔊 CD 3.22 Complete the sentences with -*ever* words. Then listen and check.

1. *A* Do you really understand what engineers do?
   B Well, I didn't until now. I mean, _____ someone said they were studying engineering, I never really understood what they were doing.
   C I do – well, kind of. My friend's an electrical engineer, and he told me that _____ I use like a cell phone or satellite TV or _____, that's the kind of thing he's worked on.

2. *A* Do you have what it takes to be an engineer?
   B Sure. _____ there's a problem at home, I can usually fix it.
   C Me? Absolutely not. _____ way I look at it, I'm not cut out to be an engineer.

3. *A* Do you think engineering could be an exciting career?
   B Oh, definitely. _____ says it's boring doesn't know what they're talking about. I mean, _____ field of engineering you look at, there's something interesting.
   C It depends. I mean, designing things for space stations or _____ sounds fun.

4. *A* Do you ever think about how roads and bridges and _____ actually get built?
   B Yes. _____ I see a new bridge or skyscraper or _____ being built, I think _____ designed all that must be a genius. It's amazing how it's all planned and managed.
   C Yeah. _____ you think of high-rise buildings, you have to admire _____ built them.

About you

C Group work Take turns answering the questions. Who knows the most about engineering? Who would be most suited to a career in engineering?

Lesson B *Incredible feats*

1 Vocabulary in context

A 🔊 CD 3.23 **Read the article. Why was constructing the bridge so challenging?**

The Millau Viaduct in southern France has been called "the freeway in the sky." On stormy days, it looks as though it is floating above the clouds. No wonder. When constructed, it was the world's tallest road bridge at 343 meters (1,125 feet) at its highest point above the River Tarn. Never before had engineers attempted to build a bridge of this size and scale. At the outset, little did they realize how much the project would push the boundaries of engineering to its limits. Nor did they know how many problems they would face. However, not once did the engineers fail to find a solution.

The viaduct is a four-lane highway across one of the deepest valleys in France. Not only does it ease the congestion of the north–south routed traffic between Paris and Spain, but it has become one of the country's most celebrated projects – a landmark in itself.

Engineers faced three challenges in building the viaduct. They had to:

- **construct** the tallest **concrete** bridge piers (supporting towers) in the world;
- **assemble** and **maneuver** a 36,000-tonne (40,000-ton), 2.5-kilometer (1.5-mile) freeway, rolling it out to **position** it onto the top of the towers;
- **erect** seven massive **steel** pylons, each weighing 700 tonnes (770 tons), and **install** 11 pairs of steel cables.

In addition, not only did this dangerous work have to be done way above the ground at a height taller than the Eiffel Tower, but it had to be completed in four years! Nowhere else on Earth had engineers accomplished a project of this magnitude **in** such **a short time frame**. By comparison, one of the longest bridges in the world – the Akashi-Kaikyo in Japan – took 10 years to complete. However, under no circumstances could the project **fall behind schedule**. Any **delays** would have cost the construction company $30,000 a day in penalties. Not only did they **complete** it **on time**, but the viaduct opened a month **ahead of schedule**.

The biggest challenge of all, apart from **engineering** the bridge to be strong enough to withstand the elements, was to make it blend into the beautiful landscape. Only by **elevating** the highway so far above ground and slimming down the towers and road deck were the architects able to achieve such a delicate and stunning visual impact.   [more]

Word sort

B **Complete the chart with vocabulary in the article. Add other items you want to learn. Then tell a partner about engineering feats you know of.**

materials	build	move	schedules	other
	construct			

"Well, one that comes to mind is the airport they constructed in Hong Kong. They built an island to put it on."

Vocabulary notebook

See page 103.

2 Grammar Emphasizing ideas

Figure it out

A Underline the sentences in the article that express the same ideas as the sentences below. Then read the grammar chart.

1. They not only completed it on time, but the viaduct opened a month ahead of schedule.
2. Engineers had never before attempted to build a bridge of this size and scale.
3. They didn't realize how much the project would push the boundaries of engineering.

Negative adverbs and word order

Grammar extra
See page 161.

If you use a negative adverb (e.g., *never, not*) to start a sentence for emphasis, put the verb before the **subject**. Use *do* or *does* for simple present and *did* for simple past verbs.
Not only **does it ease** *traffic congestion, but it has become a landmark.*
Not once **did the engineers fail** *to find a solution.*
Never *before* **had engineers attempted** *to build a bridge like this.*

Use the same inversion after *little, rarely,* and *only* + prepositional phrase.
Only *by elevating the highway* **were the architects able** *to achieve the stunning visual impact.*

Writing vs. Conversation
The inverted forms are about three times more common in formal writing than in conversation.

B ◀))CD 3.24 **Rewrite the sentences starting with the words given. Make any other necessary changes. Listen and check. Then close your book. How much information can you remember?**

1. They not only had to erect seven towers taller than the Eiffel Tower, but they also had to make sure the towers were at exactly the right point. *Not only . . .*
2. They supplied the concrete by building a concrete factory on-site. *Only . . .*
3. Engineers have rarely constructed freeways out of steel. *Rarely . . .*
4. Engineers had never before built such a tall bridge. *Never before . . .*
5. No one had positioned a road onto towers in this way. *Nor . . .*
6. They didn't realize how difficult it would be. *Little . . .*
7. You never hear of projects like this going according to schedule. *Never . . .*

3 Listening Other amazing feats

A ◀))CD 3.25 **Listen to three extracts from a documentary. What project is being described? Number the pictures 1–3. There is one extra.**

☐ the Queen Mary 2   ☐ Palm Islands, Dubai   ☐ Churaumi Aquarium, Japan   ☐ Channel Tunnel, Britain / France

B ◀))CD 3.26 **Listen again. Answer the questions about each project.**

1. What was the main challenge of the project?
2. What specific aims were engineers trying to accomplish?
3. What world record did it break at the time?
4. How many people use the facility annually?

C **Pair work** **Choose an engineering feat from the lesson or another you know about. Prepare a presentation to give to the class.**

Lesson C *It makes no sense whatsoever.*

1 Conversation strategy Supporting ideas

A **What are the biggest challenges engineers will face in the next century? Make a list.**

Not only will there be more people, but there'll be more cars. So building roads will be a challenge.

B 🔊 CD 3.27 **Listen. What challenges do Sonia and Scott talk about?**

Sonia   I was just listening to a report on the radio about engineering challenges for the next century.

Scott   Yeah? Let me guess. Is one of them building a colony on Mars? I mean, it makes no sense whatsoever, but . . .

Sonia   No, and in view of the fact that it takes about seven months to get there, that's a long way off.

Scott   Right. OK. Well, let's see, um, considering the price of gas, maybe finding cheaper sources of fuel?

Sonia   Yeah, there were a couple about energy – like making solar energy economical. But there's one that's kind of surprising, given the weather.

Scott   Uh-huh. Yeah?

Sonia   Providing access to clean water.

Scott   Oh, right. That's pretty basic considering we're in the twenty-first century. But I guess it makes sense in light of the fact that some places got no rain at all last year. I mean, none whatsoever.

Sonia   Yeah, they were saying one in six people don't have access to clean water for whatever reason.

C **Notice** how Sonia and Scott use facts to support their opinions and thoughts, using expressions like these. Find the examples in the conversation.

> *considering*
> *given (that / the fact that)*
> *in view of / in light of (the fact that)*

D 🔊 CD 3.28 **Listen. Complete the sentences with the expressions you hear.**

1. _____ the world's population is growing, I predict there'll be a crisis over water one day.
2. For some regions, access to water should be relatively easy, _____ the technology to extract water from underground already exists.
3. Having clean water is a really pressing problem, especially _____ something like 80 percent of illnesses in developing countries are linked to poor water conditions.
4. _____ over 90 percent of the world's water is in the ocean, we should find a way to use more sea water for drinking water.
5. _____ everyone needs water, you'd think more people would be concerned about it.
6. _____ how precious clean water is, we should pay more for it and people should be fined if they waste it.

About you **E** **Pair work** Discuss the statements in Exercise D. What are your views?

A I think there will definitely be a crisis over water supplies in the future.

B Especially considering it's such a basic need. Some people say it will even lead to conflicts.

2 Strategy plus *at all, whatsoever*

◄)) CD 3.29 You can use **at all** or **whatsoever** to emphasize a negative phrase.

Whatsoever is more emphatic. It is mostly used after **no . . .**, **not any . . .**, or **none**.

Some places got **no** rain **at all**. I mean, **none whatsoever**.

In conversation . . .

Whatsoever is typically used after *none, nothing,* or these nouns: *(no / any) problem(s), reason, sense, evidence, doubt(s), impact, effect.*

aquifens. ✶

About you

Find two responses for each comment. Write the letters a–f. Then practice in pairs. Continue the conversations.

1. Engineering is so important, yet it's not a subject you can take in high school. __D__ __F__
2. It seems that either money or politics gets in the way of finding solutions to most problems. __A__ __C__
3. It takes years before engineering breakthroughs affect most people's lives. __B__ __E__

> a. Right. But there's no doubt whatsoever that we can solve these issues.
> b. Yes, a lot of them have no impact on us whatsoever.
> c. Right. It makes no sense whatsoever. I mean, we should just get on with it and sort these things out.
> d. I know. There are no classes in it at all. There was nothing whatsoever like that when I was a kid.
> e. Well, I don't see much evidence at all for that. It depends what advances you mean.
> f. Yeah, and there shouldn't be any problem at all including it in the curriculum.

3 Strategies *More priorities*

A Circle the correct options to complete the conversations. Circle both options if they are both correct. Then practice with a partner. Practice again, using different expressions.

1. *A* I wonder what some of the other engineering challenges are. Do you have any ideas?
   B Well, mapping the brain would be a huge breakthrough. I mean, **given** / **considering** that we know so little about diseases like Alzheimer's.
   A Oh, there's no doubt **whatsoever** / **in view of the fact that**. If they could treat brain disorders, that would be huge. I mean, they have no cure **whatsoever** / **at all** for migraines, even. → *Bad headech.*

   important.

2. *A* What's the most *immediate* challenge, do you think?
   B Well, they need to update a lot of the infrastructure in many cities. **Considering** / **In light of** the fact that so many of the subways and sewers are so old, that should be a priority.
   A True. And there's no reason **considering** / **at all** not to do that now. They know how to.

3. *A* Do you think developing space technology and exploring Mars is a priority?
   B I don't know. I don't think it has **any impact whatsoever** / **given** on our daily lives. Though I guess studying asteroids might be good, **in view of** / **given** that we've been hit by asteroids in the past.

   Big rock in space

About you

B Pair work Ask and answer the questions in Exercise A. Give your own answers.

Speaking naturally

See page 142.

Lesson D *Robotics*

Debris ← sidince (handwritten)

1 Reading

A Prepare What do you know about robots? How are robots used? Make a list. Then scan the article to see if your ideas are mentioned.

Robots are used in the medical field for things like keyhole surgery. (handwritten)

B Read for main ideas Read the article. Then check (✓) the best title for the article.

1. ☐ Robots cause unimaginable problems   3. ☐ Home is where your robot is
2. ☑ The future is here and it's robotic

1 Robots are probably not high on the list of priorities for the average consumer. The nearest they might come to a robot is a robotic vacuum cleaner, which maneuvers its way around the home picking up dust. For most people, not only is the thought of interacting with a humanoid robot in their kitchen highly unlikely, but it also seems a little absurd. Some even consider it positively creepy, which may in part be because people are unsure how to relate to a robot. Such reluctance might also be explained by the ethical dilemmas posed by using robots instead of real people for certain tasks. Is it acceptable, for example, to have robots babysitting our children or looking after our elderly?

2 Robots have of course played a critical part in society for decades. In the 1960s, robots transformed the automotive industry by performing hazardous and repetitive tasks and working more efficiently and more accurately than humans. They could also work longer hours, which undoubtedly had an enormous impact on the profitability of the industry. Since then, industrial robots have been deployed in various manufacturing and electronics industries. Many of the products we purchase have been assembled or handled in some way by robots. Little do consumers realize how much their lives are actually already influenced by robotics.

3 If you consider the robotics industry today, there doesn't seem to be a field that is *not* influenced by robotics in significant ways. Indeed, robotics now plays a role in everything from agriculture and forestry to mining and construction – even to warfare.

Medical robotics

4 For years now, surgeons have been using robots in performing different types of operations. Not only is robotic surgery less invasive, but recovery for the patient is much quicker. More recent groundbreaking developments may have a profound impact on identifying and treating

→ spreads quickly. (handwritten)

serious diseases. For example, ETH Zürich researchers have developed micro-robots that are the size of bacteria. While more research needs to be conducted, possible applications include carrying medicine to specific areas of the body and treating heart disease.

Search and rescue

5 Whatever challenges responders face when they arrive at a large-scale disaster site – for example, after an earthquake – one of the greatest is determining where victims may still be trapped. Germany's Fraunhofer Institute has been developing a robotic "spider" that can easily move through the debris of collapsed buildings and send rescuers live images or even sense hazards such as leaking gas. The advantages of using robots as opposed to humans in these situations are obvious.

Ocean exploration

6 U.S. Navy-backed research has produced a robotic "jellyfish" that can power itself using hydrogen from seawater. Possible applications

include monitoring oceans for signs of pollution or for security purposes, and for exploration of otherwise inaccessible ocean waters.

7 However you look at it, robots will increasingly be part of our lives in the future. The field of robotics is rapidly expanding, and scientists are forging ahead with developing robots that can see, speak, think, and even make decisions based on the environment around them. The applications of robotics seem unlimited, and certainly the general public might perceive the advantages of using robots in specialized areas. The question remains: How accepting will we be of having robots rather than humans, as caregivers for our families?

C **Understanding inference** Do the statements below agree with the information in the article? Write Y (Yes), N (No), or NG (Information not given).

1. The average consumer really wants to get a robot for their home. _1_ No
2. It's generally more efficient to use robots in industry. yes 2
3. Patients who have robotic surgery live longer. NG
4. The robotic spider decides where it should go to find victims of earthquakes. NG
5. The robotic jellyfish can go to places where humans can't normally go. yes 6
6. Robots will always play a limited part in our lives in the future. No 7

2 Focus on vocabulary Verbs

A Find verbs with similar meanings to the verbs in bold. Rewrite the questions, using the correct forms of the verbs and making any other changes needed.

1. Given that robots have no emotions, can we really **communicate** or **connect with** them? (para. 1)
2. If you were to **do** a survey of friends, do you think they would want a robot in their home? (para. 4)
3. Can you **recognize** the ways in which humanoid robots are lacking? (para. 4)
4. What industries do you know of where robots are **used**? What jobs do they **do**? (para. 2)
5. How do you think robots will **change** the workplace in the future? (para. 2)
6. How would you **decide** if robots could make good caregivers or teachers? (para. 5)
7. Will we need to **watch** robots to make sure that they don't become more powerful than humans? (para. 6)

About you **B** **Pair work** Discuss the questions above. Think of as many ideas as you can.

3 Listening *Is she for real?*

A Read the questions about a humanoid robot. Can you guess the answers?

1. ☐ How did they build "her"?
2. ☑ What can "she" do?
3. ☐ How much did she cost to build?
4. ☐ How do people react to her?
5. ☑ What applications does she have?
6. ☐ What are the ethical issues of "human" robots?
7. ☑ Do people want robots as friends?

B ◀))CD 3.30 Listen to a radio interview. Which questions does the guest answer? Check (✓) the boxes.

C ◀))CD 3.31 Listen again. Write one detail to answer the questions you checked in Exercise B.

Geminoid F

4 Viewpoint Applications for the future

Group work Imagine there are no technological barriers whatsoever. How could robots be useful? Discuss your ideas about specific applications. What are your top 10 ideas?

"You could have a robot that mows lawns – kind of like a robot vacuum cleaner. The thing is you'd have to make sure it didn't cut down all your flowers."

> **In conversation . . .**
>
> You can use *The thing is . . .* to introduce ideas or problems.

Writing *A good alternative*

In this lesson, you . . .

- write a classification essay.
- express alternatives.
- avoid errors with *would rather / rather than*.

Task   **Write an essay.**
Can robots replace human beings in all activities? Give reasons and examples in your response.

A   Look at a model Look at these extracts from an essay. Think of a topic to add to each paragraph.

> . . . There are a number of fields in which robots can and should be used as opposed to human beings. These can be classified into the following types: dangerous activities; tasks requiring extreme precision; tedious, repetitive work; and activities that require huge computing power. One area is in heavy industry, where robots are already used instead of human beings. Not only can they do dangerous or unpleasant jobs, they are also more efficient. Another example of where robots are a good alternative to humans is in space exploration. . . . Yet another is . . .
>
> . . . On the other hand, there are some fields where a robot, however smart, would be no substitute for a human being. One example of this is caring for people in hospitals. Although robots can now perform surgery, human caregivers rather than robots are best at satisfying the psychological needs of patients. In fact, most patients would rather be cared for by a human caregiver than a robot. An additional area is . . .

Classifying

There are a number of . . .
One is . . . Another . . . Yet another . . .

They can be classified into the following types: . . .

They can be divided into four groups / categories. The first is . . .

B   Focus on language Read the chart. Then underline the expressions for stating alternatives and preference in the paragraphs in Exercise A.

Stating alternatives and preference in writing

You can use these expressions to write about alternatives.
*Robots are used in industry **in place of / instead of / rather than** humans.*
*Human caregivers **as opposed to** robots are best at caring for patients.*
*Robots are a good **alternative to / substitute for** humans in space.*

Would rather, be preferable to, and *be no substitute for* express preference.
*Most people **would rather** have a human caregiver **than** a robot.*
*Robots **are no substitute for** humans in some areas.*

In writing . . .

Rather than joins nouns, verbs, prepositional phrases, adjectives, or adverbs. Notice the verb forms after *rather than*.

*Rather than **use / using** humans for these tasks, we should use robots.*

C   Complete the sentences with expressions from the chart. How many correct answers are there?

1. In jobs where conditions are dangerous, robots are the obvious substitute human workers.
2. The construction industry could easily use robotic devices instead of human beings.
3. There are many industrial jobs where robots would be a better than humans.
4. Manufacturers would rather use robotic technology because it preferable employing people.
5. instead of using human mechanics, some companies now use robots that repair themselves.
6. In teaching, however, rather than use robots as teachers, we should always employ humans.
7. Robots are no substitute for people when it comes to jobs such as hotel receptionists.

D   Write and check Now write your essay as described in the Task above. Then check for errors.

Common errors

Do not use *prefer* after *would rather.*
***I would rather be** cared for by a robot.* (NOT *I would rather prefer to be . . .*)

Avoid using *rather* before *than* in basic comparisons.
*Robots are more suited to heavy work **than** humans.* (NOT *. . . work rather than . . .*)

Vocabulary notebook *How do you do it?*

Learning tip   Ask a question

When you learn new vocabulary, put it into a
question to ask yourself. Thinking of the
question and answer can help you remember it.

Q What's made of steel in the kitchen?
A The silverware / knives and forks.

A   Answer the questions. Use the words in bold in your answers.

1. Is there any **concrete** in the building where you live? _____ yes _____
2. Are you good at **maneuvering** a car into a small space? _____
3. Are you usually able to **complete** your assignments **on time**? _____
4. Is there an **elevated** highway near your home? _____
5. Have you ever tried to **assemble** flat packed furniture? _____

B   Write questions and answers for these words.

1. construct _____
2. erect _what is erected in front of town hall?_ _____
3. engineer _____
4. install _____
5. position _____
6. fall behind schedule _____
7. delay _____
8. in a short time frame _____
9. ahead of schedule _can you finish test ahead of schedule_

**C   Word builder Find the meanings of these words from the article on page 96. Write questions and
answers for them.**

| to blend into   to float   a landmark   a landscape   a lane   a penalty   a pylon   a viaduct |

A How can new buildings blend into the natural environment?
B Well, using materials in the same colors as those naturally found in an area can help.

**D (Focus on vocabulary) Read the questions below. Replace the verbs in bold with words from the box.
Then write your own answers to the questions. Refer to Exercise 2A on page 101 to help you.**

| conduct   deployed   determine   identify   interacting   monitor   perform   relate to   transform |

1. What's the best way to **decide** which courses you should take in college?
2. What single thing would **change** your life **completely**?
3. How do you **get along with** people generally? Are you good at
   communicating with others?
4. What jobs in your home would you let a robot **do**?
5. Are you able to **recognize** your own strengths and weaknesses?
6. Have you ever had to **do** a survey for a school project?
7. Which industries are robots best **used** in?
8. How does your boss or professor **watch and check on** your performance?

Checkpoint 3 *Units 7–9*

1 Is life easier now?

A Rewrite the underlined parts of the sentences, starting with the words in bold. Then complete the missing parts of the expressions.

In this _____ age, many young people may think that life is hard. They **not only** find it difficult to get work, but that it takes time _____ even to get an interview. Young people have **never before** found it so difficult to buy their first home. But maybe we need to _____ think for a moment, because it's **only** by looking back in history that we are able to gain a different perspective.

In the 1930s, people were accustomed to the _____ downs of the stock market, but when it crashed on October 29, 1929, it initiated the Great Depression. The U.S. had **never before** experienced such a catastrophic economic loss, which was coupled with a drought and failure of crops. The Depression **not only** affected the economy, but it also had a huge social impact. People had **rarely** had so little money. It was a time of great pain _____.

Unemployment rates rose above and _____ anything seen previously. Many young men **not only** had to wait to find work before marrying, but many, sick _____ of not being able to find work, migrated in the thousands to other states. Divorce rates had **rarely** been as low as in the 1930s. However, _____ wives often ran away from their marriages. Homelessness became a huge problem. Some people were able to find a roof over their heads **only** by moving in with their relatives.

History shows us that _____ later things can change, and for the 1930s generation, they did – slowly _____. We'll have to _____ see what the next decades will bring us. But one thing is for sure: we move back _____ between good times and hard times.

B Pair work Do you think life is difficult for young people? In what ways is life today easier than a hundred years ago? Summarize your points with expressions like *At the end of the day.*

"*. . . When all is said and done, life is a lot easier today than a hundred years ago.*"

2 Learning lessons from history

Cross out one word to correct the underlined phrases. Rewrite sentences beginning with a bold phrase as a cleft. Rewrite the *italic* sentences without using *if*.

View: How do we approach problems in the world needs to change. We should analyze precisely what are the problems are. Then we should consider whether have there have been similar problems in history. What we do we fail to do is learn lessons from history.

Comment 1: **Sir Winston Churchill said,** "Those who fail to learn from history are doomed to repeat it." **When we are faced** with a world crisis, we look back and consider how did it happened. **Only several decades ago,** our country suffered a crisis that threatened our security. Yet most people have no idea why do things like that happen. **When people's lives are directly affected,** they pay attention to what's going on in the world.

Comment 2: If we had learned anything from the twentieth century, this century might be more peaceful. We should look back before any crisis looms. If we don't, we are doomed. And if you should think our problems are new, think again. If you ask any historian, they'll tell you the same problems occur throughout history. If I were in a position of influence, I'd make history a required subject every year of school.

3 Improve your relationships

A Complete the article with *whatever, whenever, whoever, whichever, however,* and *wherever.* Then replace the words in bold with one word with a similar meaning.

Problems with a relationship? _____ you look, you'll find advice. But have you tried these tips?

1. _____ you do, don't ignore a problem – no matter how **unimportant** it may seem. If it's a **small** issue, talk it through right away. _____ is at fault, ask what *you* can do to help solve the problem. You'll notice an **instant** change in attitude from your partner.

2. _____ you have an argument, figure out what it is *really* about. Many times they seem to be about something "**on the surface**," but often there's a deeper problem. So focus on _____ *that* problem might be, and _____ you are having an argument about the same old topic, don't just fire off a **quick** answer. Try a different response. You might see a **quick** change in the direction of the argument and a **clear** difference in the outcome. Bad moods are **common**. If your partner is in a bad mood, just remember it's probably **for a short time**. Remember that while there's a **small** chance it's about you, most likely it's not. So _____ it's **obvious** that he or she needs some space, give it to them.

3. _____ the problem, _____ you solve it, use it as a life lesson. Solving even **tiny** problems can create **deep** and lasting changes in your relationships in the future.

B Pair work Discuss the advice in Exercise A. What other advice do you have? Use expressions like *considering* and *in light of (the fact that)* to support your opinions.

A *However you look at it, you can't really ignore any problem in a relationship.*
B *Right. I mean, given the fact that you live with someone day after day, it's important to solve problems.*

4 Construction projects

A Complete the paragraph with words and expressions. Use the cues given to help you.

Many modern buildings are made of steel and _____ (materials). Sometimes they are _____ (built) or _____ (put together) in one place and then brought to the construction site to be _____ (moved) into position or _____ (put up). After that, all the services need to be _____ (put in). Construction scheduling is a huge challenge. Even though companies agree to complete projects _____ (quickly), their schedules often _____ (are late). This can be because of a _____ (lateness) in getting materials or because the project is complex. For example, roads that are _____ (lifted up) above cities are particularly complex. However, companies often have to pay penalties if the project is not _____ (finish punctually).

B Use the verbs given with perfect infinitives. Then add the expressions in the box. There may be more than one correct answer. Do you have similar views about your city?

don't get me started   in that case   let's not go there   then   what I'm saying   whatsoever

Everything's different now. If you look at old photos, the city _____ (seem / change) completely. The old stores _____ (appear / go – I mean, there are none left _____. The old neighborhoods _____ (be supposed to / be) really beautiful, so _____, why did they demolish all the old wooden houses? It's terrible. But _____. I _____ (would love / meet) the planners and asked, "Why did you destroy the character of the city, _____?" They also took out all the trolley cars, which _____ (be said to / be) more environmentally friendly than cars. We need to think about the environment. But _____. We've just lost so much. That's _____.

Unit 10 Current events

In Unit 10, you . . .

- talk about news and how it is reported.
- use continuous infinitives to report ongoing events.
- use the subjunctive to write what should happen.
- use *this* and *these* or *that* and *those* in conversation.

PRESS

Lesson A *Breaking news*

1 Vocabulary in context

A Look at the four headlines. What do you think they are about?

    a. *Region still struggling to recover*
    b. *Conflict over the economy*
    c. *Bomb squad too late*
    d. *New contender to enter race?*

B ◀)) CD 4.02   Read the home page of an online news site. Write the headlines in Exercise A in the news articles. Are there any similar events in the news at the moment?

| HOME | U.S. | WORLD | POLITICS | JUSTICE | ENTERTAINMENT | LIVING | TRAVEL | OPINION | MONEY | SPORTS > |

1. _____ A _____

Efforts to **contain the oil spill** on the south coast appear to be working. But the oil giant responsible for the disaster could be facing more difficulties. Local businesses were rumored yesterday to be **considering legal action**, claiming for loss of income and livelihood. "People are going to be suing people over this," said one fisherman. A spokesperson for the oil company said they are committed to **compensating victims** affected by the spill. [Full story]

2. _____ C _____

A blast in the downtown area has caused extensive damage. Investigators are not sure what **caused the explosion** but have not **ruled out the possibility** that it was a terrorist attack. Three people were reported to have been acting suspiciously in the financial district, and police were said to be searching for a red pickup truck that was seen in the area. A **bomb went off** in the same area two years ago. [Full story]

3. _____ D _____

Three years after becoming the first female senator from her state, a young politician may be preparing to run for office in the upcoming presidential election. While the senator seems not to be **announcing** her **campaign** just yet, an appearance on a Sunday morning talk show has **fueled speculation**. [Full story]

RELATED The president's press secretary announced that the president will be **undergoing routine surgery** later this week and might not be able to greet a trade delegation of Chinese officials. [Full story]

4. _____ B _____

Investors might have been worrying unnecessarily after the **stock market plunged** to an all-time low last month. **Stocks** are now **making** a modest **recovery** as **markets** are said to have been gaining in confidence over the last two weeks. However, there are still concerns over the state of the economy and the huge deficits. Protesters are said to be planning more demonstrations in the capital. The marches seem to have been going peacefully so far. However, police say that they will be **mobilizing riot squads** if **tensions escalate**. [Full story]

Word sort

C Make a chart like this of the collocations in bold in the article. Then take turns telling the news stories in Exercise B to a partner.

verb + noun	noun + verb
contain the oil spill	a bomb goes off

Vocabulary notebook
See page 115.

2 Grammar Reporting events in progress

Figure
it out

A How are the ideas below expressed in the article? Underline the sentences in the article, and compare them with the sentences below. Then read the grammar chart.

1. They say protesters are planning more demonstrations in the capital.
2. There were rumors yesterday that local businesses are considering legal action.
3. It seems the marches have been going peacefully.
4. It's possible investors have been worrying unnecessarily.

Continuous infinitive forms

Grammar extra
See page 162.

Continuous infinitives describe events as ongoing, temporary, or possibly incomplete.
*Efforts to contain the oil spill appear **to be working**.*
*The senator seems **not to be announcing** her campaign just yet.*
*Police were said **to be searching** for a red pickup truck.*
*Markets are said **to have been gaining** confidence.*

Modals can be followed by *be + -ing* or *have been + -ing*.
*The president **will be undergoing** routine surgery.*
*Investors **might have been worrying** unnecessarily.*

Writing vs. Conversation

In writing, continuous infinitive forms with *to* often come after the verbs *seem, appear, be supposed to, have to*. They are less common in academic writing. In conversation, they are also often used after *be going to, need, want, (have) got to*.

B Complete the news reports using continuous infinitives of the verbs given with or without *to*. Sometimes there is more than one correct answer.

1. The president of an international microchip corporation may _____ (prepare) to step down. Over the last year, his health appears _____ (deteriorate), and the company is now rumored _____ (search) for a successor. A company spokesperson said, "We are going to _____ (make) an announcement soon."
2. After a month of protests, which seem _____ (have) little effect, steel workers agreed yesterday to go back to work. The workers might _____ (try) to get a bigger pay increase, but the company refused to negotiate and appeared _____ (not listen) to their demands.
3. An actor from a popular sitcom might _____ (not appear) on the show again. TV executives are believed _____ (consider) legal action after the actor failed to show up for filming on several occasions. When told the show may _____ (cancel) his contract, the actor said, "You've got to _____ (joke)!"
4. A senator who was filmed last week at a nightclub when she should _____ (attend) government meetings would make no comment today. An opposition spokesperson said that she was supposed to _____ (represent) voters in her state that evening.

HMM. IT SAYS HERE THAT NEW COFFEE YOU'RE DRINKING MAY BE KEEPING YOU UP AT NIGHT.

3 Viewpoint

Pair work Choose a story that's in the news at the moment. Prepare a news report to present to the class. Give as much detail as you can.

"Fans of the biggest sitcom on television may have been protesting unnecessarily. The show's producers announced that they are going to be bring the show back for at least one more season."

Lesson B *"Old" news*

1 Grammar in context

A Where do you get your news from? Conventional, mainstream sources or via social networking? Do a class survey.

"I tend to read the headlines on my phone every morning."

B ◀))) CD 4.03 Read the editorial column. What is "old" news? How does the writer regard it?

Why it is essential that "old" news survive

In the United States, in the trial of a celebrity on a murder charge, a judge demands that the jury reach its verdict. On the other side of the world, a devastating earthquake strikes. In Europe, the winning goal is scored in a crucial soccer game. All three events are instantly broadcast around the world – not via conventional news media, but through text messages, microblogs, social network postings, emails, and blogs that are passed on, person to person, within seconds. The major news organizations receive the same news from their reporters, but because of their insistence that everything be written and edited to broadcast standards, by the time it is broadcast or posted on the Web, it has become "old" news, if only by a few minutes.

In a world where readers and viewers get news via their smartphones and social media, it is important that the story be instantly available. Meanwhile, the requirement that a journalist check the facts more conscientiously can mean precious time is lost. In the case of major breaking news, the mainstream news organizations may insist that a controversial story be investigated, even if this means a delay in broadcasting some of the details. In dangerous situations, it may be advisable that a foreign correspondent not go to the scene immediately. It is essential that the reputation of the organization not be damaged and that the safety of the reporter be guaranteed.

In light of this situation, there is a danger that the major news organizations are perceived as a source of old news, which only a few might turn to for the fuller details of events they already know about. However, it is essential that there be a place for news that, while slower, is ultimately more measured, in-depth, and trustworthy. Ultimately, this comes down to money and whether the public is prepared to pay for such meticulously researched content. It is crucial that this issue be taken seriously by all consumers of news before we lose something precious.

C Pair work Discuss the questions.

1. Why are conventional news sources sometimes slower?
2. What qualities does "old" news have?
3. Do you recognize the picture the editorial paints of news? Do you think it's accurate?
4. What do you think is the real purpose of the editorial? What does it want you, the reader, to do?
5. What do you think about the recommendation?

2 Grammar Describing what should happen

A Write the form of the verb given that the editorial writer uses to express these ideas. Then read the grammar chart.

1. The judge demands that the jury _reach_ its verdict. (reach)
2. The requirement that a journalist _check_ the facts can mean time is lost. (check)
3. It is important that the story _be_ instantly available. (be)

The subjunctive ⬇

Grammar extra
See page 163.

The subjunctive uses the base form of the verb. Use it for all persons – including third person singular – after certain verbs, nouns, and adjectives. You can use it to refer to demands, suggestions, and recommendations; to say what is important; or to say what should happen in an ideal world

Verbs: *demand, insist, require, request, ask, suggest, recommend*	*The judge demands that the jury **reach** its verdict. They insist that everything **be edited**.*
Nouns: *demand, requirement, insistence, suggestion, recommendation*	*The requirement that a journalist **check** the facts can mean time is lost.*
Adjectives: *important, crucial, necessary, advisable, essential*	*It is important that the story **be** instantly available.*
The negative form is *not* + verb.	*It is essential that its reputation **not be damaged**.*

Writing vs. Conversation

The subjunctive is rare in conversation. People say:
*The judge asked the jury **to reach** its verdict.*
*It's important that the story **should be / is** accurate.*

B Read the comments below. Then complete the editorial extracts that reflect these views. Use the subjunctive form of the underlined verbs in the comments.

1. Parents say: "Our kids aren't aware of world events." "They're not exposed to 'proper news' early enough." "We want schools to teach current events." "They should make it a priority."

Parents are demanding that their children ___be___ well-informed about world events. Many feel it is important that children from sixth grade on _exposed_ to reputable news sources. Their insistence that the school curriculum _teach_ students current events is right. It is our recommendation that every school _make_ this a priority.

2. Students say: "Local news needs to change." "They should include more news about us." "The local TV station should have reports on our activities." "Don't ignore us."

Students feel it is essential that the news media's attitude toward young people _changed_. Their recommendation that the news _____ more items that are relevant to their concerns seems justified. Student leaders have suggested that our local TV station _have_ more coverage of student politics as one example. We would recommend that their suggestions _not be ignored_.

3. Media experts say: "Newspapers shouldn't die." "They should change their business model." "The consumer should pay more for access to online news."

It is crucial to the well-being of society that newspapers _not die_, but they do need to change. The suggestion that the traditional business model _be changed_ should be taken seriously. It is time to insist that the consumer _pay_ more for access to high-quality news reports.

C Write an editorial about an issue that you feel strongly about. Share it with the class.

Lesson C *Those news tickers*

1 Conversation strategy Highlighting topics

A How often do you listen to or watch the news? Are you a "news junkie"?

B ◀))CD 4.04 Listen. How do Jill and Kyung get their news?

Jill	Have you noticed how some people seem almost addicted to news? Like, this guy at work, he has all these news apps on his phone, but he never knows what's going on, really.
Kyung	Yeah. My girlfriend, she watches news channels all the time. But I don't think she really listens, you know what I mean? It's just background noise.
Jill	I know. Those TV channels, they just repeat the same news over and over. It drives me crazy, hearing the same thing all the time.
Kyung	Me too. And those news tickers, they're another thing I hate. It's so distracting, trying to listen with those things going across the screen at the same time.
Jill	Yeah. Public radio, that's what I like. They have some really interesting in-depth reports, too.
Kyung	Speaking of which, did you hear that report about that huge investment company? It seems to be going under.

C **Notice** how Jill and Kyung highlight the topics they talk about. Sometimes they put the topic at the start of a sentence and then use a pronoun. Sometimes they put the topic at the end. Find more examples in the conversation.

> *My girlfriend, **she** watches news channels all the time.*
> ***It** drives me crazy, **hearing the same thing all the time.***

In conversation . . .

When speakers put a topic at the end, it's usually after an evaluative comment such as *It drives me crazy*.

Note: These structures are for use in conversation only. Do not use them in writing.

D ◀))CD 4.05 **Guess the missing topics in these sentences. Then listen and write the topics.**

1. _weather forecast_, that's another thing people listen to but can never remember afterwards.
2. _the news_, these days, it always seems to be reporting what's going to happen. It's annoying.
3. _Economic_, that's beyond me. I don't understand anything about the markets and trade.
4. _Radio_, it's more informative than TV news. The reports are just more in-depth.
5. _headlines_, they're all I read these days. I never have time to read the full articles or news stories.
6. It's fantastic, having _news app_ on your phone. You can keep up with the news wherever you are.
7. It takes up so much airtime, _sports_. Especially if you're not interested in football or whatever.
8. They're so dirty and difficult to handle, _news papers_. I don't miss them at all.

About you **E** **Pair work** Discuss the statements in Exercise D. Do you agree?

2 Strategy plus *this, that, these, those*

◀)) CD 4.06 You can use **this** and **these** to introduce and highlight important information.

This guy at work, he has all **these** news apps.

Did you hear **that** report?

You can use **that** and **those** to refer to something specific, which you have mentioned or expect your listener to know about.

You can use *that* and *those* to sound negative about a topic.

Those news tickers, they're another thing I hate.

A ◀)) CD 4.07 **Complete these comments with *this, that, these,* or *those*. Use the cues in parentheses. Then listen and check.**

1. There's ___that___ show on the radio called *Radio Lab*. It has ___these___ really interesting, creative reports on things like time, or ants, or numbers. It's so cool. Do you listen to the radio much? (*highlight*)
2. There were all ___these___ students in my high school who had no idea what was going on in the world. (*highlight*) To them, international news was boring. Do you follow international news?
3. You know ___this___ talk show host on late night TV? I don't like her interview style. (*sound negative*) I don't think talk show hosts should be aggressive. What do you think?
4. I hate ___those___ magazines that make up news like celebrity gossip or stuff that you *know* isn't true. (*be specific*) Don't you?

About you

B **Pair work** **Ask and answer the questions at the end of each comment above.**

3 Strategies and listening *Journalism*

A **Look at some of the issues in journalism. What do you think they refer to?**

"The first issue is probably about the fact that news is often reported instantaneously."

1. ☐ The speed at which news is reported
2. ☐ The cost of publishing news stories
3. ☐ The increase in the number of news sources
4. ☐ 24-hour rolling news reports are superficial.
5. ☐ The use of graphic photos
6. ☐ The influence of reporters on events

B ◀)) CD 4.08 **Listen to a radio show. Which trends do the speakers refer to? Check (✓) the topics in Exercise A.**

C ◀)) CD 4.09 **Listen again. Circle the correct option to complete each sentence. Then discuss the expert's views with a partner. Do you agree?**

1. The radio presenter suggests that journalists' work is often _____.
   a. mundane   b. risky   c. boring   d. fun
2. The expert says that journalists often publish their reports _____.
   a. as events take place   b. through agencies   c. 24 hours later   d. before something happens
3. The expert suggests that the reason news organizations use some pictures is _____.
   a. they want to shock   b. it's ethically right   c. to show the truth   d. to compete
4. The expert believes that journalists can _____.
   a. change situations   b. have a huge impact   c. have limited influence   d. give no personal views

Speaking naturally

See page 142.

Lesson D *Reporting the news*

1 Reading

A Prepare Are some sources of news more trustworthy than others? In what ways?

"I think the news on public radio is pretty reliable because . . ."

B ⬇ Read for main ideas Read the article. What kinds of information does the writer question in terms of its accuracy? Why is information sometimes not accurate?

Establishing the truth: How accurate are news reports?

1   Following one of the worst natural disasters in recent U.S. history – Hurricane Katrina – journalists and newscasters swarmed the area to report on the extraordinarily terrible events. There were stories of chaos: widespread looting, gunshots, murders, and other violent crimes. While there was indeed disorder, it turned out that much of the initial reporting was either exaggerated, misleading, or plain wrong. The murder victims didn't materialize, and it became apparent there was no widespread increase in violent crime, either.

2   This episode raises some important questions. How does such "news" get reported? Can we believe what we hear on breaking news, or is news reporting so overstated that we are being at best misinformed and at worst deceived? How do we ultimately know whether any of the so-called facts in a news report are true or misrepresented? And perhaps more importantly, how can we verify what we read or hear in news reports?

3   In the case of Hurricane Katrina, a complex mix of circumstances may have created a degree of misinformation. Immediately after the storm, power outages and breakdowns in communications systems caused news "blackouts," making reliable information extremely difficult, if not almost impossible, to establish. News was spread by word of mouth, and it seems that facts became distorted as they were passed along. However, some of the blame may also lie with how news organizations operate. On the air 24/7, they are under pressure to fill airtime and win viewer ratings by being the one with the "hottest" or latest story. It is easy to see how, under such pressure, events are reported without the facts being painstakingly checked.

4   Such distortions are not limited to headline news events. During an election year, one takes for granted that candidates try to boost their ratings in the opinion polls in an effort to swing the race. The public is used to hearing claims from candidates, such as how their policies have led to an increase in manufacturing jobs or how the opposition has created massive national debt. What the public is never quite certain of is what is truth, half-truth, or untruth. Not surprising, then, that an entire industry exists to answer these very questions. Enter the fact-checkers, who check the claims that are made and the accuracy of the statistics that are presented.

5   Indeed, websites have sprung up whose business is purely and simply to check information in the public sphere – whether it be in a news report, a magazine article, or an urban myth. Other consumer sites aim to reduce the level of deception in politics, and some claim to be able to show the extent to which you can believe certain speechmakers. Cable networks also realize that the public is increasingly concerned about being able to trust what they hear, and use slogans to impress on their viewers the fact that they present honest news that is balanced and without bias. While many have jumped on the bandwagon of truth, one enterprising website has done the complete opposite. Rather than publish verifiable facts, it prides itself on featuring satirical news stories which are completely fabricated. Unfortunately, not all media outlets have realized this, and on occasion they have cited reports from the website as though they were true. Sorting fact from fiction just became even more of a challenge.

Reading tip

Writers sometimes start an article with a short story to illustrate what they are going to write about.

C **Understanding idioms** What does the writer mean by saying . . .

1. breakdowns in communications systems caused news "blackouts"? (para. 3)
2. news was passed by "word of mouth"? (para. 3)
3. in an effort to "swing the race"? (para. 4) *influence political candidates*
4. websites have "sprung up"? (para. 5)
5. many have "jumped on the bandwagon" of truth? (para. 5)

D **Read for inference** Check (✓) the statements that the writer would agree with.

1. ☐ Hurricane Katrina caused an increase in crime.
2. ☒ There are several reasons why the facts are sometimes misrepresented.
3. ☒ It is difficult to tell truth from fiction in modern news reporting.
4. ☐ It is only major events that are not reported truthfully.
5. ☒ The general public needs consumer websites to know if politicians are telling the truth.
6. ☐ These websites really make politicians more truthful.
7. ☐ It is much easier these days to determine if information is accurate.
8. ☐ The news on one satirical news website is more truthful than from other media outlets.

2 Focus on vocabulary Truth or fiction?

Tip

Prefixes sometimes help you understand meanings: *mis-* often means "badly."

A **Find alternative ways in the article to express the ideas below. Compare with a partner.**

Talking about truth . . .
make sure something is true (para. 2)
find out (facts) (para. 3)
truth or correctness (para. 4)
believe in (para. 5)

. . . and lies
giving a wrong impression (para. 1)
exaggerated (para. 2)
lied to (para. 2)
presented in a false way (para. 2)
wrong information (para. 3)
changed to be untrue (para. 3)
an untrue story (para. 5)
made up (para. 5)

B **Make a chart like the one below of the words you found in Exercise A. Add other forms. Write (–) if you cannot make the word into a noun, an adjective, or a verb.**

Noun	Adjective	Verb
verification		

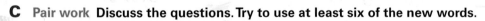

World NEWS

About you

C **Pair work** Discuss the questions. Try to use at least six of the new words.

- Does the situation the article describes apply to news organizations you follow?
- Do you always trust everything you hear or read?
- Have you ever found something in the news to be exaggerated or misleading?
- Do you think news stories about celebrities are fabricated? What else is?
- Which news channels do people trust most?
- Do you enjoy satirical news websites or TV shows? If so, which ones?

Writing *In short, . . .* *Reman Ahmad Fawzi*

- summarize an article.
- choose singular or plural verbs.
- avoid errors with verbs in relative clauses.

Task   **Write a summary.**

Write a summary of the article on page 112 in no more than 150 words.

A   **Look at a model** Read the summary below of the article on page 112 and the notes. Cross out two sentences in the summary that are not suitable. Then circle the correct verbs.

Writing a summary

Use your own words.
Include main points only.
Do not add new ideas.
Do not add an opinion.

uncountable noun

It is crucial that news reporting be accurate. The dramatic news report(s) after Hurricane Katrina, some of which **was / were** later shown to be inaccurate, **is / are** an example of the difficulties of news reporting. The reason(s) for inaccurate news coverage **varies / vary**. In complex situations, news **is / are** easily misreported, owing to a variety of factors. Social networks seem to be taking over news reporting. People often **pass / passes** on inaccuracies in word-of-mouth reporting, while in places of conflict, there can be failures in power and communications. News organizations **bear / bears** some responsibility for inaccurate reporting because they do not always verify facts. Political reporting and campaigning **is / are** also in danger of misleading the public and **has / have** led to the need for professional fact-checkers. The number of websites which **checks / check** facts in the news **has / have** grown as a result of increasing public concern.

B   **Focus on language** Read the chart. Then complete the sentences below with simple present verbs.

Subject-verb agreement in writing

Use singular verbs after uncountable nouns and most singular nouns that refer to a group.
News is easily misreported. **Information needs** to be checked. **The public is** concerned.

Use a singular verb if the main noun in a phrase is singular, but not in expressions that mean "a lot of."
The **number** of websites . . . **has** grown.   BUT   **A number of** websites **have** appeared.

Use a plural verb after noun *and* noun, when the main noun is plural, and after an irregular plural noun.
Political **reporting and campaigning are** in danger of misleading the public.
The **reasons** for inaccurate news coverage **are** varied. **People pass** on inaccuracies.

1. People _need_ to be able to trust the organizations that _broadcast_ news. (need / broadcast)
2. The main reason for inaccuracies _is_ that news reports and broadcasts _are_ live. (be)
3. The number of reporters who _give_ accurate accounts of stories _grows_ every year. (give / grow)
4. Accurate news and information _are_ hard to find. The pressure on reporters _is_ huge. (be)
5. A number of journalists _have not_ always _reported_ news accurately. (not report)
6. The population generally _wants_ to know the truth, even if the truth _is_ not easy to hear. (want / be)
7. The use of social networks _affects_ news reporting. (affect)

C   **Write and check** Write a summary of the article on page 112. Then check for errors.

Common errors

Be careful with the verbs in relative clauses.
The number of websites which **check** *news* **has** *grown. (NOT . . . checks . . . . have)*

Vocabulary notebook *Trust your instincts.*

Dictionary tip

Read all the examples in a dictionary entry for a word. They often give clues to collocations.

surgery /'sɜr·dʒə·ri/ *n* [C/U]

the treatment of injuries or diseases by cutting open the body and removing or repairing the damaged part, or an operation of this type:

[U] *He had undergone open-heart surgery two years ago.*

[U] *I'm recovering from back surgery, so it's going to be awhile before I can ride a horse again.*

[C] *She has undergone several surgeries and will require more.*

A Which two verbs go with each noun in bold below? Circle a, b, or c.

1. a. contain	b. hold	c. prevent	**an oil spill**
2. a. rule	b. contemplate	c. consider	**legal action**
3. a. compensate	b. create	c. protect	**victims**
4. a. mobilize	b. trigger	c. cause	**an explosion**
5. a. explore	b. edit	c. rule out	**the possibility**
6. a. run	b. announce	c. determine	**a campaign**
7. a. fuel	b. make	c. cause	**speculation**
8. a. do	b. make	c. see	**a recovery**

B Find two verbs in the box that can be used to complete each sentence below.

ask for help

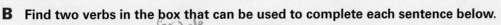

arise	called in	escalate	explode	go	go off	mobilized	plummet	plunge	start

1. Bombs can ___explode___ or ___go off___.
2. The stock market can ___plunge___ or ___plummet___.
3. Protest marches can ___started___ or ___go___ peacefully.
4. Riot squads can be ___called in___ or ___mobilized___.
5. Tensions can ___escalate___ or ___arise___.

C Focus on vocabulary Complete the vocabulary notes with words from Lesson D on page 113. Look for words with similar meanings to the words in bold.

1. **confirm** or **prove** or ___verify___ the accuracy of a story, someone's identity
2. **find out** or ___establish___ the facts, the truth, someone's identity
3. **believe (in)** or ___trust___ your instincts, your judgment
4. **exaggerate** or ___overstate___ the impact or benefits of something
5. **lie to** or ___deceive___ the public, consumers, voters
6. **not tell the truth about** or ___misrepresent___ information, facts, someone's position or view
7. paint an **unclear** or ___distortion___ picture or give a **false** or ___wrong___ impression
8. create or perpetuate an **untrue story** or an urban ___Myth___
9. **make up** or ___fabricate___ evidence, stories, an account, a report

11 Is it real?

In Unit 11, you . . .

- talk about whether information is true or not.
- use *be to* expressions to talk about the future.
- use passive verb complements.
- express concerns with expressions like *That's my concern.*
- give your opinion using *To me.*

Lesson A *Imagined threats?*

1 Grammar in context

A What kinds of threats to society are there? What could disrupt life as we know it? Make a list.

B ◀》CD 4.10 Read the blog. What threats does it mention? Are any of the threats on your list?

WHAT ARE WE TO BELIEVE?

Recently I saw a trailer for a TV documentary that is to air later this week. It's about families known as "preppers." These are people who are so convinced that life as we know it is to end or that civilization is about to collapse that they are preparing for the day it happens. So they're stockpiling food, water, and survival equipment, which no one is to touch until the day when some unknown disaster occurs – like the failure of the national grid, a natural disaster, even an asteroid strike – which they say is bound to happen eventually. I have to admit: If society were to collapse tomorrow, or if food and energy supplies were to be threatened, they are certainly better prepared than my family. We have barely three cans of baked beans and a pack of birthday candles between us. If we are to survive a catastrophe, we'd better shape up.

If the doomsayers are correct, the world as we know it is to end sooner than we think – which kind of got me thinking about what threats to our lives are real and which are imagined.

For example, remember Y2K? At the turn of this century, there was a great panic that computer systems around the world were about to crash because of the way computers recognized dates. The Year 2000, or Y2K, as it became commonly known, was set to be the biggest systems failure the world had ever experienced. It never happened.

Another perceived threat is an asteroid strike. Is one imminent? If so, shouldn't we all be panicking? Didn't the last one wipe out the dinosaurs? Well, according to experts at NASA*, earth is not about to be hit by an asteroid. They do say that there's bound to be debris from space falling on us at some point, although given the fact that around 70 percent of the earth's surface is water, there's little chance it's going to fall on me as I head for the supermarket.

There's always some disaster that's about to happen. And it truly is hard to know what's real and what's not. So what's the average family like us to do? Maybe the next time I go to the supermarket, I'll buy a few more cans of baked beans and some large white regular candles. Just in case.

END OF WORLD AHEAD

*National Aeronautics and Space Administration

C **Pair work** Discuss the questions.

1. What kind of blog is this? Instructive? Lighthearted? Informative?
2. What kinds of things are "preppers" stockpiling? What other things might they need?
3. Why does the writer suggest we ought to be panicking? Do situations like that cause you to panic?
4. Have you prepared in any way for problems that may arise in the future? How?

2 Grammar Talking about the future

Figure it out

A Find the underlined ideas in the blog and rewrite the sentences. Then read the chart.

1. Life as we know it will end.
2. Civilization is going to collapse very soon.
3. It's certain there will be debris from space.

Expressions with *be to* ⬇

Grammar extra
See page 164.

You can use *be to* to refer to the immediate future, especially events that are fixed or decided.
A TV documentary **is to air** later this week.

You can also use *be to* in conditional sentences and for hypothetical events in the future.
If we **are to survive** a catastrophe, we'd better shape up.
If society **were to collapse**, these people are well prepared.

Be about to means something will happen very soon; *be bound to* or *be set to* suggest certainty.
Civilization **is not about to collapse**. There**'s bound to be** debris falling on us.

These expressions can also be used to talk about the future as it was seen in the past.
They said the world **was to end** in 2012. It **was bound to happen**, they said.

B Complete the sentences from a survey using the words given. Then ask and answer the questions. Do situations like these concern you?

1. If scientists are right, a global flu pandemic _____ (bound) occur sooner or later. Some years ago, a flu virus that _____ (set) affect millions of people turned out to be less disastrous than predicted. If another pandemic _____ (be) occur, would you panic?

1. A super volcano in North America _____ (set) explode sometime in the future. It's not known when, but an eruption is 40,000 years overdue if past patterns _____ (be) be repeated. If you _____ (about) travel to that area soon, would you cancel your trip?

1. Doomsayers predict that cyber-warfare _____ (bound) happen soon. They're not the only ones who think that computer systems _____ (set) fail as a result of infiltration. Security experts say that if cyber-terrorists _____ (be) attack, we would not be prepared.

3 Viewpoint *Are you prepared?*

Group work Discuss the questions below.

In conversation . . .
You can introduce what you say with an adverb (e.g., *clearly, fortunately*) to show your attitude.

- Have you ever had to evacuate a building for any reason? Do you know what you're supposed to do in a fire drill?
- If communications systems were to shut down around the country, what would you do? How would it affect you?
- Do you know what people are to do if utility supplies shut off for any reason? What problems would the loss of utilities be bound to cause?
- If you were to hear of an impending crisis (such as a hurricane), how would you prepare?
- What supplies should people have ready in these situations?

"Interestingly enough, we had to evacuate our office building one time. Luckily, it was OK in the end."

Lesson B *Hard to believe*

1 Vocabulary in context

A 🔊 CD 4.11 **Read the article. What is Frank Abagnale known for — now and in the past?**

Why Frank W. Abagnale deserves to be admired

Frank Abagnale is a well-respected businessman, but **turn back the clock** several decades and you will find a notorious past – a past that he probably never expected to be **turned into** a Hollywood movie. But it's his work over the last four decades with the FBI* and other agencies – after he **turned his back on** a life of crime – that he'd rather be remembered for.

As one of the world's most respected authorities on security and fraud prevention, Abagnale is the person to **turn to** when you need to understand the crimes of check forgery and embezzlement. That's because he was an expert at these activities. In his youth, Abagnale was an extraordinary con artist, successfully conning people into thinking he was an airline pilot, a pediatrician, and a college professor – without ever being qualified in any of these fields. He lived a jet-setting lifestyle, but it **turned out** that he had funded all his activities by forging checks across the globe. He successfully avoided being apprehended for several years but was finally caught at the age of 21 by French authorities. He served prison time in three different countries. It was a **turning point** in his life.

Abagnale recalls being devastated by his parents' divorce, shortly after which he started his life of deception. His crimes, committed between the ages of 16 and 21, earned him a 12-year U.S. prison term, which seems to have been considered harsh even back then. He ended up being released early after agreeing to assist U.S. federal law enforcement agencies. It was an offer Abagnale was smart enough not to **turn down**, and it allowed him to **turn over a new leaf** in his life.

Even if you can't **turn a blind eye** to his past, Abagnale deserves to be admired for the way he **turned** his life **around**. On his website, he states that he regrets being drawn into illegal and unethical activities. He comments, too, on the movie *Catch Me If You Can*, which is loosely based on his life. Abagnale wants it to be known that it's not a true biography. Indeed, many of the events appear to have been exaggerated, which can only be expected. After all, it is a movie.

*the Federal Bureau of Investigation – a U.S. government agency

CHECK FRAUD

B **Find idioms and phrasal verbs with *turn* in the article that have the meanings below.**

Word sort

1. stop being involved in _____
2. become _____
3. stop a bad habit _____
4. ignore _____
5. a moment of change _____
6. refuse _____
7. go back in time _____
8. become apparent _____
9. make something better _____
10. go to, approach _____

C **Pair work Discuss the questions. How many *turn* expressions can you use?**

1. Why does Frank Abagnale have a "notorious" past? Why is he now a respected authority on security?
2. When did he begin his life of deception? How did he turn his life around?
3. What do you think about the way Abagnale turned over a new leaf?
4. Have you seen *Catch Me If You Can*? If not, would you like to?

Vocabulary notebook

See page 125.

2 Grammar Information focus

Figure it out

A Which of the two options in each sentence is the idea that is expressed in the article? What's the difference in meaning between the two options? Then read the grammar chart.

1. It's his work for the FBI that Abagnale would rather **remember / be remembered for**.
2. He has a notorious past, which he never expected **to be turned / to turn** into a movie.
3. Many of the events appear **to be exaggerated / to have been exaggerated**.
4. He regrets **drawing others / being drawn** into illegal activities.

Passive verb complements ⬇

Grammar extra
See page 165.

Base forms, infinitives, and *-ing* forms can have passive forms after some verbs and expressions.

Base form	*He'd rather* **be remembered** *for his work with the FBI.* (= i.e., that others remember him.) *He'd rather* **remember** *his work with the FBI.* (= He prefers to remember it himself.)
Infinitives	*Abagnale deserves* **to be admired**. (= Other people should admire him.) *A 12-year prison term appears* **to have been considered** *harsh even then.*
-ing form	*He avoided* **being apprehended** *for several years.*

Use base forms after *had better, would rather*, and modal verbs.
Use infinitives after *appear, claim, deserve, expect, love, etc., seem, want, 'd like*.
Use *-ing* forms after *avoid, be worth, enjoy, love, etc., mind, recall, remember, regret*.

B Complete what these people say about a movie of their lives. Use passive verb complements of the verbs given. Sometimes there is more than one correct answer.

If they made a movie of my life, . . .

1. I'd rather _____ (play) by Chris Rock than anyone else. I want _____ (remember) for my humor, and he's a funny guy. I wouldn't mind _____ (play) by Eddie Murphy, either.
2. One thing I'd really like _____ (know) for is being kind to people. I'd rather _____ (remember) for that than for the hours I spend at work.
3. I took my math exams three times to improve my grade. That deserves _____ (include) in a movie about me!
4. Don't show my first job – I never expected _____ (fire). I hate _____ (tell) what to do and I argued with my boss. I was right, but it wasn't worth _____ (fire) for.
5. One story about me that should never _____ (tell) is the time I stole money from my mother's purse. Fortunately, it seems _____ (forget). I'm sure she'd rather not _____ (remind) of it in the movie.
6. I've always avoided _____ (make) to do things that I don't want to do. That's one thing I'd like _____ (say) about me.
7. I'd like _____ (give) the chance to direct the movie. I might _____ (nominate) for "best director." I'd enjoy _____ (present) with an award!

About you

C Imagine a movie being made of your life. Make the sentences above true for you. Then share your ideas with a partner.

"I think one thing I'd really like to be known for is being a good friend."

Speaking naturally

See page 143.

Lesson C *That's my concern.*

1 Conversation strategy Expressing concerns

A A "white lie" is often told to be tactful or polite. In what kinds of situations might someone tell a "white lie"? Would you ever call someone on telling a white lie? (= point it out)

"For example, if an older person asked me to guess their age, I might say they're younger."

B ◀))CD 4.12 **Listen. What does Tania think about telling lies? How about Tom?**

Tania	You know, it's interesting. A friend of mine was telling her 12-year-old son about how it's not good to tell lies, and then he caught her telling a lie.
Tom	He did not.
Tania	Oh, yeah. They were going into an amusement park, and she told them he was 11 to get the reduced rate. And her son called her on it.
Tom	Well, yeah. I mean, that doesn't seem right.
Tania	Yeah. And she's like, "It's just a white lie." I guess, to her, it was no big deal. But you know, I'm not comfortable with that. To me, it was a lie.
Tom	Yeah, very much so, but . . . did you tell her that?
Tania	No. I just laughed it off.
Tom	See, that doesn't sit quite right with me.
Tania	But what are you supposed to do? Say, "That's wrong"?
Tom	Yeah, but I mean, if you don't say anything, that's kind of a lie, too. That would be my concern, anyhow.

C **Notice** how Tania and Tom use expressions like these to express their concerns. Find the examples they use in the conversation.

That's not good.	*I'm not too happy about (that).*
That's my concern.	*I'm not comfortable with (that).*
That doesn't seem right.	*That doesn't sit right with me.*

D ◀))CD 4.13 **Listen. Complete the conversations with the expressions you hear.**

1. *A* You know what I don't like? When people realize they've done something wrong, and then they don't tell the whole story – you know, to try and hide it. ___not comfto___ ___with the___
   B Yeah. ___dot good___. That's kind of like lying, too, when you don't tell the whole story.

2. *A* What do you do if you find out your friend's boyfriend is cheating on her? Do you tell her?
   B No. ___that doesn't seem right___. I mean, it's not your business. It's better not to get involved.
   A Yeah, but ___nightmare___ – not saying something.

3. *A* So if someone asks you, "Does this look good?" and it looks awful, what would you say? I mean, you can't say it looks terrible. You'd hurt their feelings. ___that would be___ ___my concern___
   B Yeah, but you can still say it looks awful but in a tactful way. Like, "Your other one looks way better."

About you **E** **Pair work** **Discuss the conversations above. What are your views?**

2 Strategy plus *To me, . . .*

◀))) CD 4.14 You can use **to me** to mean "that's how it seems to me," "that's my view."

To me, it was a lie.

You can also use **to** + other pronouns or nouns.

To her, / To my friend, it was no big deal.

A ◀))) CD 4.15 **Listen to five people talk about white lies. Number the responses 1–5.**

☐ Right. And you don't want to risk your friendship over something so minor. To me, it's not worth it.

☐ Maybe to them, it's a way of trying to make friends, like saying, "Look, I'm worth knowing."

☐ Yeah. To him, that's not a lie. He's just telling a story, and he's getting a bit carried away.

☐ Very much so. In any case, is that really a lie? To me, it's just a case of believing in yourself.

☐ I agree. Saying something's nice is a relatively minor thing to me. Like, it doesn't hurt anyone.

About you

B ◀))) CD 4.16 **Pair work** **Listen again and discuss each response. Do you agree with the speakers?**

3 Listening and strategies Online lies

A ◀))) CD 4.17 **Read the start of a conversation. Can you guess the missing words? Then listen and write the missing information.**

A Do you think most people post things on social network sites that are untrue?

B Not sure. I know I have. I've listed a _fake B.r_, and I actually use a _name_. And to me, that's OK. I'm just protecting _identity_. I mean, some people change things like their marital status. But that doesn't sit right with me – saying you're single when you're actually married.

A So have you ever changed other information, like, you know, your _qualifiction_ or . . . ?

B ◀))) CD 4.18 **Listen to the rest of the conversation. How do the speakers answer the questions below?**

1. Why is it easier to lie online than in person?
2. What's the biggest lie people tell face-to-face?
3. What kinds of white lies do people tell on online dating sites?
4. Are men or women more likely to tell white lies?
5. How can you tell if someone is lying in person? What do they do?

About you

C **Pair work** **Discuss the questions in Exercises A and B. What are your views? Give examples of people you know or stories you've heard.**

A I know people who have posted stuff on their profiles that's not true. But it seems silly to me.

B Well, the problem is everyone has access to that information and . . .

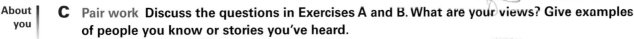

Lesson D *Artistic fakes*

1 Reading

A Prepare Look at the title of the article and the photographs. Brainstorm 10 words that you might read in the article. Make a list.

painting
forgery

B 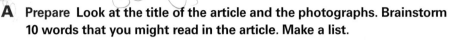 **Read for main ideas** Read the article. What techniques are used to authenticate art?

Authenticating ART

1 When a work of art sells at auction for millions of dollars, the buyer needs to be certain of its authenticity. Establishing this is not always straightforward, and therefore it is not uncommon for forged works of art to change hands for large sums of money, earning the forger or corrupt dealer huge profits. Forgery can be a lucrative business. Museums, galleries, and private collectors all over the world have repeatedly been taken in by art forgeries despite their best efforts to authenticate the artwork, as this almost unbelievable story illustrates.

2 Several decades ago, a New York art dealer bought three watercolors, which he believed to have been painted by the famous Russian artist Marc Chagall. The fact that they were fakes may never have come to light had the dealer not met with the artist that very same day, entirely by chance. Chagall reportedly declared the paintings to be fake immediately on seeing them. The man who sold the art, and who also happened to be the forger, served several years in prison as a result of his dishonesty.

3 However, most dealers are not this fortunate, and in most cases experts are unable to rely on the word of the actual artist to determine whether a piece of artwork is authentic. In the past, it was art experts and academics who were the main sources for authentication, rather than scientific proof. Other methods of authenticating art include tracing its ownership, a laborious and often unreliable process, especially if the work is several centuries old.

4 While these methods of verifying a work of art remain important, experts also rely on a variety of other techniques, such as analyzing the handwriting of the artist's signature. More technological approaches include carbon dating the pigments in the paint or the age of a canvas. In one case of a painting whose origin was uncertain but thought to be that of Leonardo da Vinci, a high-resolution multi-spectral camera was used to identify a faint fingerprint on the canvas. The fingerprint was then matched to another on a known work of da Vinci's. Carbon dating of the canvas also matched with material of the same period – around 1500. With such techniques, the painting's authenticity seemed to have been confirmed, although there are still those who fiercely contest it.

5 More recently, experts have turned to digital-imaging techniques to examine works of art in fine detail, such as the brushstroke patterns in a painting. In one study, analysts scanned 23 genuine van Gogh works into a computer and studied the number of brushstrokes they had, their length and how steadily they had been made. Statistical models were then developed to create a unique "signature" of the work. Works of art that were known to have been forged were found to have more brushstrokes when compared to genuine works.

6 The difference in value between a forgery and a genuine piece can run into millions of dollars, so there's a lot at stake. Not only that, but anyone who appreciates art wants to see the handiwork of the original artist and not be fooled by the copycat efforts of a forger. However, experts now have a growing arsenal of forensic techniques, which may well make it harder to pass off forged works of art in the future.

Reading tip

Writers often use the first paragraph of a text to set out a problem to which the rest of the text will offer solutions.

C Read for detail Answer the questions about the article.

1. What is not uncommon in the art world?
2. How was the Chagall forgery uncovered?
3. Why has authenticating art been unreliable in the past?
4. How can experts tell if a van Gogh painting is genuine?
5. Why is it important to be certain about a work of art's authenticity?

D Read for inference Are the sentences below true (T) or false (F) or is the information not given (NG)? Write T, F, or NG.

1. It's easy to make money from forging art. ___ NG
2. The New York art dealer was a longtime friend of Marc Chagall. NG
3. The New York art dealer had arranged to meet Marc Chagall after he bought the paintings. F
4. Few experts are as lucky as the New York art dealer. F
5. Experts all agree that the da Vinci painting is authentic. F
6. Van Gogh's signature was analyzed on 23 of his paintings. NG

② Focus on vocabulary Words in context

Tip

If you don't understand a word, look back or ahead in the text for clues to help you.

A What do the words in bold mean? Which parts of the article help you guess their meaning? Explain your guesses to a partner.

1. Forgery can be a **lucrative** business. (para. 1)
2. Collectors all over the world have repeatedly been **taken in** by art forgeries. (para. 1)
3. The fact that they were fakes may never have **come to light**. (para. 2)
4. . . . **tracing** the ownership of a piece of art can help to determine if it is an original work. (para. 3)
5. . . . the process can be very **laborious**. (para. 3)
6. However, experts now have a growing **arsenal** of **forensic** techniques . . . (para. 6)
7. . . . (it) may well make it harder to **pass off** forged works of art. (para. 6)

About you

B Pair work Take turns using the words and expressions in Exercise A to say something you have learned about the topic of art forgery.

③ Listening *Fakes of art!*

A CD 4.19 Listen to a radio profile of artist John Myatt. Why is he no ordinary artist?

B CD 4.20 Listen again. Complete the sentences in no more than four words.

1. A collection of John Myatt's watercolors sold out in _less 2 month_ months.
2. The story of John Myatt's life is a case of truth being _streng im fiction_.
3. Myatt co-wrote a song _____ called "Silly Games," which was a hit.
4. When his wife left, he had _2 young children_ to support.
5. Soon after, he put an ad in a magazine offering to paint _fake works of art_.
6. An auction house sold one of his paintings for _40,000_ dollars.
7. He went to prison for _12 months_.
8. A police investigator persuaded Myatt to _paint_ again.

About you

C What do you think of Myatt's story? Should he have been given a longer sentence?

Writing *So what if it's fake?*

In this lesson, you . . .
- report other people's views and give your own.
- use academic conjunctions and adverbs.
- avoid errors with *provided that*.

Task | **Write an opinion essay.**

Producing or selling fake designer goods is illegal. Yet many people buy them. Is it possible to stop these illegal enterprises?

A **Look at a model** Read the extracts from six essays. Which say that selling fake goods can be stopped (Y)? Which say it can't (N)? Write Y or N. Do you agree with the arguments they make?

1. I would argue that sellers of counterfeit products are unlikely to be stopped irrespective of any efforts to do so given the demand for cheap goods. ___ (No)

2. Clearly, people are attracted to fake goods regardless of the economic consequences. Yet if the law were enforced, this industry could be shut down. _Y_

3. It is inevitable that this activity will continue given that there is a market for fake goods. _N_ (Y)

4. The law can be changed, assuming that there is enough political will to do so. ___ (Y)

5. I consider buying fake goods to be a form of stealing in view of the fact that it deprives the designers of income. However, it would be naïve to think that it can be stopped. _Y_

6. This activity can be stopped provided that the authorities take decisive action. _N_

B **Focus on language** Read the chart. Then circle the expressions used in the extracts above.

> ### Conjunctions and adverbs in academic writing ⬇
>
> "If": as long as, assuming (that), provided / providing (that) ; "But + despite this": Yet
> *This activity can be stopped **as long as** the authorities take decisive action.*
> *Counterfeiting is a serious problem. **Yet** people are attracted to cheap, fake goods.*
>
> "Because": considering (that), in view / light of [the fact (that)], given (that)
> *It will continue **in view of the fact / given that** there is a market for fake goods. / **given** the demand.*
>
> "Despite": regardless of, irrespective of, no matter (who / what / how / etc.)
> *People buy fake goods **regardless of / irrespective of / no matter** how much it hurts the economy.*
> ***regardless of / irrespective of / no matter what** the consequences.*

C **Complete the sentences with appropriate expressions.** There may be more than one answer.

1. People buy fake goods to save money _regardless of_ how much harm they are doing to the industry.
2. _In view of_ the time that designers put into creating their work, we should pay the full price.
3. It is illegal to buy counterfeit goods. _No matter_ some people continue to do this.
4. People think it is acceptable to buy fake goods _as long as_ they are for their own personal use.
5. _In view of the_ legitimate businesses lose massive profits from the sale of counterfeit products, it is imperative that the law be enforced.

D **Write and check** Write the essay in the Task above. Then check for errors.

> ### Common errors
>
> Don't use *provided that* to give reasons.
> *Counterfeit items should not be sold **given that** this is illegal.* (NOT ~~provided that~~. . .)

Vocabulary notebook *Use it or lose it.*

Friend: Have you read The Hunger Games?
Me: No, but they turned it into a movie, and I saw that.

A Complete the conversations with the expressions from the box. You may need to change the form of the verbs.

turn back the clock	turn down	turn out	turn over a new leaf	turn to

1. *A* How was your summer?
   B Actually, it _turned out_ great. It was a little busy, but it was fun.

2. *A* How are things going?
   B Really well. Actually, I've _turned over a new leaf_ and started going to the gym every day.

3. *A* Did you grow up around your cousins?
   B Yeah. I remember being devastated when we moved away. I wish I could _turn back the clock_. They were good times.

4. *A* So, are you close to your parents?
   B Oh, yeah. They're the first people I _turn to_ when I need help.

5. *A* You know, I didn't get into college. They _turn down_ my application.
   B Oh, that's too bad. Well, something else is bound to come along.

How do we turn?

The top collocations with *turn* include *turn out / into / to / around / down / upside down / over / off / up, twists and turns.*

B Use the expressions below to write your own conversations.

a turning point	turn down	turn your back on
turn a blind eye to	turn something around	

C Word builder Find the meanings of these expressions. Then write a conversation using each one.

turn inside out	turn into	turn upside down	turn up somewhere

D (Focus on vocabulary) Complete the paragraph with the words in the box. Refer to Exercise 2A on page 123 to help you.

arsenal	forensic	lucrative	taken in
come to light	laborious	passing off	tracing

Passing off fake goods as original designer products is a _lucrative_ business. While some consumers may be _taken in_ by these products, many buy the goods knowing they are fake. _Tracing_ the criminals who make the goods is not always easy. The work is _laborious_ and requires _forensic_ investigations. However, as more of these products _come to light_, law enforcement is adding to its _arsenal_ of tactics to deal with the problem.

Psychology

In Unit 12, you . . .

- talk about independence, attraction, and the brain.
- use objects + *-ing* forms after prepositions and verbs.
- use reflexive pronouns and *each other / one another*.
- explore arguments with expressions like *at the same time*.
- use expressions like *to put it mildly* and *to put it bluntly*.

Lesson A *Being independent*

1 Grammar in context

A In what ways should young adults be independent? Tell the class.

B ◀))CD 4.21 **Listen. What experience did each person have of becoming independent?**

BECOMING INDEPENDENT

In psychology, young people between the ages of 17 and 22 are often characterized as experiencing "early adult transition." At this age, they might leave home to attend college, get their first job, or think about starting their own family. It's a time when young people start to separate from their family attachments and become truly independent. We asked readers to tell us about their experiences of becoming independent.

"Actually, I've always been independent. My parents raised me and my brother that way. They always insisted on us making our own decisions. I guess they were big believers in children being responsible for themselves and their own choices. Like I remember us setting off on a trip one time, and it was snowing, and I wouldn't wear a coat. And I was *frozen* and sobbing. And I remember my mom saying, 'It's your own fault.' She's always hated people complaining about things that are their own fault."
CHRIS, 24

"Interestingly enough, I didn't find it hard leaving home. I think actually my parents had a much harder time dealing with me becoming independent. But at the time, they encouraged me to leave without me realizing how difficult it was for them. My mom said later that she and my dad dreaded me leaving and hated the thought of them becoming 'empty nesters.' But for me, it was all just a big adventure."   LARRY, 22

"I left home with little experience of being independent. I'd always depended on my parents being there and doing everything for me. Leaving home was a big shock to me. I couldn't cook, didn't know how to do laundry. I mean, there's nothing wrong with children relying on their parents. But it's a balance. I wish mine had been more supportive of me doing things by myself."   PAULA, 46

About you

C **Pair work** **Discuss the questions.**

1. What do you think about Chris's mother's philosophy?
2. Do you know any parents that have suffered from becoming "empty nesters"?
3. Why do you think some parents find it hard when their children leave home?
4. Do you think Paula's experience is common?
5. Whose experience is most similar to your own or is most likely to be?

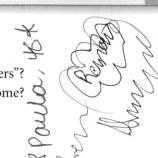

2 Grammar Describing complex situations and events

Figure it out

A Circle the correct options to complete the sentences. Then read the grammar chart.

1. My parents always insisted on **we make / us to make / us making** our own decisions.
2. She hated the thought of **become / them becoming / them to become** empty nesters.
3. I remember my mom **say / saying / to say**, "It's your choice."

Objects + -ing forms after prepositions and verbs

Grammar extra
See page 166.

You can put a noun or pronoun between a preposition and an -ing form, or between some verbs and an -ing form. The noun or pronoun is the object of the preposition or verb and the subject of the -ing form.

verb + preposition	They always **insisted on us making** our own decisions.
adjective + preposition	There's nothing **wrong with children relying** on their parents.
noun + preposition	They were big **believers in children being** responsible for themselves.
verb (e.g., *love, hate, not mind, recall, remember*)	I **remember us setting** off on a trip. My mom and dad **dreaded me leaving**.

Writing vs. Conversation

In formal writing and speaking, possessive determiners are often used before the -ing form.

*They dreaded **my** leaving*

B Rewrite the underlined parts of the sentences. Use an object and an –ing form. Then ask and answer the questions with a partner.

1. *A* How independent were you when you were a kid?
   B Very. I remember that my brother took me off to explore the neighborhood. My parents weren't really concerned about the fact that we might get lost or fall or anything.
   C Not at all. My parents were really protective. They couldn't even deal with the fact that we went away for summer camp. I hated the fact that they fretted so much.

2. *A* Do you think it's good for young children to be independent?
   B Well, I'm a supporter of the idea that kids should learn to be independent at a young age. I didn't mind that my dad told me to get a job when I wanted a new bike. I was only 12, but I did. There's nothing wrong with the idea that kids should have to do things for themselves.
   C Well, I'm not so sure. I'm a big believer in the idea that kids need to be kids. I don't like the thought that they grow up too early. I don't recall that my parents gave us much responsibility. It resulted in the fact that they raised two happy, carefree kids.

3 Listening "Helicopter" parents

A ◀)) CD 4.22 Listen to the conversation between a mother and her college-age son, Mark. What do they both think of "helicopter" (i.e., overprotective) parents? Do they agree?

I DON'T MIND MY MOM BEING CONCERNED, BUT WHY DOES SHE HAVE TO BE SO LITERAL?

B ◀)) CD 4.23 Listen again and complete the sentences.

1. Mark remembers parents storming into class and . . .
2. Mark's mom recalls moms rushing in if kids . . .
3. Mark says his roommate's mom insists on . . .

C Pair work What are your views on helicopter parents? Do you know any?

Lesson B *Love is blind.*

1 Vocabulary in context

A 🔊 CD 4.24 **Listen to the podcast. What happened to Dr. Epstein? Why is it ironic?**

HOME   LATEST POST   TOP POSTS   LEAVE POST   SEARCH BLOG

Who are YOU talking to?

Robert Epstein could rightly describe himself as an expert in human relationships. One might even say a leading expert, if being a former editor of *Psychology Today* is anything to **go by**. However, he proved himself to be as vulnerable as the rest of us when it comes to matters of the heart. A cousin **talked him into** trying online dating, and he **picked out** a photo of an attractive young woman on a dating website. She hadn't written much about herself on her profile, but he liked the photo and wrote to introduce himself. She replied, revealed herself to be Russian, and though her English wasn't good, they started getting to know each other through regular email correspondence. Her letters were warm and affectionate, and he felt that they were attracted to each other. Epstein found it odd that she didn't respond to specific questions, in particular to his suggestion that they might meet. Then, after they had been writing to one another for two months, the realization dawned on him. So he wrote a nonsense message of random characters, to which she replied as usual. The reason for her evasive replies suddenly presented itself. It turned out that he had been conversing with a so-called "chatterbot" – software that interacts with humans on the Internet. As he himself put it, he'd been "had." The clues that should have **given "her" away** were all there, but he had failed to **pick up on** them.

One might think oneself immune to such tricks – that one's judgment would be better – but Epstein's story shows that even the smartest people can fool themselves into thinking they are communicating with a real person. Any one of us might **go about** finding our life partner in this way, and Epstein estimates there are thousands of chatterbots on the Web. So in case you think you could never **be taken in** by a chatterbot yourself, think again. History does repeat itself. At least it did in Dr. Epstein's case. Some time later, he was again fooled by a dating site chatterbot. Interestingly enough, instead of keeping it quiet and **putting it behind him**, Epstein used his experiences in his work, **playing down** in interviews and articles the fact that he corresponded with a chatterbot twice. (He is, after all, also an expert in human-computer interaction.)

In the end, it **comes down to** this: No matter how smart we are, we all want to be loved – and love, as they say, is blind.

About you

B **Rewrite the underlined phrases with phrasal verbs from the article. You may need to change the verb forms or word order. Which sentences do you agree with? Compare with a partner.**

1. If his profession is anything to be considered, this shouldn't have happened to him.
2. He shouldn't have let his cousin persuade him to try online dating.
3. He couldn't have known when he chose the photo that it was a fake.
4. The poor English in the emails should have revealed "her" secret immediately.
5. It's odd that he didn't notice the fact that it wasn't a real person sooner.
6. It's a matter of someone looking for love, and anyone can be fooled by a chatterbot.
7. It could happen to anyone if they know how to do online dating.
8. If it had happened to me, I'd try to stop being upset by it. Or I'd try to make it seem less serious.

Word sort

C **Make charts of phrasal verbs like this. Add other verbs you know. Compare with a partner.**

Verb = GO	Meaning	Example sentence
go by	consider, judge, take into account	If you go by his experience, . . . If his experience is anything to go by, . . .
go on	happen	He didn't understand at first what was going on.

Vocabulary notebook

See page 135.

2 Grammar Referring to people and things

Figure
it out

A Which of the two options is the meaning given in the article? What would the other option mean? Then read the grammar chart.

1. Epstein wrote to the woman in the photo to introduce **himself / him**.
2. If you think you could never be taken in **yourself / yourselves**, think again.
3. People fool **one another / themselves** that they're communicating with a real person.

Pronouns

Grammar extra
See page 167.

Use reflexive pronouns when the subject and object of a sentence refer to the same person or thing.
*He could rightly describe **himself** as an expert in human relationships.*
*She hadn't written much about **herself** on her profile.*
*One might think **oneself** immune to such tricks, but history often repeats **itself**.*

Reflexive pronouns can also be used for emphasis.
*As he **himself** put it, he'd been "had."*

Use *each other* or *one another* when the subject does something to an object and the object does the same thing to the subject.
*They wrote to **each other** / **one another** for months.*

Common errors

Don't confuse *each other* with *themselves, ourselves, yourselves.*
*Helen and I looked at **each other**.*
= She looked at me and I looked at her.
*We looked at **ourselves** in the mirror.*
= I looked at my reflection. She looked at hers.

B Complete the conversation with appropriate pronouns.

A Have you ever been taken in by someone?

B Not that I can think of. But did you ever see that movie *Catfish*? It's about this guy and someone he met online. They wrote to _____ for months. And she'd described _____ as this young woman and sent him these songs that she said she'd written. And he kind of convinced _____ that he was really attracted to her.

A Oh, I've heard those stories, where people fall in love online and then when they meet, they find _____ in this awkward situation where they don't really like _____ at all.

B I know. See, I don't think I'd ever let _____ get into a situation like that. But anyway, he started picking up on these weird things, like that she hadn't written the songs _____. And even though they'd seen photos of _____ and spoken to _____, he realized something wasn't right. So he talked _____ into driving across the country to meet her. Anyway, I don't want to spoil the ending! You'll have to see the movie _____. I guess the story _____ isn't that unusual, but it was interesting that they were able to document it.

3 Viewpoint *It's easy to be taken in . . .*

Group work Discuss the questions.

In conversation . . .

You can use *As a matter of fact* to give new or surprising information.

- What are some ways that people get taken in by others online?
- Can you get to know someone online? Is it the same as meeting face-to-face?
- How can people protect themselves from situations like the ones in the lesson?
- Do you consider yourself an expert on relationships?
- Do you know anyone who falls in love easily?

"People get taken in by those lottery emails. I got one myself last week, as a matter of fact."

Speaking naturally
See page 143.

Lesson C *I can see it from both sides.*

① Conversation strategy Exploring arguments

A Do you ever judge people by their appearance? How do you form an impression of someone?

B ◀))CD 4.25 Listen. What does Sydney think about judging people by their appearance? How about Nate?

Sydney	We were talking in class today about how much appearance matters in society.
Nate	Yeah?
Sydney	Yeah. Apparently, they say that more attractive people do better in job interviews, and they earn more. I mean, it seems unfair – to put it mildly – that the good-looking ones are more likely to get hired and promoted.
Nate	Well, I suppose if you look at it from an employer's perspective, the people who make an effort to look good are probably the ones who make more of an effort at work.
Sydney	Possibly. But at the same time, surely your skills and education are more important than how you look.
Nate	True. They always say, "Never judge a book by its cover." But equally, shouldn't we try to make ourselves look as good as we can?
Sydney	I suppose. But to put it bluntly, there's something not right about employers only hiring people that are attractive.

C **Notice** how Sydney and Nate use expressions like these to consider different aspects of an argument. Find examples in the conversation.

> **Considering different points of view:**
> *I can see it from both sides.*
> *If you look at it from someone's point of view / perspective, . . .*
>
> **Giving different information with the same significance:**
> *at the same time, by the same token, equally*

D ◀))CD 4.26 **Read Speaker A's views below. Then listen and complete the various responses. Which views, if any, do you agree with? Discuss the ideas with a partner.**

1. *A* They say you're more likely to stop and help attractive people on the street. That's awful, really.
   B Yeah, but _____ people probably don't do it deliberately. It's probably just instinct.
   C Actually, _____ , you might not feel *safe* stopping and helping a stranger.
   D I guess _____ . I think we're all probably influenced by looks in some way.

2. *A* You should always trust your first instinct about someone, don't you think?
   B Well, it depends. I mean, instincts can be right. But _____ , sometimes you need time to get to know someone new. Like, I don't like it when people think I'm unfriendly because I'm shy. _____ , I guess I prefer people who are more friendly than I am.
   C Well, _____ . Trust your instincts *and* give people the benefit of the doubt.
   D Yeah. I mean, what if you just met them on a bad day? You should either trust your instincts and hope you're right, or _____ , you can be cautious and let them prove you wrong.

2 Strategy plus *To put it mildly*

🔊 CD 4.27 You can use **to put it mildly** to show that you could say something in a stronger or more extreme way.

> I mean, it seems unfair – **to put it mildly** – that . . .

When you want to be very direct about what you say, you can use **to put it bluntly.**

> But **to put it bluntly**, there's something not right about it.

In conversation . . .

Other expressions are *to put it simply / politely / crudely.*

About you | Match the two parts of each comment. Write the letters a–e. Then discuss the views with a partner. Do you agree?

1. They often say people choose a life partner who looks like them. _____
2. People are often suspicious of people who look and dress differently. _____
3. TV is responsible for our obsession with looks. _____
4. People should make an effort to look good. _____
5. Some people care too much about their appearance. _____

a. Though that seems like the last reason to marry someone, to put it mildly.
b. To put it simply, the media just creates unrealistic expectations.
c. To put it bluntly, they should be more concerned with their personality.
d. I mean, to put it bluntly, there's nothing worse than people looking like a mess.
e. Which is pretty shallow, to put it politely. I personally think it makes people interesting.

3 Strategies Stereotypes

A 🔊 CD 4.28 **Read the information. Circle the best expressions in the people's reactions. Then listen and check.**

1. *Researchers say certain names on résumés receive more callbacks than other names.*
   Mindy That seems ridiculous, **to put it mildly / equally**. Why should a name matter?
   Leo Actually, people probably react to names all the time. I mean, **at the same time / to put it bluntly**, they might draw conclusions, for example, about a guy with a feminine name like Lee.
   Harriet Well, **I can see it from both sides / by the same token**. Either those interviewers are stereotyping people, or maybe it's that they really don't think the person is suitable for the job.

2. *Employers often consider elderly people as less productive and are therefore less likely to employ them.*
   Yvette That's not fair. I mean, older people have a wealth of experience to contribute. **At the same time / To put it mildly**, it's true they might not be able to do physically demanding work.
   Grant Well, **I can see it from both sides / if you look at it from an employer's perspective**, I think it's justified because, um, older people are more likely to have health issues. **To put it simply / Equally**, they're more likely to get sick.
   Susan Well, **I can see it from both sides / to put it bluntly**: Older people may cost a company more, but they're probably reliable.

About you | **B** **Pair work** **Discuss the information and views in Exercise A. Do you agree? What other stereotypes do people have? Are stereotypes ever justified?**

> "I have to say it seems unfair, to put it mildly, to judge someone by a name.
> After all, you don't choose your name."

Lesson D *Brain matters*

1 Reading

A Prepare Which statements do you think are true? What do we know about the brain?

1. Scientists have a clear understanding of the brain.
2. The brains of men and women are different.
3. Brains don't fully develop until the age of 12.
4. Girls are better at language than boys.

B Read for main ideas Read the article. Were your guesses in Exercise A correct? How is the brain different across gender and age?

THE DEVELOPING BRAIN

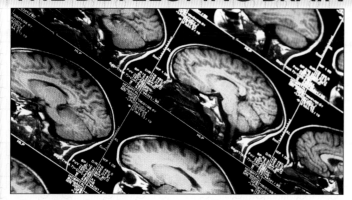

1 At the heart of psychology is understanding behavior, and understanding behavior has much to do with understanding the brain, an endeavor that has proved somewhat elusive. However, as neuroscientists become more efficient at mapping the brain, and as they gain more insight into how the brain develops and functions, scientists believe they may be closer than ever to an understanding of why we behave in the way we do. Differences in behavior as we age and between genders may well be accounted for by the physical state of and changes in our brains.

2 At the age of six, the brain is about 95 percent of its adult size. Over the coming years, it continues to thicken and develop extra connections. Around the age of 12, it is believed that the areas of the brain that are used most will strengthen in terms of neural connectivity. Cells in the brain that are not used tend to wither and die. The implications are enormous. What you do with your brain in your teen years may well determine how your brain functions for the remainder of your life. If a teen spends endless hours watching TV, the neural connections that help the brain process TV are what will

strengthen. It is clear, therefore, that how young people spend their time really is of great importance.

3 Surprisingly, and contrary to earlier beliefs, the brain is still developing even in the early twenties. Areas of the brain that are related to emotion, decision making, reasoning, and problem solving are still not fully matured. This may go some way toward explaining impulsive behavior in teens and why vehicular accident rates in young people are significantly higher than those among older people. Young people just don't have the capacity, that is, the set of skills necessary, to make complex judgments while driving.

4 There are also differences in the way brains develop across gender. It appears that girls are ready to process more challenging information earlier than boys, with the area of the brain responsible for this activity peaking at the age of 14 to 16 in boys, a full two years later than girls. In addition, studies have demonstrated that girls and boys process language input in different parts of their brains. Girls typically tend to display stronger language skills than boys. Girls have more brain matter dedicated to language skills. "If there's more area dedicated to a set of skills, it follows that the skills will be more refined," says David Geary, PhD, professor of psychological sciences at the University of Missouri.

5 This kind of research raises important questions about how boys and girls should be taught in schools to maximize their learning. For example, the idea of single-sex education should perhaps be taken into consideration. Experts say that we would do well to revisit the timing of the subjects taught in school, given that some parts of the brain develop before others. Additionally, what we understand about the adolescent brain should perhaps inform public policy and the laws we make with regard to the minimum driving age.

C Read for detail Complete the sentences. Then compare with a partner.

1. Mapping the brain is important because _____.
2. How your adult brain works may largely be a result of _____.
3. In their early twenties, young people probably still don't have the skills to _____.
4. The brains of young girls and boys differ in that _____.
5. Understanding the brain may have a social impact – for example, in areas of _____.

D Paraphrase Read the sentences below. Underline the sentences in the article that they paraphrase.

1. After the age of six, the brain continues to mature.
2. How you use your brain as a youngster may well impact the efficiency of your brain as an adult.
3. The brain is still not fully grown in early adulthood, which is the opposite of what was previously believed.
4. Male and female brains mature differently.
5. It is worth thinking about educating male and female students in different schools.

2 Focus on vocabulary *be, do, go, have, take*

A Find the expressions in the box below in the article on page 132. What do they mean? Rewrite the questions using the expressions. Change the forms of the verbs if necessary.

be at the heart of	be of great importance	have to do with	would do well to
be close to	go some way toward	take into consideration	

1. Do you think how we behave **relates to** how our brains are hardwired at birth?
2. What do you think **is the key to** understanding how people behave? Do you think we **are near** an understanding?
3. Do you think lawmakers **should** reconsider the legal age for driving as a result of this research?
4. What aspects of the teenage brain and behavior should schools **think about**?
5. Do you believe that understanding the teenage brain **is essential**? Why?
6. Do you feel the article **gives part of** an explanation of why teens behave differently from adults?

About you **B Pair work** Ask and answer the questions in Exercise A.

3 Listening *Understanding the brain—outcomes*

A ◀))CD 4.29 Listen to four experts lecture about brain research and how it impacts their areas of expertise. Choose the most likely profession of each speaker. Circle a, b, or c.

1. a. education consultant
2. a. marketing consultant
3. a. education consultant
4. a. psychiatrist

    b. management consultant
    b. chef
    b. mathematician
    b. education consultant

    c. IT consultant
    c. psychologist
    c. management consultant
    c. specialist in aging

B ◀))CD 4.30 Listen again. How will research impact these areas in the future according to the experts? Complete the notes using as many words as you need.

Lecture 1: What is the research certain to affect?

Lecture 2: What are we coming closer to understanding?

Lecture 3: What may we be able to design in the future?

Lecture 4: What will be easier to treat in the future?

About you **C Pair work** Discuss the impact of the research in the different fields mentioned. Which field do you think would benefit most from research? In what ways?

Writing *Twice as likely*

In this lesson, you . . .
- discuss statistics.
- make statistical comparisons.
- avoid errors with *twice*.

Task | **Write a report with a recommendation.**

Write a report on safety issues for a social studies class, and make some recommendations for state policy. Use at least one statistic to support your argument.

A **Look at a model** Which of the sentences do you think are true? Then read the report and check.

a. Girls use phones more than boys while driving.
b. Girls are less likely to eat while driving than boys.
c. Boys talk to people outside the vehicle more.
d. Boys are less likely to turn around while driving.

Per mile driven, teen drivers have four times as many crashes as adult drivers.* According to research by the AAA Foundation for Traffic Safety, teen girls are . . .

- twice as likely as teen boys to use a cell phone while driving.
- nearly 50 percent more likely than males to reach for an object in the vehicle.
- nearly 25 percent more likely to eat or drink while driving.

The same report shows that teen boys . . .

- are roughly twice as likely as girls to turn around in their seats while driving.
- communicate with people outside of the vehicle twice as often.

*Centers for Disease Control

B **Focus on language** Read the chart. Then underline the statistical comparisons in Exercise A.

Statistical comparisons in writing

You can make comparisons with adjectives, adverbs, nouns, or pronouns.
Girls are **twice as likely as** boys to use a cell phone.
Teens are **four times more likely** to have a crash **than** adults.
    OR   **as likely** to have a crash **as** adults.
Boys communicate with people outside of the car **twice as often / much**.
Teen drivers have **four times as many** crashes **as** adults. OR **four times more** crashes **than** adults.
    OR   **four times the number of crashes** that adults do.
The cost of insurance for teens can be **five times as much as** for adults.

Writing vs. Conversation

You can use *more* or *as* in phrases like *six times more / as likely*. *More* is more frequent than *as*. *As* is more frequent in writing than in conversation.

C Complete the sentences with the information given. Then write the report in the task above.

1. Sixteen-year-old drivers are _____ to be in a fatal crash when there are three or more young passengers in the car _____ when they are driving alone. (four times / likely)
2. A 16-year-old is only _____ to be involved in a fatal crash with one young passenger in the car. (3% / likely) However, a 17-year-old driver is _____ be involved in a fatal crash. (66% / likely)
3. With an adult passenger over 35, teen drivers are _____ when they are alone. (twice / safe)
4. Boys turn around in their seats while driving _____ girls. (twice / times)
5. Girls use a cell phone while driving _____ boys. (twice / often)
6. If there is loud talk, teen drivers are _____ to have a serious incident. (six times / likely)
7. Insurance costs for a 16-year-old driver can be _____ for an 18-year-old. (twice / much)

D **Write and check** Write the report in the Task above. Then check for errors.

Common errors

Don't use *twice* + a comparative adjective.
They are **twice as safe** with an adult. (NOT They are ~~twice safer~~ . . .)

Vocabulary notebook *Pick and choose*

Learning tip   Thesaurus

In writing, you often need to refer to the same idea more than once, so it's a good idea to learn different ways to express the same meaning. Create your own thesaurus.

pick out, choose, select, decide on
If I were asked to pick out one book from my favorite author,
I would choose The Handmaid's Tale.

A   **Replace the bold expression in each essay extract to avoid the repetition. Use a word or an expression in the box, and make any other necessary changes.**

be a matter of	minimize	persuade	proceed	show their true feelings

1. Charismatic individuals can often **talk** other people **into doing** things they don't want to do. It can be difficult to resist someone who is good at talking people into things.
2. Some people are good at hiding how they feel and not giving anything away. Their expressions do not **give them away**.
3. Many people would like to find the right partner but do not know how to **go about it**. For example, they don't know how to go about finding places to meet people.
4. When it comes down to finding a partner, it is not always easy to make the best choice. Also when it **comes down to** deciding whether or not to get married, you need to be sure.
5. It is important to play down your shortcomings and **play down** your failures in job interviews.

> ### Dictionary tip
>
> Some expressions are too informal for writing. Check in a dictionary. If it says "spoken" or "informal," don't use the expression in formal writing.
>
> **hit it off**
> INFORMAL
> to like someone and become friendly immediately

B   **Match the expressions in bold with the words and expressions on the right. Write the letters a–d. Then rewrite the sentences using the alternatives.**

1. It's not always easy to **pick up on** other people's moods. ____
2. If you only **go by** looks, you may choose the wrong partner. ____
3. It's easy to **be taken in** by people who seem sincere. ____
4. You have to **put** difficult or unpleasant experiences **behind you**. ____

a. stop being upset by
b. be fooled
c. take into consideration
d. notice

C   **Word builder Find the meaning of the expressions in bold, and write a word or expression with a similar meaning. Which are too informal for writing?**

1. It may be necessary to **brush off** criticism. _____
2. Life can **get to** people sometimes. _____
3. Some people never **hit it off**. _____
4. Often it is better to **give in**. _____

D   (**Focus on vocabulary**) **Match the expressions on the left with the ones on the right. Write the letters a–f. (See Exercise 2A on page 133 to help you.)**

1. be at the heart of ____
2. have to do with
3. be close to ____
4. be of (great) importance ____
5. go some way toward ____
6. would do well to ____

a. be near
b. be essential
c. should, be advised to
d. relate to
e. be the key to
f. help, make progress with

Checkpoint 4 *Units 10–12*

1 Change in the workplace

A Change the underlined verbs to continuous forms. Then complete the sentences with reflexive pronouns. One blank needs *each other* or *one another*.

be undergoing

Economists say that society will <u>undergo</u> some critical changes in the near future, especially in the workplace. Women seem <u>to graduate</u> in larger numbers than men, although they appear <u>not to take</u> as many graduate courses in science, business, and engineering. Women also appear <u>to have gained</u> momentum in the workplace _____ . They are said <u>to gain</u> in confidence, according to a study by N. Scott Taylor of the University of New Mexico, and now rate _____ as equal to men in terms of leadership qualities. Ask any young professional woman today if she can see _____ in a top job in 15 years from now, and she'll likely say yes. Given that employers will <u>need</u> a more highly educated workforce, it's likely that we are going to see more women in top jobs. What's more, an increasing number of women might well <u>earn</u> more than their spouses. A man who sees _____ as a "traditional" male partner and thinks he ought <u>to earn</u> more than his partner is more likely to feel the relationship _____ is not satisfactory. However, men with "progressive" attitudes are more likely to have high-quality relationships, where respect for _____ is more important than income.

B Pair work Discuss the information in Exercise A. Highlight the topics you talk about.

"It's interesting, more women are graduating from college. I wonder why that is?"

2 Pick out the real problem.

A Add a word to each bold expression. Then complete the sentences using the verbs given. Some need passive verbs.

1. *Q:* Would you <u>turn</u>_____ **your back** on an old friend if she <u>were to do</u> (be to / do) something really bad? A friend of mine was recently arrested for stealing from her employer. She _____ (be to / go) to court next month. She's trying to _____ **it down**, but when it **comes** _____ **to it**, I don't want to **be** _____ **in** by someone who's dishonest.
   A: If your friendship _____ , (be to /continue), then your friend should face up to what she's done. You can't **turn back the** _____, but anyone can **turn over a new** _____ and **turn their** _____ **around**. Tell your friend how you feel. She may appreciate having someone to **turn** _____. Then try to **put it** _____ **you**.
2. *Q:* A friend is trying to **talk me** _____ setting up a business with her. I don't want to **turn** the offer _____ , but I'm not sure. She spends a lot of money and I don't. I know I won't be able **to turn a** _____ **eye to** that. I don't know how to _____ **about** telling her. She's beginning to **pick** _____ **on** my reluctance, though.
   A: This is a common problem, if my inbox is **anything to** _____ **by**. It could **turn** _____ to be a success, or it could **turn** _____ a nightmare. If we _____ (be to / believe) the statistics, many new businesses fail in their first year. Therefore, you are right to be cautious. Maybe you've reached a **turning** _____ **in your lives** and friendship. Your email **gives** _____ one thing – you have different attitudes toward money. You need to talk. Otherwise, it _____ (be bound to / end) in failure.

B Pair work Discuss the problems and solutions above. Use expressions like *to me, I can see it from both sides,* and *at the same time* to express different points of view.

3 A true story

A Complete the story using the verbs given. Many have passive verb complements.

Maybe every young person _wants to be known_ (want / know) as a hero, but very few people get the opportunity. As he left for work one morning, pilot Chesley Sullenberger probably _____ (not expect / call) a national hero later that day. Passengers on Flight 1549 _____ (recall / terrify) as their plane headed into the Hudson River. A flock of geese _____ (appear / suck) into the plane's engine. Sullenberger landed the plane safely on the water. He also made sure that every passenger and crew member was safely out of the plane before leaving the aircraft himself. For this above all, perhaps, he _____ (deserve / admire). It was an incident that many passengers no doubt _____ (would rather / forget). However, it is a feat that the industry _____ (need / remember) for many years to come.

B Pair work Retell this comment on the story. Use *that* and *those* to refer to ideas your partner knows and *this* and *these* to introduce or highlight ideas. Add *to put it mildly* in two more places.

       those   to put it mildly

"I'm sure ~~the~~ passengers were pleased ₌when the plane landed safely. The geese caused a few problems. Just think what could have happened if the pilot hadn't been so skilled. The guy must have nerves of steel. He must have analyzed the problem instantly to bring the aircraft down safely. Then he made sure all the people were safe. I read a story recently about a pilot who fell asleep, which is scary, and some passengers woke him up."

4 In the news?

A Replace the underlined words in the reports with expressions from Unit 10, Lesson A. Then complete the verb phrases to express the ideas given in brackets [ ].

               greet a delegation

1. The failure of the president to <u>meet a group</u> of foreign heads of state this week has <u>encouraged rumors</u> about the state of her health. She <u>had</u> surgery earlier this year. However, it is thought that doctors are insisting **on** _her having_ [= insisting that she should have] more surgery before they can **agree to** _____ [= agree that she can carry out] her normal duties. This comes in a week when her main political rival <u>stated</u> he was running for office. Analysts say with the political uncertainty, there is **a danger of** _____ [= that the stock market be affected]. They say they cannot <u>exclude the idea</u> **of** _____ [= idea that the economy may collapse]. Stocks <u>fell sharply</u>.

2. A bomb <u>exploded</u> near a central market in the capital early this morning. There were no injuries. A protest group has said it <u>was responsible</u>. If these protests continue, it could result **in** _____ [= have the result that the government will take action]. Riot squads may be <u>put on the streets</u>. A government spokesperson said that victims will be <u>paid damages</u> and that the protest movements need to be <u>controlled</u>. It is thought the government is already <u>preparing a legal case</u> against one group.

B Complete the sentences from an editorial column with an appropriate verb in the subjunctive.

1. The requirement that every student _____ an advanced English exam to graduate is a good one.
2. It is essential that everyone _____ English well.
3. Our recommendation is that English exams _____ harder.
4. Colleges should demand that any student who fails _____ in college for another year.
5. It is crucial that our country _____ better at English than neighboring countries.

C Pair work Do you agree with the editorial in Exercise B? What subjects do you think should be mandatory? Signal your concerns with expressions like *That doesn't sit right with me*.

Unit 1, Lesson C Stressing auxiliaries for emphasis

> People often add the stressed auxiliary verbs *do, does, did,* or stress the full form of the auxiliary verbs with *be* or *have* (e.g., *am, was, have,* and *had*) to emphasize an idea.
>
> *I'm not surprised John didn't come to the party, but I **am** surprised he didn't call! I mean, I **had** asked him to let me know if he couldn't come, so I really **did** think he would call me.*

A 🔽 Read and listen to the information above. Repeat the example sentences.

B 🔽 Read the conversation. Rewrite the phrases in bold to emphasize the speakers' ideas. Then listen, check, and repeat.

    I do know

A **I know** computers help people learn, but **I think** they often make it difficult to concentrate.

B Well, at one point **I worried** that using computers in class was a mistake, but now I don't.

A Yeah, no. I mean, **it's been shown** that math students learn algebra faster on a computer.

B And **it's true** that students often pay more attention to a good computer program. . . .

A But **I've noticed** that students spend a lot of time doing other things instead of studying.

B Yeah, **I'd hoped** that wouldn't happen, but there are lots of distractions on the Internet.

About you | **C** Pair work Practice the conversation. Then discuss the ideas. Which do you agree with?

Unit 2, Lesson A Stress in noun phrases

> Notice the stress in these noun phrases. The primary stress is on a word after the noun or pronoun. The main noun or pronoun gets the secondary stress.
>
> ▪   ◼   ▪   ◼   ▪   ◼
> *information online*   *attitudes toward privacy*   *information considered private*
>
> ▪   ◼   ▪   ◼   ▪   ◼
> *people on social networks ads requesting private information something to worry about*

A 🔽 Read and listen to the information above. Repeat the phrases.

B 🔽 Listen. In the bold phrases, underline the syllable with the secondary stress and circle the syllable with the primary stress. Then listen, check, and repeat.

1. I often feel that **attitudes toward privacy** are changing for the worse. It seems like **information once considered private** is now shared freely on social networks.

2. I ran into a problem after checking out some **products on the Internet**. On every website I went to, I got all these **ads for similar products**.

3. Someone hacked into my email, probably because I used a **password based on my birthdate**. Now when I choose passwords, I never choose **anything obvious**.

4. I have maximum privacy settings on my social networks so my boss won't see the **photos posted by my friends**. That really is **something to think about**.

About you | **C** Pair work Have you or has anyone you know had these problems? Tell your partner.

Unit 3, Lesson C **Stress in expressions of contrast**

> **Notice which words are stressed in these expressions introducing a contrasting view.**
>
> *It's important to get a college degree, **but even then**, you won't necessarily find a job.*
> ***Having said that, though**, your chances are better if you finish college.*
>
> *There's a lot of competition for jobs these days. **But then again**, there always has been.*
> ***Even so**, the competition is probably more intense now than ever.*

A Read and listen to the information above. Repeat the example sentences.

B Listen. Circle the stressed word in each bold expression. Then listen, check, and repeat.

1. I think you should attend the best college that accepts you. **Having said that, though**, you need to make sure you can afford the housing and tuition costs.
2. I think it's great that people have a shorter workweek than they used to. **But then again**, many people now work two jobs in order to earn enough money to live on.
3. More people are working overtime, **but even then**, many have a hard time paying their bills.
4. I think it's good that people are getting married later, when they're more mature. **But even so**, the divorce rate doesn't seem to be going down.
5. There *is* competition for jobs. **Having said that**, there aren't enough candidates for some jobs.

About you **C** Pair work Discuss the comments. Which views do you agree with?

Unit 4, Lesson C **Stress in adding expressions**

> **Notice which words are stressed in these expressions that add information.**
>
> *Overfishing decreases the fish population, **not to mention** that many fish are killed by pollution.*
> ***On top of that**, fish consumption continues to increase every year.*
> ***What's more**, no one seems interested in finding a solution to the problem.*
> ***In any case**, someday people will have to consume less fish, or there won't be any left to eat.*

A Read and listen to the information above. Repeat the example sentences.

B Listen to these conversations. Circle the stressed word in each bold expression. Then listen, check, and repeat.

1. *A* No one seems to agree on the causes of global warming. **What's more**, they don't agree on any solutions, either.
   B I suppose it's hard to identify the causes, but **in any event**, we need to do something.
   A I agree. I mean, we need to prepare for higher temperatures, **not to mention** extreme weather events like hurricanes. And **on top of that**, there's rising sea levels.
2. *A* The world uses way too much oil, and **what's more**, demand is increasing every year.
   B Yeah. **Not to mention** the fact that the supply of oil is decreasing pretty quickly.
   A And **on top of that**, people aren't trying very hard to develop different energy sources.
   B You're right. **In any case**, we'll need to do something soon. We're running out of oil.

About you **C** Pair work Practice the conversations. Then discuss the issues. What's your view?

Unit 5, Lesson C   Stress in expressions

> **Notice that in these expressions, which introduce different perspectives on an issue, the primary stress is on the determiners, and the secondary stress is on the verbs.**
>
> ■   ■
> *One way to look at it is that space exploration is a good investment.*
>
>   ■   ■
> *I don't really agree.* **Let me put it this way**: *If money's limited, you need to set priorities.*
>
>   ■   ■
> **To put it another way**: *As long as people are hungry, we can't waste money on space.*

A 🔽 Read and listen to the information above. Repeat the example sentences.

B 🔽 Listen to these conversations. In the bold expressions, circle the primary stress and underline the secondary stress. Then listen, check, and repeat.

  1. *A* I think we need to cut back on government spending, including education.
      B Well, yes, but **look** at it **this** way: Education is the key to our children's future.
  2. *A* I think we spend too much on infrastructure – you know, highways, bridges, and things.
      B Well, **one way to look at it is** investing in infrastructure creates jobs, which we need. **To put it another way**, it makes the economy grow.
  3. *A* They should eliminate taxes on gasoline. Gas costs too much these days.
      B Well, I'm not too sure. **Let me put it this way**: Taxes help lower consumption. Or **to look at it another way**, if we don't tax gas, consumption rises and it'll cost more.

About you   **C** Pair work Practice the conversations. Then discuss the ideas. Who do you agree with, Speaker A or Speaker B?

Unit 6, Lesson A   Prepositions in relative clauses

> **Notice how the prepositions before the relative pronouns are reduced. Notice also which word has the primary stress in each phrase.**
>
>   ■   ■
> *Online coupons bring in new customers,* **some of whom** *become regular customers later on.*
>
>   ■   ■
> *These coupons generate income for gyms,* **many of which** *have equipment that isn't used for long periods during the day.*

A 🔽 Read and listen to the information above. Repeat the example sentences.

B 🔽 Listen and repeat these sentences. Pay particular attention to the weak forms of the prepositions and the stressed words in the bold expressions.

  1. Online coupons don't always work for small restaurants, **most of which** have low profits.
  2. The steep discounts, **some of which** attract lots of customers, often don't continue long term.
  3. Restaurants get paid a low fee for their meals, **half of which** goes to the coupon website.
  4. Coupons attract particular types of people, **many of whom** never return for a full-price meal.
  5. Often a restaurant's regular customers, **all of whom** pay full price, get annoyed that others are getting better deals.

About you   **C** Pair work Discuss the ideas in the sentences. Which do you agree with?

Unit 7, Lesson B   **Binomial pairs**

Notice how *and* and *but* are reduced in these binomial expressions. Notice also that the primary stress is on the second word of the pair and the secondary stress on the first.

I'm **sick and tired** of getting work calls at night. When I'm home, I need **peace and quiet**.

I suspect that, **slowly but surely**, phone calls will become an issue between me and my wife.

A Read and listen to the information above. Repeat the example sentences.

B Read the conversation. Circle the bold words that have the primary stress. Underline the bold words with secondary stress. Then listen, check, and repeat.

A Guess what! I just quit my job. I gave notice on Friday.

B Really? I thought you were going to **wait and see** if things got better.

A Yeah, but you know, **slowly but surely**, things were getting worse, so . . .

B Well, you and your boss certainly had your **ups and downs**.

A That's for sure. I mean, I went **above and beyond** most of the other staff, and he'd still criticize me. I just got **sick and tired** of it.

B Yeah. But did you **stop and think** what you might do? I mean, now you have no job to go to.

A Well, actually, I might do a PhD now that I have the **time and energy**!

About you

C Pair work Practice the conversation. Then discuss the situation. Did Speaker A do the right thing? Why, or why not?

Unit 8, Lesson A   **Saying perfect infinitives**

Notice that in perfect infinitives, *to* is not reduced, but *have* is reduced.

My grandfather seems **to have had** an extremely interesting career as a journalist.

I'd like **to have known** him, but he died before I was born.

I'd like **to have spoken** to him about his experiences in war zones.

A Read and listen to the information above. Repeat the example sentences.

B Listen and repeat these sentences. Pay attention to the pronunciation of the perfect infinitives.

1. I'd like **to have studied** math with Einstein. He's said **to have been** a great teacher.
2. I would love **to have gone** to the moon with Neil Armstrong.
3. People seem **to have lived** much simpler lives 100 years ago – certainly less stressful.
4. My grandparents' generation seems **to have had** more time to spend with family.
5. We're supposed **to have made** great progress in how we handle conflict, but I'm not so sure.
6. People are said **to have lived** healthier lives until about 20 years ago.

About you

C Pair work Discuss the sentences. Do you agree?

Unit 9, Lesson C   Intonation of background information

Expressions that give background information, or information you expect your listener to know, have a fall–rise intonation: *considering . . ., given (that / the fact that) . . ., in view of (the fact that) . . ., in light of (the fact that). . . .*

Space exploration is expensive. **Considering the cost**, *it makes no sense at all to go to Mars.*

It makes no sense at all to go to Mars, **considering the cost**.

A Read and listen to the information above. Repeat the example sentences.

B Listen to this conversation. Circle the stressed words where the fall-rise intonation starts in the underlined parts of the sentences.

A I'm getting worried about the storms we've had recently, given all the damage.

B Well, in light of rising sea levels, I think this is just the beginning. Frankly, I think it's time for people to start moving away from the coasts.

A Maybe. But what are we going to do about places like New York, Bangkok, and Rio? We can't just move entire cities, given the huge populations.

B No, but we could build sea walls for protection, given how serious this is.

A I don't think that's going to happen anytime soon, considering the incredible cost.

B But in view of the fact that 15 of the world's 20 largest cities are in flood zones, we can't ignore the problem. We have to find ways to protect the people in these cities.

About you **C** Pair work Practice the conversation. Which ideas do you agree with?

Unit 10, Lesson C   Stress and intonation

Notice how longer sentences can be broken up into parts. Each part has a primary stress, where the intonation changes, and often a secondary stress as well. Notice also the fall–rise intonation for background information and falling intonation for new information.

My **girlfriend**, */ she's* **always watching** */ those* **cooking shows**.

[Background]   [New]   [New]

A Read and listen to the information above. Repeat the example sentences.

B Each phrase has two stressed syllables shown in bold. Listen and circle the syllable with the primary stress.

1. Those **shop**ping **chan**nels, / I **nev**er **watch** them. / **They** can be ad**dic**tive.
2. This **friend** of **mine**, / he's **al**ways on his **smart**phone, / **check**ing the **finan**cial news.
3. The **weath**er **chan**nels, / now **they're** useful. / The **weath**er re**ports** / are **con**stantly up**dat**ed.
4. The **cook**ing **chan**nels, / **they're** a **lot** of fun. / You can **learn** to **cook** / **sim**ply by **watch**ing them.
5. My **moth**er and **fath**er, / they **leave** the TV on / pretty **much** all **day**. / I **guess** they **like** it / when there's **background** **noise**.

About you **C** Pair work Rewrite each comment with your own information. Discuss with your partner.

Unit 11, Lesson B Stress in longer idioms

> Phrasal verbs are usually stressed on the particle. However, in idioms that are phrasal verbs with a noun object, the object has the primary stress.
>
> ■ ■
> I **turned around** and looked in the mirror.
>
> ■ ■ ■ ■
> I realized that I needed to **turn my life around**.   BUT   I **turned it around**.

A 🔽 Read and listen to the information above. Repeat the example sentences.

B 🔽 Listen. Circle the word that has the primary stress in the bold expressions. Then listen, check, and repeat.

1. Have you ever known anyone who was in a bad situation but was able to **turn his life around**?
2. Have you ever needed to **turn your back on** friends who were doing things you didn't approve of?
3. If you knew some friends were cheating on exams, would you **turn a blind eye to** what they were doing? Or would you **turn them in** to the teacher?
4. Have you ever wanted to **turn over a new leaf** for any reason?
5. Do you ever feel you want to **turn back the clock** to a time when life was more fun?
6. Have you ever regretted **turning down an opportunity** of some kind?

About you **C** Pair work Take turns asking and answering the questions

Unit 12, Lesson B Stress with reflexive pronouns

> Notice how reflexive pronouns are stressed when they are used for emphasis. They are generally unstressed in other cases.
>
> Once my parents found **themselves** in trouble because some harassing emails had been sent from their computer. They **themselves** hadn't sent the messages, of course.
>
> I **myself** have never had a problem with my email. But once I let **myself** be tricked into giving money to a con artist on the street.

A 🔽 Read and listen to the information above. Repeat the example sentences.

B 🔽 Listen. Circle the stressed reflexive pronouns. Then listen, check, and repeat.

1. People allow **themselves** to taken in by the same scams again and again. If you think you'll never get taken in **yourself** think again. History repeats **itself**.
2. I wouldn't describe **myself** as terribly cautious, but I never open emails if I don't recognize the sender. I've never had a virus **myself**, but I just want to protect **myself**.
3. You have to be careful not to let **yourself** be fooled when you meet people online. They often say things about **themselves** that are simply untrue.
4. My brother got so upset with **himself** because he was spending too much time on social media, so he deleted all his accounts. It was a decision he made **himself**.

About you **C** Pair work Read the comments aloud. What do you think of the ideas they express?

❶ More on auxiliary verbs to avoid repetition

- You can use auxiliary verbs to avoid repetition of these verb tenses and forms.

Simple present or past	*I don't often take risks, but my best friend **does** all the time.*
Present or past continuous	*I was hoping to graduate last year. One of my friends **was,** too.*
Present perfect (or continuous)	*I've been thinking about settling down, but my friends **haven't**.*
Past perfect (or continuous)	*I'd never had straight A's till this year, though my friends all **had**.*
Modal verbs	*My dad can't understand why I want to travel, but my mom **can**.*

Use auxiliary and modal verbs to complete what these people say about the different topics. Use the same tense and form as the first verb.

1. *Work:* Well, I was trying to get a job in TV. Actually, I know a couple of other people who _____ , too. But I'm finding it difficult to get *any* job, as many people _____ these days.
2. *Family:* I've never really thought about starting a family, and I know my husband _____ either. I'm getting so involved in my career at the moment, as we all _____ , I guess.
3. *Relationships:* I hadn't really met anyone serious until now, though a couple of my friends _____ . I mean, I can really imagine getting married now – I just hope my girlfriend _____ !
4. *Social life:* It's funny. Some of my friends are going to parties still, but I _____ . I'm not interested. I want to do other things with my life now. I think my closest friend _____ , too.
5. *Hobbies:* I haven't had much time to do anything, but my wife _____ . She's been learning how to edit videos. I don't often use my computer now; well, I _____ a bit but not a lot.
6. *Travel:* My sister and I went to Italy last fall. I hadn't gone overseas before that, and she _____ , either. We had a fabulous time. Now I want to go away again – and my sister _____ , too.

❷ *too, either, so, neither,* and *(to) do so*

- You can use auxiliaries with *too, either, so,* and *neither* to show similarity. After *so* and *neither,* change the order of the auxiliary and subject.
  *I am saving for a trip, and **my best friend is, too**.* OR . . . *and **so is my best friend**.*
  *She doesn't enjoy her work, and **I don't, either**.* OR . . . *and **neither do I**.*
  *She can't afford to go away next year, and **I can't, either**.* OR . . . *and **neither can I**.*

- Use *(to) do so* to avoid repeating a verb + object or complement.
  *Learning to play sports has given me confidence and will **continue to do so** for many years.*
  *Many people want to buy their own home but are not in a **position to do so**.*
  *A lot of people want to publish novels but are **unable to do so**.*
  *Anyone who wishes to take a career break **can do so** if they plan it carefully.*

Complete the bold phrases with an auxiliary and the sentences with *(to) do so*. Then write another way to state the bold phrases using *so* or *neither*.

1. To get ahead in your career, you often have to move to another city. I don't really want to uproot my family, and **my wife** _____ , **either,** but if necessary, we'll _____ .
2. A friend asked me to go to a debate club last year with him, and you know, I was happy _____ . And actually, I'm glad I did. I can speak much more confidently now, and **my friend** _____ , **too**.
3. It's easier than ever now to take a year off before college if you can _____ .
4. My friend's thinking of studying in Paris. **I** _____ , **too,** if I can get the money _____ .
5. I've always wanted to go on a cycling tour, but I've never had the time _____ . But finally my sisters and I are planning to go next spring. I'm looking forward to it, and **my sisters** _____ , **too**.

1 **More on using *to* to avoid repeating verb phrases**

- You can use *to* to avoid repeating an infinitive verb phrase when it is clear what you mean.
  Use *to* after *choose, deserve, expect, hate, hope, like, mean, intend, need, prefer, want, 'd like.*
  *I've never written a journal. I keep meaning **to**. / But I hope **to**. / I'd prefer **not to**.*

- You don't need *to* after *agree, ask, promise, forget, try,* or *after want, like, wish* in *if* clauses.
  *"I want to get my novel published. I've tried **(to)** but can't." "I'll look at it if you **want / like / wish**."*

- When you use *be* in the first clause, including in the passive, use *to be* in the second clause.
  *My parents **aren't** interested in poetry, and they've never pretended **to be**.*
  *In college, I **was asked** to enter a short-story contest, though I didn't expect **to be**.*

Complete the comments with *to* or *to be*. Write parentheses where *to* is not needed.

1. A classmate asked me to comment on her poems. Well, I promised ___(to)___ , and I really tried
   _____ . But they were really bad. After a month, she asked, "Did you read them?" I said,
   "Sorry, I forgot _____ ."

2. My friend has entered a few writing contests. She's never won, though she always expects _____ .

3. I'd love to see a Shakespeare play in English. I've always wanted _____ , and I intend
   _____ one day.

4. I was voted the best fiction writer in high school, though I didn't deserve _____ .

5. You can borrow my e-reader if you want _____ . I lost some books off it. I didn't mean
   _____ , but . . .

6. I'm just not very good at writing, and I'll never hope _____ , really. I'll stick to math!

7. My sister wants to work in publishing. Well, she hopes _____ .

8. I think I'm going to have to play the lead role in the school play, but I'd prefer not _____ .

2 **More on *one / ones* to avoid repeating countable nouns**

- You need to use *one / ones* after *the, the only, the main, every,* and after adjectives.
  *I read six plays last week – a **long one** and five **short ones**. **The one** I liked best was the **long one**.*

- You don't need *one / ones* after *which,* superlatives, *this, that, either, neither, another, the other.*
  *"Can I borrow a book?" "Sure. **Which (one)** do you want? You can take **this (one)** or **that (one)**."*

- Don't use *one / ones* after *these, those, my, your, Dan's,* etc., *some, any, both,* or numbers.
  *"**Both (books)** are good. They're both **mine**." (NOT . . . ~~my ones~~.)*

- In formal English, especially writing, use *that / those* or a possessive instead of the *one / ones.*
  *Keats's poems are better than **those of Byron / Byron's**.*

> **Common errors**
> Notice the spelling of *ones.*
> *I love books. The **ones** I like best are . . .*
> (NOT . . . ~~once / one's I like~~)

Replace the underlined words with *one / ones* if possible or make other changes to avoid repeating.

1. *A* Can I take a look at one of your magazines? I mean,
   these <u>magazines</u> on your desk.
   B Sure. Which <u>magazine</u> do you want to read?
   A Either <u>magazine</u>. Oh, actually, I'll take a look at that <u>magazine</u>. It's an expensive <u>magazine</u>.
   B Actually, that's the only <u>magazine</u> worth reading. It's the <u>magazine</u> I prefer, anyway. The other
   <u>magazine</u> doesn't have very many interesting articles.

2. *A* My literature classes are fun. Are your <u>literature classes</u>? I have three <u>literature classes</u> a week.
   B Well, Mrs. Brown's classes are the hardest <u>classes</u>. She said in her lecture last week, "My class is
   more demanding than Mr. Smith's <u>class</u>." And honestly, the homework is hard. I mean, listen to
   this: "The works of J.K. Rowling are as important as <u>the works</u> of Shakespeare. Discuss."

1 Adjectives after nouns

- Adjectives usually come before nouns, but these adjectives often come after nouns:
  available, possible, concerned, responsible, involved, necessary, extra.
  *Cybercrime is a problem, and the people **responsible / involved** should be punished.*
  *There are various antivirus programs **available**.*
  *Look for the easiest solution **possible**.*

- Adjectives come after nouns in measurements and after indefinite pronouns.
  *Social media sites are only about a **decade old**.*
  *There's **nothing unusual** about getting spam mail.*
  ***Anyone interested** in protecting themselves from cybercrime should talk to an expert.*

- Adjectives with complements come after nouns.
  *One action **worth taking** is changing your password regularly.*
  *Websites **full of personal data** can be targets for identity thieves.*

Unscramble the sentences. Put the adjectives after the nouns.

1. a great deal of / personal information / Some people / have / available online
   Some people have a great deal of personal information available online.
2. with doing this / wrong / don't think / They / there's anything
3. your personal data / any means / eager to get / However, hackers / will try / possible
4. responsible for hacking / It can be / the people / to find / difficult
5. may "lose" / People / confidential information / what hackers / are doing / unaware of
6. The victims / problems with / concerned / their credit / may end up having
7. the steps / You need to / take / necessary / to protect yourself

2 Negative phrases after nouns

- Phrases that come after nouns can be negative. You can add *not* after the noun.
  *Some information can be hidden from people **not in your group of "friends."***
  *Individuals **not willing to give personal information** shouldn't have to do so.*
  *Emails **not to trust** often have the subject "Hi."*
  *Credit card numbers are one example of the kind of data **not to be shared**.*
  *Social networking sites can be a mystery to anyone **not belonging to one**.*
  *Any computer **not protected by antivirus software** is vulnerable.*

A Complete the sentences using the words given. Sometimes there is more than one answer.

1. These days anyone_____ (not / wish) to have their information online may find it impossible.
2. Computers _____ (not / protect) by antivirus software are unsafe.
3. If you think you've been hacked, there are some warning signs _____ (not / ignore).
4. There are some basic rules for first-time users _____ (not / familiar) with social networks.
5. Your phone number is one example of information _____ (not / post).
6. Don't allow people _____ (not / in your contacts list) to read your profile.
7. Another thing _____ (not / do) is to post photos of yourself doing silly things.
8. Remember that your problems at work are a subject _____ (not / discuss) on social media sites.
9. Online ads _____ (not / click) on are the ones that say you won a prize.

About you

B Choose a sentence from Exercise A that you agree with. Explain why.

I agree. It's almost impossible for people not wishing to have their information online to stop it from happening. Every time you sign up to a website you have to give personal information.

❶ More on two-part conjunctions

> • You can use two-part conjunctions to combine nouns, adjectives, and verbs.
>
> | | |
> |---|---|
> | **Nouns** | My TV can play **either DVDs or** Internet **movies**.
Both the mouse and the keyboard are wireless.
My friend has **neither a TV nor a computer** in her home.
The kitchen has **not only a self-cleaning oven but also a robot** that cleans the floors. |
> | **Adjectives** | Some high-tech products are **either very expensive or very complicated**.
Housework is **both boring and tiring**.
Housecleaning with modern appliances is **neither difficult nor time-consuming**.
Using a microwave to cook is **not only simple but also fast**. |
> | **Verbs** | You can **either raise or lower** all the blinds with a remote control.
My alarm clock **both flashes** lights **and sounds** an alarm to wake me up.
Older cell phones **neither play** music **nor take** pictures.
I'd like a robot that **not only cleans** the house **but also cooks** the meals. |

> **Common errors**
>
> Don't use *neither . . . nor* when you have already used a negative verb. Use *either . . . or*.
> We do not have **either** a dishwasher **or** a washing machine. (NOT ~~We do not have neither a . . .~~)
> If you use a modal verb, put it before the first conjunction.
> My TV **can either** stream movies **or** play DVDs. (NOT My TV ~~either can stream~~ . . .)

Rewrite the sentences using the two-part conjunctions in parentheses.

1. Many features in high-tech homes are convenient. They are innovative. (both . . . and)
   Many features in high-tech homes are both convenient and innovative.
2. In high-tech homes, one control manages temperature. It manages lighting. (both . . . and)
3. Remote computers can control the central systems. Smartphones can control them. (either . . . or)
4. In new, high-tech homes, cooking is simpler. It is more efficient. (not only . . . but also)
5. Refrigerators list their contents. They suggest recipes for the foods available. (not only . . . but also)
6. Cookbooks won't be needed anymore. Recipe cards won't be needed anymore. (neither . . . nor)
7. A computer displays the recipes on your kitchen counter. It reads the recipes aloud. (both . . . and)

❷ Two-part conjunctions with phrases and clauses

> You can turn on the oven **either from work or in the car on the way home**. (phrases)
>   **either before you leave work or as you drive home**. (clauses)
> High-tech homes are good **not only in summer but also in winter**. (phrases)
>   **not only because they are innovative but they also make life easier**. (clauses)

A Rewrite the sentences using two-part conjunctions to combine phrases and clauses.

1. You can control the systems when you're at home. You can control them when you're somewhere else. (either . . . or)
2. With a sophisticated security system, you can monitor your house at work. You can monitor your house on vacation. (both . . . and)
3. A high-tech home can adjust the temperature when it gets cold outside. It can adjust the temperature after it warms up. (not only . . . but also)

About you

B Write three sentences about a home you'd like to live in. Use two-part conjunctions.

I would like to live in a home that has both a modern kitchen and a nice entertainment system. . . .

1 **Clauses with prepositions and conjunctions + *-ing***

- Clauses with prepositions (e.g., *after, by*) + *-ing* or conjunctions (e.g., *while, when*) + *-ing* are common in writing. The subject of the *-ing* clause and the main clause should be the same.
  After completing *my masters, I felt pressured to study for a PhD.* (Formal: **On / Upon completing** . . .)
  By taking *extra classes, and* **without telling** *anyone, my sister was able to graduate early.*
  Many students take on part-time work **while studying** *for their masters.*
  I changed careers and became a writer **after having worked** *in accounting all my life.*

Complete the blog. Use *-ing* clauses with the words given.

(After / spend) _____ my college years at home, I was ready to set off into the world.
So, (after / graduate) _____ , I flew to New York on a one-way ticket. (In / look back)
_____, I feel I became truly independent (upon / board) _____ the plane. However,
(while / stay) _____ with a friend for a week, I felt the initial excitement begin to wear off.
Luckily, I had gotten in touch with her (before / leave) _____ home. But I didn't want to
overstay my welcome. I also realized, (when / go) _____ for my first job interview, how much
pressure I felt. I had to find a job *and* a place to live quickly. I soon found a paid internship at a
design company (by / make) _____ dozens of phone calls, and shortly (after / start) _____
work, I was invited to rent a room in a colleague's apartment. (Since / come) _____ to New
York, I have felt the pressure of city living, but I enjoy it. Of course, I've often felt homesick, but
(by / make) _____ use of social media, I keep in touch with people. I also make sense of my
experience of post-college life (through / write) _____ this blog.

2 **Passive forms of participle and time clauses**

- Passive participle clauses can start with a past participle or *having been* + past participle.
  Clauses that start with *being* + past participle are not common.
  Presented *with a chance to change careers, my father bought a café.* (= when he was presented)
  My boss doesn't have many friends, **compared to** *his co-workers.* (= if he is compared)
  Having been born *in the country, she found it hard to live in the city.* (= because she had been born)

- You can use prepositions or conjunctions before *being* + past participle or *having been* + past participle.
  Use only the conjunctions *when, while, as, if,* and *though* before a past participle.
  After being laid off, *most workers moved to other cities to find employment.* (more common)
  After having been laid off, . . . (less common)
  When told *that the company was closing, most people felt relieved.* (NOT ~~After told~~ . . .)

Rewrite the underlined clauses with a participle or time clause, as in the chart above. In two cases, you need to delete *and* from the sentence.

Before he was elected, a politician said that if more women managed corporations and more men stayed at home with their families, the world would be a better place. I heard the speech while I was employed at a bank, and I took it to heart. At the time, my wife, who held a higher position than me, and I were expecting our first child. She was faced with the prospect of interrupting her career, and she suggested that I should be the primary caregiver. So, I was given the chance to take care of our child, and I immediately agreed to do so. As I had been raised in a traditional family, I knew my parents would pressure me to pursue my career. Indeed, when they were informed of our decision, they were clearly disappointed. Twelve years later, I still believe I made the right choice. In fact, I feel fortunate, if I am compared to many of my friends. When I'm asked if I made the right choice, I say it's the best decision I ever made. My wife agrees. She is now the president of a large company.

1 More on *so* and *such*

- You can use *such* before some nouns to add emphasis. It means "big."
  *It makes **such a difference** to keep your desk neat. Mine was **such a mess**. I was **such an idiot**.*

- With some nouns, *such* can refer forward to what will be mentioned.
  *Organize your time in **such a way** that you have time for a social life.*

- You can use *so* and *such* with determiners and pronouns: *so much / many / few / little; such a lot.*
  *In my first semester, there were **so many** parties that served pizza and soda. I ate **so much** (pizza) and drank **such a lot** (of soda) that I gained weight.*

- You can use *so much* as an adverb and before comparative adjectives and adverbs.
  *I enjoyed college **so much**. It was **so much better / more fun** than I expected. The time went by **so much more quickly** than I thought it would.*

Use *so* or *such* to complete the posts on a website about the challenges of marriage. Then write a post of your own on the topic of marriage using *so* or *such*.

1. There's no _____ **thing** as an easy marriage. It was _____ **much harder** at first than I imagined. I worked _____ **a lot**, and my husband and I spent _____ **little** time together that we almost broke up.

2. Getting married had _____ **an impact** on some of my friends. They had a lot of arguments at first, but my husband and I didn't have _____ **many**. You just have to take responsibility for making things work

3. I've always loved my single life _____ **much** that I can't imagine getting married. Married life has been _____ **a disaster** for some of my friends, and I've seen _____ **many** of them get divorced.

4. I've enjoyed being married _____ **much** more than I thought. It's been _____ **a great experience**. My advice is to live your life in _____ **a way** that nothing takes precedence over your marriage.

2 More on *even* and *only*

- *Even* and *only* usually go after *be*, after an auxiliary verb, or before a main verb.
  *Semesters **are only** 14 weeks. I'**ve even** made friends. I **only called** home a few times.*

- *Even* and *only* can also go before other words or phrases to add emphasis.

Nouns / pronouns	*The test was easy – **even weak students** passed. **Even I** got an A.*
Numbers	***Only one student** got a B.*
Adverbs	*I worked **even harder** in my last year. I missed class **only once**.*
Prepositions	*It was hard, **even in** the first week. It got easier **only after** spring break.*
Conjunctions	*I was tired **even before** classes started. I was tired **only because** I was sick.*

Note: *She **only missed** two classes because she was sick* can have two meanings.
You can make the meaning clear by moving the position of *only*.
*She missed **only** two classes because . . .   She missed two classes **only** because . . .*

About you

Cross out the incorrect uses of *even* and *only*. Then answer the two questions about yourself.

A Do you remember your first job? I remember mine. I was nervous, **even** after the first month. But that's **only** because my boss **only** was so scary. She used to yell at everyone.

B Oh, that makes you feel **even** worse, if you have a boss like that.

A Yeah. I think **only** there was **only** one person that my boss liked. And **even** he **even** didn't like her. I **only** stayed in that job three weeks. Then I moved to another city. Have you ever had to move?

B Um, just once. We moved when I **only** was eight, and that was **only** because Dad got a new job. My parents **even** hadn't considered it before – they hadn't **even** been on a vacation.

1 More on the future perfect

- The future perfect describes events that at a future point will be in the past, or in a time leading up to that future point in time. It can emphasize the completion of the events.
  *In two months, it will be winter and many birds **will have migrated** south.* (The migration is complete.)

- Time expressions, especially with *by*, are often used with the future perfect to show the time by which an event will be complete, e.g., *by then, by that time, by the time (that) . . ., by 2030, by the end of the century, by the age of six, within 30 days, within a decade, within the next 20 years.*
  ***Within the next 10 years,** many species **will have become** extinct.*

- The future perfect has a passive form – *will have been* + past participle – but it is not very common.
  *In the time it takes you to do this lesson, hundreds of sharks **will have been killed**.*

Complete the time expressions with *by* or *within*. Then rewrite the verbs in bold using either the active or passive form of the future perfect.

_____ the time our children reach adulthood, hundreds of species **disappear** off the face of the planet. Onc study estimated that _____ 2050, 37 percent of terrestrial species **die out** or will be in danger of extinction. That is well over a third _____ the next 30 years.

Sea life is also in danger._____ the time that sea levels rise 50 centimeters (about 20 inches), one-third of nesting beaches in the Caribbean **lose**, leading to the decline in turtle populations. _____ the end of this century, it is believed that seawater temperatures **rise** enough to affect the food supply of some ocean species. This impacts various species in different ways. For example, it is believed that _____ only a few decades, the reproductive cycle of the sperm whale **affect**, which threatens the very survival of the whale itself.

2 The future perfect for predictions and assumptions

- You can use the future perfect to state predictions or assumptions about the present or to say what you think has happened in the past. It suggests you are certain.
  *No doubt you **will have read** about the melting ice caps.*
  *Many people **will not have seen** the recent documentary about this.*

- The negative with *won't* with this meaning is mostly used in speaking and informal writing.
  *"A lot of people **won't** even **have heard** about it."*

Rewrite the underlined parts of the blog using the future perfect.

will not / won't have heard

It is unlikely that there is anyone who has not heard about the threat to certain species on the planet. No doubt you have reacted to the news that species such as polar bears are under threat. But what can we as individuals do? In recent years, perhaps you have noticed the appeals for help that come in the mail or that are on TV. They are certainly having an impact on my children. I'm sure that in addition to sending donations to various charities, you have heard about the "adopt an endangered animal" programs. I suspect what you haven't realized is how expensive these "adoptions" are. Not that I mind donating $50 for my child to adopt an orangutan or a Sumatran rhino. It's all for a good cause. And no doubt donations have saved some obscure species from the brink of extinction, and certainly the programs have motivated many children to become involved. What I hadn't expected was for a cuddly stuffed toy version to arrive in the mail. Now my daughter wants the entire collection, which is all very well – except there are more than 100 endangered species that she can sign up to help!

❶ Formal prepositional expressions

- Some prepositional expressions are very frequent in academic writing. You can use them instead of more common prepositions to make your writing sound more formal.

after	One desert spread **subsequent to / following** the introduction of new farming practices.
before	Delegates will meet **ahead of / in advance of / prior to** the conference.
with	Talks will take place **in conjunction with / alongside** an exhibition on deserts. Small mammals, **together with / along with** larger ones, survive in harsh climates.
about	There is concern **with respect to / with regard to / regarding / in relation to** agriculture.
because of	It is classified as a desert **owing to / in view of / on account of / given** its lack of rainfall.

Circle the correct expressions to complete the paragraph. Then rewrite each sentence using an alternative expression from the chart above. More than one expression is possible.

Environmental concerns, especially **with regard to / in advance of** desertification, are growing. Desertification is a huge problem **prior to / with respect to** loss of habitats and agricultural land. **Given / Alongside** the problems that desertification causes, the United Nations adopted a convention in 1994. This convention proposed returning land to its original state (land rehabilitation) **in conjunction with / owing to** programs of sustainable land management. Many countries signed up to the convention **on account of / together with** the economic problems that desertification was causing. Projects that have emerged **prior to / following** the adoption of the convention include the mapping of desertification using satellite imagery **together with / on account of** a variety of educational programs. **In view of / Subsequent to** the severity of the issue, it appears that much more still needs to be done.

❷ More on *the fact that*; prepositions + perfect forms

- The prepositional expressions *apart from, because of, besides, by virtue of, despite, due to, except for, including, in spite of, in view of, owing to, thanks to,* and *given* are often followed by *the fact that.*
  The Antarctic is classified as a desert **in view of the fact that** it has low rainfall.
  Despite the fact that it is extremely cold, Antarctica is a desert.

- Prepositions can be followed by *having* + past participle to refer to events in a period of time up to the present or up to a point in the past.
  The government takes credit **for having initiated** a tree-planting program to halt desertification.
  Agricultural practices were criticized **as having been** partly responsible for the growth of deserts.

Complete the sentences. In some, you need to add *the fact that*; in others, add *having*.

1. The Atacama desert is considered *the* driest region by virtue of _____ some parts have no rain.
2. Apart from _____ it is so dry, much of the land is also at high elevation.
3. It is surprising that over a million people are recorded as _____ settled there given _____ it is so arid.
4. Population centers developed in several areas despite _____ it is so inhospitable.
5. Teams of astronomers operate observatories in the desert due to _____ its skies are so clear.
6. Crops can now be grown owing to _____ farmers have developed irrigation systems.
7. Communities in northern Chile no longer import water into the region thanks to _____ they can now collect water from fog. Lives have improved.
8. A Canadian development team can be credited for _____ helped to develop this system.

① Adverbs in present and past passive verb phrases

- In present and past passive verb phrases, adverbs usually go after the verb *be*. In negative statements, adverbs usually go after *not*. This is the most frequent position for most adverbs.

Simple present passive	**Present continuous passive**
*New discoveries are **apparently** made every day.*	*GPS software is **continually** being upgraded.*
Simple past passive	**Past continuous passive**
*Asbestos was **widely** used until the 1960s.*	*Alternatives were not **yet** being developed.*

- Some adverbs usually go before *not*, e.g.: *also, still, just, probably, certainly, reportedly,* attitude adverbs.
  *Alternatives were **simply** not developed until later.   Alternatives were **still** not being developed.*

- Adverbs that describe the participle (e.g., to say "how" or "how much") often go before it.
  *Some inventions are not being **widely** reported or are being **completely** ignored by the media.*

Write the adverbs given into the underlined verb phrases.

Vaccinations <u>are required</u> *often* for entry to kindergarten. (often) For many parents, it's a nuisance. Yet where would we be without them? One of the first vaccines <u>was invented</u> in 1776 by Edward Jenner, a British country doctor. (originally) A milkmaid <u>was heard</u> to say that she would never develop smallpox because she <u>was infected</u> with the cowpox virus. (reportedly / already) Jenner understood the significance, and thanks to him, a vaccine for smallpox <u>was discovered</u>. (fortunately)

Jenner's smallpox vaccine <u>is being used</u> today, but his work <u>was not recognized</u>. (still / initially) However, smallpox vaccines <u>were used</u> around the world and were even made compulsory by law, until 200 years later, when the disease <u>was eradicated</u>. (increasingly / eventually) The last case of smallpox <u>was recorded</u> in 1977. (finally)

While vaccines <u>are not being developed</u> for every disease, they <u>have been approved</u> for many life-threatening ailments. (currently / already) As a result, children <u>are being protected</u> from disease, which has to be anything *but* a nuisance. (effectively)

② Adverbs in perfect verb phrases

- Adverbs usually go after *has / have / had*. Some can also go before for emphasis.
  In negative statements, adverbs usually go after *not*.
  *Some progress has **clearly** been made.* OR *... **clearly** has been made.* (more emphatic)
  *The difficulties of research had not **always** been understood.*

- Adverbs that describe the participle to say "how" or "how much" often go before it.
  *Scientists have not always been **widely** praised. Some have even been **sharply** criticized.*

- *Still* goes after *has / have / had*. In negative statements, *yet* goes after *not* or at the end of a clause.
  *Liquid water has **still** not been found on Mars. Liquid water has not **yet** been found on Mars.*
  OR *Liquid water has not been found on Mars **yet**.* (less formal)

Read the clues. Write the underlined words in the correct order. Can you guess the product?

1. A variation of this product <u>widely been used has</u> for millennia – since 4000 B.C.E., in fact.
2. A number of my friends said they thought that it <u>had invented originally been</u> by the Egyptians.
3. However, the first "recipe" for the product as we know it today <u>been had created apparently</u> by the Chinese. Historians say it <u>used had been obviously</u> to protect bronze mirrors in the second century.
4. In addition, records show that medicines <u>had wrapped been carefully</u> in it for safekeeping.
5. A replacement product <u>yet been discovered not has</u>, unless you consider computer technology.
6. The idea we can live without it <u>not has materialized completely still</u>, but will it ever be obsolete?

Exercise 2 Answer: Paper

❶ Adverbs and past modal verb phrases

- In past modal verb phrases, adverbs like *probably, certainly,* and *definitely* often go before the modal.

  Active

  He **never** should have tried to jump.

  He **probably** should not have jumped.

  Passive

  The jump **certainly** could have been stopped.

  It **probably** should not have been allowed.

- Within the verb phrase, adverbs can go after the modal or after *have.* After the modal is more frequent.

  He should **never** have gone there.

  Something bad could **easily** have happened.

  It should **never** have been allowed.

  Someone could **easily** have been killed.

Read the post from a video website and the various comments. Put the words in a correct order. There is more than one correct answer.

In 2012, a young Russian base-jumper jumped off a tall electrical tower not knowing that his parachute wouldn't open. He crashed into the ground below and miraculously survived. He was able to walk again three months later after fracturing his legs and hip.

Comments

1. Not a good idea. He <u>easily / have / could / died</u> by jumping off that tower.

2. He <u>also / have / been / might</u> electrocuted!

3. His friends <u>probably / should / have / allowed / not</u> him to jump.

4. He <u>checked / should / have / definitely</u> his parachute before jumping!

5. He <u>been / have / crippled / actually / could</u> for life.

6. He looked nervous. He <u>have / should / probably / followed</u> his gut instinct and not jumped.

7. I <u>never / watched / have / should</u> this video. It was scary!

❷ Questions with passive past modals

- Questions with passive past modals are not very common. In writing, they are often rhetorical.

  Would these problems **have been avoided** if there had been more support?

  Should this trip **have been prevented**?

  Could more money **have been raised** in another way?

Read the excerpt from an editorial news column. Then read the comments. Complete the questions in the passive form, using the verbs given.

The youngest British woman ever to climb Mount Everest was welcomed home by her family and friends this week. Such is the danger of climbing Everest that the return of any climber must be met with relief. However, the young Briton reported treacherous conditions. She had to climb past several badly-injured people and even some who had died. She had also experienced a dangerous 100-person "snarl up," as people rushed to the summit during a period of calm weather. It raises important questions about such dangerous expeditions. For example:

1. Should people <u>have been allowed</u> (allow) to climb in such treacherous conditions?

2. Could the injured climbers _____ (help)?

3. Could more _____ (do) to make the climb safer?

4. Would deaths _____ (prevent) if people had shown better judgment?

5. In the past, should people rescued off the mountain _____ (make) to pay for their rescue?

6. Should climbers _____ (charge) for failing to help other injured climbers?

❶ Pronouns and numbers in relative clauses

- Relative clauses can start with a pronoun (*both, each, much, neither, none, several*, etc.) + *of* or with numbers and quantity words (*half, 30 percent, the majority*, etc.) + *of*.
  In 2013, we launched two new products, **neither of which** was successful. / **both of which** failed.
  The company had four directors, **each of whom** made a fortune. / **none of whom** stayed after the sale.
  There are over 2 million businesses in Canada, **the majority of which** have fewer than 100 employees.
  One company has 500 employees, **half of whom** are part-time.

> **Common errors**
>
> Don't start these types of relative clauses with *which* or *whom*.
> *There are 100 companies,* **most of which** *have one employee.* (NOT . . . ~~which most of them~~ *have* . . .)

Rewrite each pair of sentences from a report using a relative clause. You may delete words.

Consumers, most of whom are on tight budgets, are looking to save money when they shop.

1. Consumers are looking to save money when they shop. Most consumers are on tight budgets.
2. There are thousands of online coupon sites. The majority of these offer more or less the same thing.
3. So how do you know which sites to use or which information to trust? Much of it is misleading.
4. Our staff researched 10 options. Two of them are avid coupon users.
5. Two sites we researched had out-of-date coupons. Both are major players in the coupon business.
6. Our staff identified four more sites. None was easy to navigate.
7. On two sites, staff found much better deals than on other sites. Neither site is particularly well-known.
8. These two sites had coupons with discounts up to 30 percent. Each one specializes in grocery coupons.
9. Of the 10 sites we surveyed, three had too many distracting banner ads. Eighty percent offered email alerts.

❷ Nouns in relative clauses

- Relative clauses can begin with a preposition, or a noun + preposition, + *which* or *whom*.
  Imagine a world **in which** there is no profit motive and a staff **for whom** nothing is a problem.
  The end-of-year report, **a copy of which** was sent to the press, painted a gloomy picture.
  The CEO of this company, **a person for whom** I have great respect, just retired.

> **Common errors**
>
> Don't start these types of relative clauses with *which* + noun.
> *We read the research,* **the results of which** *were unclear.* (NOT ~~which results were unclear.~~)

Rewrite the underlined parts of the report as relative clauses that begin with the bold words.

in which no business fails.
Imagine a perfect economic environment <u>that no business fails **in**</u>. Unfortunately, the truth is that the rate <u>that start-up companies fail **at**</u> is high. The high failure rate, <u>and **the main reasons for** this are given below</u>, is concerning. Many owners, <u>and start-up costs are high **for** them</u>, are deterred by the risk of failure.

Reasons for failures of start-up companies

1. The frequency <u>that new businesses fail **at**</u> is high when they're started for the *wrong* reasons.
2. Many new business owners lack basic skills, <u>and **the importance** of this</u> cannot be underestimated.
   Above all, they need to be able to manage finances, <u>and **an understanding** of this</u> is critical.
3. The employees <u>that the owner entrusts the business **to**</u> often have the wrong skills.
4. A new business must have a website, <u>and **the functions** can vary</u> and <u>**without** it the business will fail.</u>
5. Many new business owners underestimate the prices <u>that their products must sell **at**</u> to make a profit.

Unit 6, Lesson B

Grammar extra

❶ other, every other, other than

- Before *other*, you can use *the, any, some, all, many, much, most, no, (a) few, every, this / that*, etc.
  One retailer outsells **all other** stores. **No other** store can compete. **Few other** stores do as well.
  There is **no other** business news. If **any other** information comes to light, it will be reported.

- You can also use these words: *several, various, numerous, whole, certain, countless*.
  Online shopping is **a whole other** problem for small retailers. There are **several other** threats too.

- *Every other* can mean "alternate" and is often used with time words (*day, week, year*, etc.).
  We go to the grocery store **every other weekend.**

- *Other than* means "except" or "apart from."
  Salesclerks need to speak a language **other than** English.

> **Common errors**
>
> Don't use *others* before a plural noun.
> *Retailers face* **other** *threats.*
> (NOT ~~others threats~~)

Use *other, others,* or *every other* to complete the sentences in this business report.

1. While many retailers are struggling, one electronics retailer outperforms all _____ stores. No _____ company attracts such a loyal consumer base. In fact, many consumers will *not* be seen with products _____ than these smartphones or tablets, which must be the envy of most _____ retailers.

2. Selling print magazines has been difficult in recent years. One magazine recently announced that it will now publish only online, and numerous _____ magazines are considering doing the same. Many _____ have simply gone out of business.

3. Maintaining sales is a problem for any small business, but supporting online sales is a whole _____ issue. Some simply don't create user-friendly sites, while some _____ often don't know how to make their sites visible on the Web.

4. While some stores are concerned about the loss of sales to online retailers, certain _____ stores are tackling the issue head-on. One retailer lets customers pick up goods that they ordered online at the store the same day. It's a huge advantage over all _____ competing stores, which deliver their goods only _____ week.

❷ More on *another*

- *Another* can mean "an additional" or "an alternative." You can use it before a singular countable noun, the pronoun *one*, numbers, and *few*, or as a pronoun instead of a singular count noun.
  I bought **another** sweater. I liked it so much I bought **another (one)** in **another** color.
  I actually bought **another three** sweaters. In **another few** weeks, I'll buy some more.

Read the blog. Find seven more places where you can replace words with *another*.

I recently bought a sweater online, but when it arrived, it didn't fit. I decided to order ~~a different~~ one [*another*] in a different size, and return the first sweater. It was a long process. I called customer service, and they promised to send me a return label. Only they didn't. I emailed them, made a second call, and then sent an additional email. Finally, I got the return label and went to the post office. I had to make a further trip, however, as I had forgotten to wrap the sweater in the original packaging. Now I have to wait an additional five days before it ships. I'll have to wait an extra couple of weeks before the refund appears on my credit card statement. Meanwhile, I ordered a new sweater, which was out of stock. Next time I'll just go to the store.

- Inversions are generally used in formal English. Use *were* + subject (+ infinitive) to describe an imaginary situation in the present or future. Use *had* + subject + past participle for the past.

  Were he to have a child, my son would take classes.   Negative: *Were he **not** to have …*

  Had they known about the classes, my friends would have   Negative: *Had they **not** known …*
  taken them.

- You can also use *If it weren't for . . .*, *If it hadn't been for . . .*, *Were it not for . . .*, and *Had it not been for* + noun phrase. They mean "If someone or something didn't exist or something hadn't happened."

  If it weren't for my parents, I wouldn't be able to continue with my education.
  OR ***Were it not for*** my parents, I . . . (hypothetical statement about the present)
  If it hadn't been for my parents, I wouldn't have been able to continue with my education.
  OR ***Had it not been for*** my parents, I . . . (hypothetical statement about the past)

A **Rewrite the underlined parts of the blog about parenting teenagers, using a structure in the chart. Start with the word in bold.**

There are many challenges associated with parenting, especially parenting teens. Some parents claim that **if** the advice in parenting magazines didn't exist, they would not know how to deal with their teenage children. If these magazines **had** existed when we were younger, we could certainly have learned from them. We relied instead on our friends for advice. Indeed, if my wife and I **had** not had the support of other parents with the same challenges, we may not have survived the journey. **If** our neighbor in particular hadn't existed, life would have been much harder. We had it tough, or so we thought. However, as you get older, you realize your "mistakes." If we **had** been able to see things from our teenager's perspective, we may have realized that it was our daughter who needed the advice – on how to handle us, her parents. Now a parent herself, she discussed this with us recently. If she **had** not done so, we may not have formed the close bond that we have today. She said:

1. If I **were** suddenly to find myself a parent of teenagers, I'd trust them to make good decisions.
2. If I **had** thought you would listen without judging me, I would have talked to you more openly.
3. If it **were**n't for the fact that you were always so busy, I would have spent more time with you.

If it **had**n't been for that conversation, we would probably have interfered too much as grandparents, too. Now we trust her decisions as a new parent. If she **were** a teenager today, our daughter would be proud of us!

B **Complete the company article extracts about its family-friendly policies. Use the words given and a structure from the chart.**

All parents complained of high childcare costs before our childcare center opened 10 years ago. Many say that _____ (it / not be) for their own parents' help, they could not have continued to work when their children were small. The center is highly valued by employees. "_____ (it / not be) for the care center, I simply couldn't do this job," is a typical comment. The costs of running this facility are high, but _____ (be) the center _____ (close), the company would lose experienced employees. Flexible working is also important. Most parents said that _____ (they / have) the opportunity to work part-time when their children were small, they would have done so. Others said they needed two incomes. One told us, "_____ (we / not keep) working, we couldn't have managed financially." Trying to juggle family life and career is still an issue. Many non-parents report that _____ (it / not be) for their careers, they might start families earlier.

Unit 7, Lesson B

Grammar extra

❶ More on *what* clauses

- Speakers often use a *what* clause as the subject of a verb to do the things below.

Describe and analyze situations	*What we're seeing is . . . What we do know is . . . What we've seen is . . . What we've found is . . . What's happening now is . . . What it comes / boils down to is . . .*
Say what is being done	*What we're doing is . . . What we've done is . . . What we're (really) trying to do is . . . What we don't want to do is . . .*
Say what is needed or wanted	*What we need to / have to do is . . . What we want to do is . . . What we're looking for is . . . What we would like to do is . . .*

Rewrite the underlined sentences in the article. Use *what* clauses and add the verb *is*.

An organization recently released a report on the state of families today. The report said, "We're seeing today the unprecedented breakdown of relationships." While the cause of the breakdowns is complex, the report emphasized, "We do know that divorce is tearing families apart." Their survey asked people, "How do you keep your relationship strong?" Here are some excerpts from the responses.

1. "We're creating more family time."
2. "My husband and I have gone to counseling."
3. "We want to stay together. We've found that it gets easier with time."
4. "It boils down to being more tolerant of other people."
5. "It comes down to small things, like doing something special for each other every day."

❷ *what* clauses with passive verbs and modals in writing

- In some *what* clauses, *what* is the subject of a passive verb.
  What was intended to be a small, quiet wedding became a huge affair.
  There may be a problem if your income falls short of **what is needed** to run your home.

- You can use these phrases in writing to define words and expressions: *what is / are called, what is / are known as, what is / are termed.*
  When planning a wedding, many couples choose **what is known as** a "full wedding package."
  My grandparents had **what is called** an "arranged introduction."

- This is a common pattern with modal verbs in object *what* clauses:
  We are always being told what we **can and cannot** do, what we **should and should not** think.

Complete the article extracts about the "worst marriage trends." Use the words given.

1. In Japan, some couples get _____ (what / know) the "Narita divorce." It's named after the airport near Tokyo and refers to the fact that the couple starts divorce proceedings on returning from their honeymoon.
2. _____ (what / consider) by most people to be a private experience after the wedding – the honeymoon – is becoming a family and friends affair. A group honeymoon, or _____ (what / call) by some a "buddymoon," is the latest "worst trend."
3. An email to four bridesmaids from a bossy bride – or _____ (what / call) a "bridezilla" – has gone viral. The bride told them what they _____ (could / wear) and what they _____ (must / do).
4. In case you're not sure _____ (what / require) to create a cost-effective wedding, it is _____ now _____ (what / term) a "drive through" ceremony. Couples are getting married at fast-food restaurants!

1 **More on perfect infinitives**

- You can use perfect infinitives after verbs in the present or past.
  He **seems to have fooled** everyone.   (= It seems now that he fooled everyone.)
  He **was said to have had** special powers. (= It was said in the past that he had special powers.)

- There are three negative forms. The first is the most frequent and the third the least frequent.
  His wealth **does not appear to have changed** him.
  His wealth **appears not to have changed** him.
  His wealth **appears to have not changed** him.

Rewrite the underlined parts in this biography. Change the *it* clauses, using perfect infinitives, and change the punctuation. Sometimes there is more than one correct answer.

Harry Houdini was known to have suffered

Near the end of his life, the great magician <u>Harry Houdini, it was known,
suffered</u> from appendicitis, for which, <u>it was said, he refused</u> treatment.
However, as part of a challenge, a Canadian student unexpectedly punched
him in the stomach, which, <u>it was believed, caused</u> Houdini a fatal injury.
It was a sad ending for a man who <u>people still think is</u> the greatest magician
of all time. As in death, his life was shrouded in mystery and, <u>it seems,
caused</u> great speculation. It was Harry Houdini himself who <u>claimed to be</u>
a native of Appleton, Wisconsin. However, he was actually born in
Budapest, Hungary, and moved to the U.S. when his family emigrated in
1878. His family, <u>it appears, wasn't</u> wealthy. But the poverty in which he
lived, <u>it appeared, did not deter</u> him from seeking success. Houdini, <u>it is
known, tried</u> all kinds of magic tricks early in his career. However, his early
tricks, <u>it seems, weren't</u> successful. He, <u>it appears, got</u> his biggest break with
an act where he freed himself from a pair of handcuffs. It was the start of an
extraordinary career as an escape artist.

2 **The perfect infinitive after adjectives and nouns**

- You can use perfect infinitives after some adjectives and nouns.
  He was **fortunate to have escaped**.   It was an **honor to have been** there.
  I'm very **lucky to have met** her.   It was a terrible **thing to have done**.
  I was **too young to have understood**.   She was the only **person to have achieved** that.

Read the information about Nelson Mandela. Rewrite the underlined parts of the sentences by using the perfect infinitive.

1. Many students today are too young <u>and didn't see</u> Nelson Mandela released from jail in 1990.
2. He is one of many activists <u>who strived</u> for racial equality in South Africa in the 1960s.
3. While he was dismayed <u>when he received</u> a life sentence in prison for his activist work, he remained true to his beliefs for a free and equal society. He spent 27 years in prison.
4. It was a remarkable accomplishment <u>when he came out</u> of jail without any anger or resentment.
5. It was also an achievement <u>that he became</u> president of South Africa in 1994.
6. It must have been an honor <u>hearing</u> his first speech after his release.
7. He is one of only two people <u>that became</u> an honorary citizen of Canada.
8. Many of the celebrities who have visited South Africa say they feel privileged <u>because they met</u> him.
9. I'm sure he was proud <u>that he contributed</u> so much to his country's history.

❶ More on cleft sentences with *it + be*

> In cleft sentences with *it + be*, the item that you focus on can be the subject or object of the next clause. When it is the object, you can leave out *who, that,* or *which.*
>
> **Subject**   *The Internet changed everything in the twentieth century.*
>   → ***It was the Internet that** changed everything in the twentieth century.*
>
> **Object**   *Martin Cooper invented **the cell phone**.*
>   → ***It was the cell phone (that / which)** Martin Cooper invented.*
>   *I remember studying **Edison** for a history project.*
>   → ***It's Edison (who / that)** I remember studying.*

Read the story. Rewrite the sentences, using *it + be* clefts to focus on the words in bold.

There were many influential figures in my past, but **my grandpa** influenced me most. When I was still an impressionable child, he took me to the Kennedy Space Center in Florida. I will never forget it as an **adventure.** I remember staring in awe at the space shuttle and riding in the simulators. However, the **exhibit** that explained how NASA needed children like me to become scientists had the biggest impact on me. I realized we have **NASA scientists** to thank for many of the things we see in daily life: baby formula, freeze-dried food, and ear thermometers. Not only that, but **NASA technology** put people into space. That **day** changed everything for me all those years ago. Looking back on my childhood, I recall **those NASA scientists** as being my heroes. Today *I'm* a scientist, and I told **my grandpa** first about my ambition to become one. **His response** convinced me. "Of course you can be a scientist. You can be anything you want to be," he said.

❷ *It + be + noun phrase in writing*

> • In writing, some cleft sentences with *it + be + noun* are used to introduce issues, e.g.:
>   *It is no coincidence that . . ., It is a fact that . . ., It is no accident that . . ., It is no wonder that . . ., It is no surprise that . . ., It is a shame / pity that . . .*
>   **It is no coincidence that** *countries with strong economies became politically dominant.*

> • Other expressions refer back to something that has just been mentioned, e.g.:
>   *It is an issue that . . ., It was a decision that . . ., It is a story that . . ., It is a system/process that . . ., It was a reminder that . . ., It was a moment that . . .*
>   *In 1919, the atom was first split.* **It was a moment that** *changed history forever.*

Complete the sentences in the article. Use *it + be* + the noun phrase given + *that*.

On July 20, 1969, the Apollo 11 spacecraft landed on the moon. *It was an event that* (an event) will forever be remembered in history, and _____ (no surprise) more than half a billion people watched it on television. During the previous decade, _____ (no coincidence) other countries had been developing rockets of their own. _____ (a period) became known as the "Space Race," as countries competed to develop superior space technologies.

In 1961, a Russian cosmonaut named Yuri Gagarin became the first human to go into space. _____ (a move) spurred President John F. Kennedy to announce a program to land people on the moon by the end of the decade. _____ (a decision) energized the entire nation. However, in 1967, during a launch test, three U.S. astronauts were killed. _____ (a tragedy) almost derailed the whole program. After an overhaul of the entire operation, the Apollo 11 mission was ready. As Neil Armstrong stepped onto the surface of the moon in 1969, he declared, "That's one small step for man, one giant leap for mankind." For those watching, _____ (a day) they will never forget, and for everyone else, _____ (a moment) defined an era.

① *whatever, whichever,* and *whoever* as subjects and objects

- *Whatever, whichever,* and *whoever* can be the subject or object of a verb.

Subject   ***Whatever** happened to the idea of building things to last?*

Object   ***Whichever (program)** you choose, make sure it's one that you're interested in.*

- Sometimes a clause with *whatever, whichever,* or *whoever* is the subject or object of a verb.

Subject   ***Whatever happens in your career** is your responsibility.*

Object   *We don't just take **whoever applies to this program.***

Common errors

Don't confuse *whatever* and *whether*. *Whether* introduces alternatives.
***Whether** you are an employer or an employee, come to our job fair.* (NOT ~~Whatever you~~ . . .)

Read the report about women in STEM professions. Complete the sentences with *whatever, whichever, whoever,* or *whether*. Sometimes there is more than one correct answer.

1. Researchers found gender bias against women in _____ jobs they chose in the fields of science, technology, engineering, and math – also known as STEM fields.

2. Women are often considered as less capable than men _____ their qualifications are.

3. _____ STEM field they pursued, women were often also seen as less likable than men.

4. High school test scores now show that _____ wants to excel in STEM subjects can do so.

5. If the school environment is right, girls can excel in _____ STEM subject they choose.

6. _____ else high school teachers may do, however, they must focus on teaching spatial skills to girls.

7. Colleges should not just accept _____ applies for STEM majors. They should actively recruit girls into these courses.

8. All students, _____ male or female, should be mentored in college.

② Patterns with *however* and *whatever*

- *However* can be used before *much / many* and before adjectives and adverbs.
*Engineering is well worth studying, **however many** years it takes, **however much** it costs.*
*We will solve the problem, **however complex** (it may be), and **however long** it takes.*

- The pattern *whatever the* + noun means "it doesn't matter what the (noun) is."
*We should make efforts to train a new generation of engineers, **whatever the cost**.*
***Whatever the reason**, engineering isn't attracting as many students as we need.*

Rewrite the underlined parts of the comments using *however* or *whatever* + an adjective or adverb, or *whatever the* + noun.

In writing . . .

The most common collocations in *whatever the* + noun are *reason(s), case, outcome, cause, merits, explanation, price, cost.*

1. It doesn't matter how much you aim to earn in life – and it doesn't matter how hard you try – you won't find a better career than engineering, in my view.

2. Engineering is a good choice, no matter what the cost is and no matter how demanding the course.

3. It doesn't matter what the cause is, there are simply not enough engineers.

4. It doesn't matter how many engineers we train, there will never be enough.

5. It doesn't matter what the financial merits are of a career in engineering, nothing beats the feeling of creating solutions to problems, no matter how challenging they are.

Unit 9, Lesson B

Grammar extra

❶ More on inversion

• Use inversion when these adverbs begin a sentence. Notice the words that begin a second clause.

Negative adverbs: *Not only . . . (but), Never, Nowhere, No sooner . . . than, No longer*
Adverbs with negative meaning: *Hardly / Scarcely . . . when, Little, Rarely, Seldom*
Only + adverb, prepositional phrase, or clause: *Only then, Only after, Only when . . .*
Expressions with *no*: *At no time, At no point, By no means, Under no circumstances*

Not only does it **wobble** as people walk across it, **(but)** it also causes nausea.
No sooner had the paint **dried** at one end **than** it needed repainting.
Hardly had construction **begun when** there were problems.
It opened. **Only then / Only after the ceremony / Only when it opened did** they **see** the problem.
At no time did anyone **raise** any objections to the construction of this bridge.

• Do not use inversion after *only, hardly,* and *scarcely* when they modify a noun, or after *In no time.*
Hardly a week went by that there wasn't a problem. **In no time, they built** the main structure.

Rewrite the information, starting with the bold negative adverb or a negative equivalent (e.g., As soon as → No sooner). Use inversions where necessary.

> **In writing . . .**
> After *Nowhere*, there is often a comparison. *Nowhere was the need for redevelopment* **more evident than** here.

There isn't a more famous sight **anywhere in the world** than the Leaning Tower of Pisa. However, its designers did not intend the tower to lean **by any means. As soon as** construction started, problems began. Work had **hardly** begun on the tower in 1173 **when** engineers noticed it was leaning. In the following centuries, it **not only** leaned farther, but it also seemed like it would collapse. It was **only after** it became unsafe in the early 1990s that authorities finally closed the tower. And it was **only then** that there was an effort to stabilize it. **As soon as** it closed, work started. A day **hardly** went by that there wasn't a danger of collapse. Nevertheless, the tower was restored. Today, the tower has **not only** reopened to the public, it has been declared safe for 200 years.

❷ Inversion with modals and in passive sentences

• After negative adverbs, the inversion with modal verbs is modal + subject + verb.
Never again would anyone **achieve** anything of this size.

• In simple present and past passive sentences, the inversion is *be* + subject + past participle.
Under no circumstances is / was this project **allowed** to be delayed.

• In present or past perfect passive sentences, the inversion is *have* + subject + *been* + past participle.
Never has / had such a large project **been completed** on time.

Unscramble the sentences, starting with the negative adverb.

Hong Kong International Airport at Chek Lap Kok is a remarkable feat of engineering.

1. attempted / nowhere before / been / a more complex airport project / had
2. nowhere in the world / an island / had / constructed / on which to build an airport / been
3. completed / been / had / a project this size / under budget / rarely
4. could / bringing in thousands of workers / only by / the project / be accomplished
5. however, under no circumstances / permitted / the project / to fail / was
6. no sooner / were / finished / than work began / the designs
7. was / not only / completed on time, / but it was finished under budget / the project

1 Simple vs. continuous infinitives

- Infinitives can be simple or continuous. The simple form describes single or repeated events in a factual way. It can also suggest that an event is complete.
  *A scientist claims **to have found** a cure for malaria. She hopes **to publish** her research soon.*

- The continuous form describes events as activities that are ongoing or temporary. It can suggest that the event is not complete.
  *The team appears **to have been working** on their research for several decades.*
  *They seem **to be making** great progress.*

Complete the infinitives in the editorial with the verbs given. Sometimes both simple and continuous forms are correct.

Weather-forecasting techniques appear to have _improved_ (improve). Certainly, the predictions of the scale and timing of major weather events, such as hurricanes, seem to have _____ (become) *have been* more accurate – fortunately so, because the frequency of strong storms appears to _be increasing / increas_ (increase). However, what we, as a society, appear not to _have been doing_ (do) is to recognize how serious forecasters' warnings are and take appropriate action. As another huge storm hits the coast, some residents of low-lying areas appear not to have _been listn_ (listen) to the reports on TV and radio that urged them to evacuate. They seem to have _had_ (hope) that the forecasts were exaggerated. Others were too poor _to move_ (move) and seem to have _had_ (have) no help from officials. Now, looking at the devastation, many are lucky to have _survived_ (survive). The whole city appears to have _stopped_ (stop) working even though officials are likely to have _been preaning_ (prepare) for a state of emergency for several days and despite the efforts of utility companies, which we believe to _be working_ (work) around the clock to restore power. They hope to _get_ (get) the city back to normal in the next few days. We are fortunate to have _had_ (have) the warnings, but many of us are unwise to have _ignored_ (ignore) them.

2 More on perfect continuous infinitives

- Verbs that are followed by perfect continuous infinitives can be present or past, active or passive.
  *The hacker **seems** to have been working alone.*
  *The economy **appeared** to have been growing steadily until 2008.*
  *The government **appears** to have been negotiating secretly with unions on a new pay deal.*
  *A terrorist group **is believed / is alleged** to have been planning attacks for several months.*

Rewrite these news excerpts without using *it* clauses.

Unemployment rates appear to have been declining / The economy is believed not to have been making

1. It appears that unemployment rates have been declining in recent months. However, it is not believed that the economy has been making a sufficient recovery.
   Twenty soccer fans were alleged to have been travelling
2. Twenty soccer fans, who, it was alleged, had been traveling to an international match with the intention of causing a riot, have been arrested and banned from all future European matches.
   are said to have been talking
3. It is said that workers' unions have been talking with employers in the auto industry this week.
4. A man was arrested after disrupting a flight en route to Miami. It is thought the man had been suffering from an anxiety attack. *The man is thought have been suffering.*
5. While it appeared that the coal mining industry had been declining in the last part of the twentieth century, it is reported that clean coal technology has been revitalizing the industry.
6. A man who, it was believed, was diving for sunken treasure has been reported missing.

5) *The coal mining industry appears to have been declining, clean coal tech. is reported to have been revitalizing.*

6) *A man who was believed to have been diving.*

① More on the subjunctive

- The subjunctive form is used for both the present and the past. It does not change.
  *An editor may require that a journalist **reveal** his or her sources.*
  *The military instisted that all reporters **leave** the war zone.*

- The negative subjunctive is *not + verb*. Do not use *do / does / did*.
  *It is often advisable that a local journalist **not report** the truth about corrupt officials.*

- Passive forms of the subjunctive are *be + past participle* and *not be + past participle*.
  *It is essential that interviewees **be treated** with respect.*
  *We requested that the exact location of the journalists **not be broadcast**.*

Read the editorial. Find 10 verbs you can change to the subjunctive form, either by deleting a verb or changing the form of a verb.

Journalists who cover combat zones often pay the ultimate price for their determination to report the news. While media outlets may not require a reporter to leave a war zone, they often encourage him or her to do so. Even so, journalists often insist that they should be allowed to stay. Typically, they request that their exact locations are not revealed to ensure their safety. While viewers demand that journalists should provide detailed reporting on conflicts worldwide, it is essential that the dangers they face in doing their work are recognized. One such courageous reporter died this week. Her family asked the media to respect their privacy. However, she herself requested that her work should not be abandoned. Indeed, in a video made shortly before her death, she said that it was critical that the plight of civilians in the cross fire is publicized. This editor asks that this reporter should not be forgotten. It is important that she is remembered for her courage in reporting the truth.

② The subjunctive and conditional sentences

- The subjunctive can also be used in conditional sentences after *on condition that*.
  *A witness agreed to testify on condition that he **remain** anonymous / he **not be named**.*

- You can use *whether it / they be . . . or . . .* OR *be it / they . . . or . . .* to introduce alternative ideas. They mean "whether we are talking about one thing or another, the issue is the same."
  *One way to read the news, **whether it be** print **or** broadcast media, is to question what you read.*
  *The problem with news reporting, **be it** live **or** recorded, is that it is always selective.*

Rewrite the underlined parts of this editorial with *on condition that, whether it be,* or *be it* (both may be possible) with the same meaning. Make any other changes necessary.

> **Writing vs. Conversation**
>
> The subjunctive is rarely used in conversation. However, *whether it / they be . . . or . . .* is more frequent in conversation than in writing.

It makes no difference if it's a television report or a printed news article, bias exists. Research shows 1 in 6 adults perceive bias in the news, both liberal and conservative. Reporting should be balanced, either in terms of reporting a range of perspectives or reflecting the diversity of public opinion. There are other problems with the way in which stories are reported, both in the use of biased language and in the fact that certain stories are given more coverage. One reporter stated, and he insisted that he did not want to be identified, that the media represent the views of the sources of their funding. Media outlets, and the issue is the same if they are transparent or not, show bias, so read as many sources as possible.

① More on *be to; be due to, be meant to*

- You can use *be to* to describe fixed events in the future, especially official or scheduled events.
  *The president **is to** host a summit of world leaders in May. World leaders **are to** meet in May.*

- You can use passive verbs after *be to* expressions.
  *Meetings **are to be held** in July, and a report **is to be published** in the fall.*
  *The government is looking at new technology, which **is about to be tested** in national trials.*

- *Be to* can be used in conditional sentences to state what is expected or assumed.
  *If we **are to** believe scientists, weather patterns are changing.* (= If we are expected to believe)

- *Be due to* suggests that the time is or was known. *Be meant to* means "what is or was intended."
  *The report **is not due to** be published until next week. Results **were due to** be announced last week.*
  *The law **is meant to** protect citizens from cyberattacks. It **was not meant to** restrict freedoms.*

Read the article and complete it with the prompts given. Use the passive where necessary.

State officials _are due to_ (due / attend) a national disaster conference next month as part of a series of events. The upcoming conference _is to consider_ (be / consider) how to cope with major disasters. "It _meant to_ (mean / teach) us how to survive," the governor stated, "in the event of a major catastrophe." With so many in the media declaring, "The world _is about to end_ (about / end)," it would serve us well to know how to survive. But how likely is such an event? The world _was due to end_ (due / end) in 2012, but it didn't. In fact, if the media hype _is to be believed_ (be / believe), disasters would have struck the world several times over in the last decade. Disaster theories have suggested that nuclear weapons _are about to be launched_ (about / launch) accidentally, that millions of people _are about to killed_ (about / kill) by a deadly virus, or that the northern United States _is about to be destroyed_ (about / destroy) by a super volcano. While much of the hype _is to be ignored_ (be / ignore), there are other real dangers if experts' warnings _are to be believed_ (be / believe). Perhaps, then, we really *should* prepare for disaster. If water supplies _were to be interrupted_ (be / interrupt), what would you do? If your family _were to be forced out_ (be / force out) of the area, where would you go? If your community _is to hold_ (be / hold) a disaster awareness event next month, attend – it could save your life.

② *be to* for orders and instructions

- *Be to* is used to give or describe orders and instructions, mostly in official notices or written instructions.
  *No one **is to use** the fire exits except in an emergency. Staff members **are not to open** windows.*
  *These doors **are to be kept** closed at all times. They **are not to be left** open.*

Read this emergency fire plan from a company website. Rewrite the plan, using *be to*.

1. Keep all fire doors shut at all times. All fire doors are to be kept shut at all times.
2. Do not tamper with fire alarms and sprinkler systems. All fire alarms are not be tampe. / All fire alarms do not be tampe.
3. If the fire alarms sound, staff members should leave all personal belongings and exit the building. are to leave
4. Staff members should not stay in the building under any circumstances. are not to stay.
5. No one should use the elevators in the event of a fire. No one is to use.
6. All staff members should meet in the parking lot. are to meet.
7. Each department head should take a roll call once staff is assembled in the parking lot. is to take.
8. No one should leave the lot until notified that it is permissible to do so. is to leave.
9. Under no circumstances should anyone return to the building without notification from the fire department. is anyone to return

Unit 11, Lesson B   *Grammar extra*

① More on passive perfect infinitives

> • Passive perfect infinitives can follow active or passive verbs. The most frequent active verbs are *seem*, *appear*, *claim*. The most frequent passive verbs are *be believed, be known, be reported, be found, be rumored, be alleged, be said*, and the expression *be supposed to*.
> *Shakespeare's plays* **appear to have been enjoyed** *by Queen Elizabeth I.*
> *Shakespeare* **is believed to have been born** *in 1564.*

Complete the sentences in the article using the verbs given. Sometimes the first verb in each pair can be present or past. Each verb phrase has a passive perfect infinitive.

The movie *Anonymous* reignited interest in the English poet and playwright Shakespeare. The plot of the movie focuses on the debate, which _*seems not have been resolved*_ (seem / not /resolve), about whether Shakespeare wrote his own plays. Few records of his personal life _*appear to have been kept*_ (appear / keep), which makes verifying his work difficult. Here are some of the issues on which scholars _*seem to have been divided*_ (seem / divide) for many years.

1. Shakespeare's plays _*are believed to have been composed*_ (believe / compose) in collaboration with other authors.
2. Secret codes about the political climate of the time _*are reported to have been hidden*_ (report / hide) in his plays.
3. The plays _*are rumored to have been written*_ (rumor / write) by his rival, Christopher Marlowe. In one study, identical word patterns _*were found to have been used*_ (find / use) by both writers.
4. In the movie *Anonymous*, the plays _*are alleged to have been written*_ (allege / write) by Edward de Vere, Earl of Oxford. A well-traveled lawyer, de Vere _*was reported to have been kidnapped*_ (report / kidnap) by pirates and left on the shores of Denmark, which was supposedly the inspiration for *Hamlet*. However, this event _*doesn't seem to have been found*_ (seem / not / find) in written sources used for the play, which raises the question: How did Shakespeare know some of the details? Many of the other places that de Vere visited _*are said to have been included*_ (say / include) in Shakespeare's plays.
5. Supporters of Shakespeare as the author of the plays dismiss these theories, saying that they _*appear to have been given*_ (appear / give) too much credibility.

② *would rather*

> • After *would rather*, you can use a passive base form.
> *He would rather* **be remembered** *for his philanthropy. He'd rather* **not be remembered** *for his crimes.*

> • Notice the patterns in comparisons.
> Passive + active: *He would rather* **be killed** *than* **give up** *his beliefs.*
> Passive + passive: *He'd rather* **be loved** *than* **(be) respected**.

Read the article and complete it with passive base forms of the verbs given.

In law enforcement, many crimes go unsolved and sometimes remain a mystery. Not so in the case of a Florida grandmother. While she would probably rather _*be known*_ (know) for her good deeds than _*be remembered*_ (remember) for her crimes, this "pillar of the community" shocked neighbors when she was arrested 34 years *after* her crimes were committed. She was sent to jail, and while it's understandable that anyone would rather _*be given*_ (give) probation than _*be sentenced*_ (sentence) to five years in prison, the woman shocked the community again. Two months later, she escaped from prison, obviously feeling that she would really much rather _*be left*_ (leave) alone to live her life out of jail than _*serve*_ (serve) a prison sentence.

Common verbs, adjectives, and nouns + object + *-ing*

- Here are some common verbs, adjectives, and nouns that introduce object + *-ing* patterns.

Verbs + prepositions	*keep, appreciate, remember, leave, mind, get, hear, see, feel, watch* *hear about, listen to, worry about, result in, count on, depend on, think of, insist on*
Adjectives + prepositions	*interested in, tired of, sick of, supportive of, worried about, wrong with, responsible for, excited about, (un)comfortable with, aware of, serious about, good about, happy with / about, fine with, grateful for, crucial / critical to, crazy about*
Nouns + prepositions	*picture / photo / video of, thought of, report of, questions of / about, probability of, possibility of, chance(s) of, danger of, worries about, way of*

I **remember my father giving** me a lot of advice.
But he also said, "I'm not **responsible for you repeating** my mistakes!"
I said, "There's no **chance of me doing** that!"

A Read the advice to parents of young adults. Rewrite the underlined parts of the sentences, using a pattern in the chart. You may need to delete or add words and change the verb forms.

After college – what then?

[handwritten: happy about their adult children moving back]
Many parents are happy if their adult children move back into their home after college, and in many families, it's expected that they will do so. For others, though, the thought that their offspring will return home raises worries that their privacy will be invaded. What's more, while parents mostly want to be supportive so their children will find their way in life, there is a limit to the financial support they can offer. *[handwritten: being / Finding / living]*

1. If you're uncomfortable that your adult children might live at home, then say so. Say you don't mind if they live with you for a fixed period of time. Then insist that they move out. *[handwritten: Them living / on them / ing]*

2. Set ground rules from the outset. If children count on the fact that their parents will do everything for them, they may never do anything for themselves. Parents often see that their children are taking advantage of them. You don't want this to leave you in a situation where you feel resentful toward your children, so speak up. There's nothing wrong if they want to do things their own way, but they are in *your* home. *[handwritten: doing / your feeling / being / them wanting]*

3. If the chances that your adult children will be financially dependent on you for a long time are high, then you should probably do something about it. You need to be serious so your kids will figure out how to manage their own money. Don't pay for everything. *[handwritten: Figuring out / about your kids]*

4. The probability that unemployed children will remain unemployed is higher if you don't insist that they pay their own way. Don't worry if your children go without luxuries or even basics. There's a good possibility that they will be more motivated to find work if they can't buy the things they want. *[handwritten: ing / on them / ing / of them being / about]*

5. If your adult children are adamant that you should support them, be firm. Say you are not responsible for the fact that they need to find work. On the other hand, say you would appreciate the fact that they do chores and work around the home in return for rent.

B Look at the sentences you rewrote. Choose six and make them more formal by using a possessive determiner (*their, your, 's*) before the *-ing* form.

[handwritten: Many parents are happy about their adult children's moving back home after college.]

❶ More on reflexive pronouns

- Reflexive pronouns are often used after *find, protect, defend, consider / see, call, ask, kill, describe, identify, pride . . . on* (= be proud), *distance, express, reinvent, introduce, see for.*
  He **prides himself on** being an expert, but even he **found himself** "dating" a piece of software.

- *Itself* is often used after *in, lend,* and *speak for.*
  Identifying who you are writing to is a problem **in itself**. (= without considering other issues)
  This tale of Internet deception **lends itself** to a movie adaptation. (= is suitable for)
  His willingness to talk openly about the event **speaks for itself**. (= is clear)

> **Common errors**
>
> You don't need a reflexive pronoun after *apologize, complain, develop, feel, relax, remember.*
> **I felt** unhappy at first, but then I began to **relax.** (NOT . . . ~~felt myself~~ . . . ~~relax myself~~)

Read the article and complete it with reflexive pronouns. If one is not needed, write an X.

Even if you pride _____ on being a good judge of character, when it comes to online relationships, ask _____ if you are sure about who you are in touch with. Meeting people online is a challenge in _____ . Many of us who have found _____ in a problematic online relationship say we didn't see it coming – even those of us who call _____ experts. People often reinvent _____ online, and email doesn't lend _____ to getting to know someone well. You may have to protect _____ from dangerous people. Take my friend Ana, who considers _____ a cautious person. This guy introduced _____ via a dating site and described _____ as caring *and* single. The relationship developed _____ , but on their first real date, he apologized _____ for being evasive, which in _____ was a warning sign. How the story ends speaks for _____ . He turned out to be married. She distanced _____ from him, but he started turning up at her home. She couldn't relax _____ and complained _____ to the police.

❷ Referring to unknown people

- If you refer back to an unknown person, you can use *he or she, him or her,* and *himself or herself.* People often say *they, their,* and *themselves,* especially after *everyone,* etc., but do not write this.
  It is up to the person **himself or herself** whether to see a doctor when **he or she** needs to.
  Everybody needs sympathy when **their** problems affect their health.

> **Common errors**
>
> Don't use *itself* for people or to refer back to plural nouns.
> The patient was in fact a doctor **herself**. (NOT The patient was a doctor ~~itself.~~)
> My friends do online dating **themselves**. (NOT My friends do online dating ~~itself.~~)

Complete the sentences. Then rewrite sentences 1–4 as you might tell a friend in a conversation.

1. Everyone should make sure that ~~his or her~~ _____ personal details are not online.
   Everyone should make sure their personal details are not online.
2. An online dater can always ask for a background check if _____ wishes to.
3. Nobody should let _____ guard down when they meet _____ date.
   Meet several times, ask to meet _____ friends, and find out where _____ works.
4. Everybody should ask _____ if _____ is a good judge of character.
   If not, ask a friend to come along and meet your new date.
5. People can protect _____ by meeting in a public place.

Illustration credits

Photography credits

Text credits

Corpus

Development of this publication has made use of the Cambridge English Corpus (CEC). The CEC is a computer database of contemporary spoken and written English, which currently stands at over one billion words. It includes British English, American English, and other varieties of English. It also includes the Cambridge Learner Corpus, developed in collaboration with the University of Cambridge ESOL Examinations. Cambridge University Press has built up the CEC to provide evidence about language use that helps produce better language teaching materials.